"[A] spellbinding memoir."
TORONTO STAR

"Koofi's story illustrates what lies beneath the chaos of this multi-factional, multilingual, complex nation caught in the current struggle between foreign nations ... and the vicious religious zealots known as the Taliban."
OTTAWA CITIZEN

"In her memoir, written with journalist Nadene Ghouri, Koofi chronicles her life from the time she was put out in the sun to die after her birth to her current place as one of the most respected people in Afghan politics. The narrative, simple but poetic at times, shows readers the long struggle against brutalities and injustice that she—and most Afghan women of her generation—have endured."
MS. MAGAZINE

"This is precisely what it's like to be a girl and then a woman in Afghanistan. Fawzia Koofi is feisty, outspoken, popular and progressive but, as this heart-wrenching autobiography shows, she is the recipient of all the brickbats her country throws at those who dare to be different. *Letters to My Daughters* is a page turner as it teases the reader to find out how Fawzia Koofi not only survived but is poised to beat the system."
SALLY ARMSTRONG,
human rights activist and journalist

"Fawzia Koofi's testament of love for her mother, her daughters, her husband and her country is a book you will not be able to put down until you're finished the final page."
TERRY GLAVIN,
author of *Come From the Shadows*

"Fawzia Koofi's voice comes to us as a powerful and moving reminder that in the midst of Afghanistan's decades of struggle, hope and humanity prevail. *Letters to My Daughters* is a compulsively good read."
SAMANTHA NUTT,
founder of War Child North America

FAWZIA KOOFI

LETTERS TO MY DAUGHTERS

Douglas & McIntyre

D&M PUBLISHERS INC.

Vancouver/Toronto

Douglas & McIntyre
An imprint of D&M Publishers Inc.
2323 Quebec Street, Suite 201
Vancouver BC Canada V5T 4S7
www.douglas-mcintyre.com

Cataloguing data available from Library and Archives Canada
ISBN 978-1-55365-876-4 (cloth)
ISBN 978-1-926812-82-3 (pbk.)
ISBN 978-1-55365-877-1 (ebook)

"A Historical Timeline of Afghanistan" on pages 271–274
adapted with permission of BBC online

Copyediting by Lara Kordic
Cover design by Setareh Ashrafologhalai & Naomi MacDougall
Text design by Naomi MacDougall
Cover photograph © Reza
Printed and bound in Canada by Friesens
Text printed on acid-free paper

To my mom, who was the kindest, most talented teacher in the world; to both my daughters, who are the stars of my life; and to all women of Afghanistan

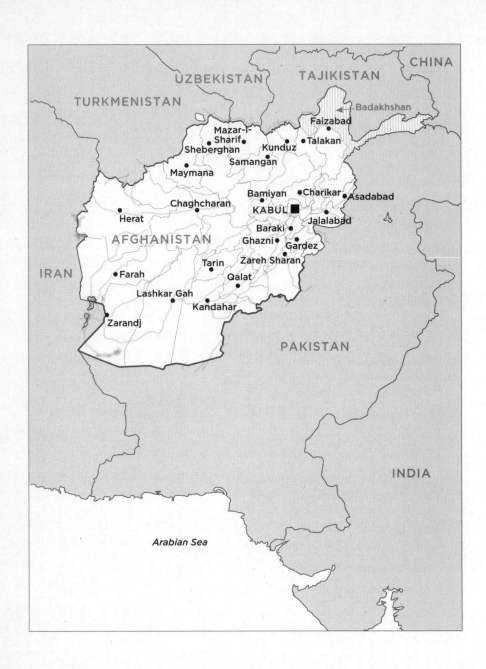

{ contents }

{ September 2010 }

THE MORNING I wrote the first letter to my daughters, I was due to attend a political meeting in Badakhshan, the province I represent as a member of the Afghan parliament. Badakhshan is the northernmost province of Afghanistan, bordering China, Pakistan and Tajikistan. It is also one of the poorest, wildest, most remote and culturally conservative areas in the country.

Badakhshan has the highest rate of maternal mortality and child mortality in the world—partly because of its inaccessibility and the crippling poverty of its people, and partly due to a culture that sometimes puts tradition ahead of women's health. A man will rarely seek hospital treatment for his wife unless her life is clearly in danger. By the time she reaches hospital—often after days of agonizing labour while travelling on the back of a donkey over rocky mountain tracks—it is usually too late to save both mother and child.

That day I was warned not to travel to Badakhshan because of a credible threat that the Taliban planned to kill me by planting an improvised bomb under my car. The Taliban dislike women holding such powerful positions in government, and they dislike my public criticisms of them even more.

They often try to kill me.

Recently, they have tried even harder than usual, threatening my home, tracking my journeys to work so that they can lay a bomb as my car passes and even organizing gunmen to attack a convoy of police vehicles assigned to protect me. One gun attack on my car lasted thirty minutes and killed two policemen. I stayed inside the vehicle, not knowing if I would emerge alive or dead.

The Taliban and all who seek to silence me for speaking out against corruption and bad leadership in my country will not be happy until I am dead. That day, however, I ignored the threat, just as I have ignored countless others. If I didn't, I could not do my job. But I felt threatened and afraid. I always do. That's the very nature of threat, as those who use the tactic know very well.

At 6 A.M., I gently woke my elder girl, Shaharzad, who is twelve, and told her that if I didn't come home after this trip of a few days, she was to read the letter to her ten-year-old sister, Shuhra. Shaharzad's eyes met mine, full of questions. I placed my finger to her lips, kissed her and her sleeping sister on the forehead and quietly left the room, closing the door behind me.

As I tore myself away from my children I knew I might well be murdered. But my job is to represent the poorest people of my nation. That mission, along with raising my two beautiful daughters, is what I live for. I could not let my people down that day. I will never let them down.

PART ONE

Dear Shuhra and Shaharzad,

Today I am going on political business to Faizabad and Darwaz. I hope I will come back soon and see you again, but I have to tell you that I may not.

There have been threats to kill me on this trip. Maybe this time these people will be successful.

As your mother, it causes me such bitter pain to tell you this. But please understand I would willingly sacrifice my life if it means a peaceful Afghanistan and a better future for the children of this country.

I live this life so that you—my precious girls—will be free to live your lives and to dream all of your dreams.

If I am killed and I don't see you again, I want you to remember these things.

First, don't forget me.

Because you are young and have to finish your studies and cannot live independently, I want you to stay with your aunt Khadija. She loves you so much and she will take care of you for me.

You have my authority to spend all the money I have in the bank. But use it wisely and use it for your studies. Focus on your education. A girl needs an education if she is to excel in this man's world.

After you graduate from school, I want you to continue your studies abroad. I want you to be familiar with universal values. The world is a big, beautiful, wonderful place and it is yours to explore.

Be brave. Don't be afraid of anything in life.

All of us human beings will die one day. Maybe today is the day I will die. But if I do, please know it was for a purpose.

Don't die without achieving something. Take pride in trying to help people and in trying to make our country and our world a better place.

I kiss you both. I love you.
Your mother

ONE

Just a Girl

{ 1975 }

EVEN THE DAY I was born I was supposed to die.

I have stared death in the face countless times in my thirty-five years, but still I'm alive. I don't know why this is, but I do know that God has a purpose for me. Perhaps it is for me to govern and lead my country out of the abyss of corruption and violence. Perhaps it is simply for me to be a good mother to my daughters.

I was the nineteenth of my father's twenty-three children and my mother's last child. My mother was my father's second wife. When she became pregnant with me, she was physically exhausted from the seven children she had already borne and depressed at having lost my father's affections to his newest and youngest wife. So she wanted me to die.

I was born out in the fields. Every summer, my mother and a host of servants would journey to the highest mountain peaks, where the grass was sweet and luscious, to graze our cattle and sheep. This was her chance to escape the house for a few weeks. She would take charge of the entire operation, gathering enough dried fruit, nuts, rice and oil to sustain the small party of travellers for the three months or so that they would be away. The preparations and packing for the trip caused great excitement. Everything was planned to the last detail before a convoy on horses and donkeys set off across the mountain passes in search of the higher grounds.

My mother loved these trips, and as she rode through the villages her joy at being temporarily free from the shackles of home and housework, able to breathe in the fresh mountain air, was obvious.

There is a local saying that the more powerful and passionate a woman is, the nicer she looks sitting on a horse in her burka. It was also said that no one looked more beautiful on horseback than my mother. There was something about the way she held herself, the straightness of her back and her dignity.

But in the year I was born, 1975, she was not in a celebratory mood. Thirteen months earlier, she had stood at the large yellow gates of our *hooli*, a large, sprawling single-storey house with mud walls, watching a wedding party snake its way down the mountain path that wound through the centre of our village. The groom was my mother's husband. My father had chosen to take a seventh wife, a girl just fourteen years old.

Each time he remarried, my mother was devastated—although my father liked to joke that with each new wife my mother became even more beautiful. Of all his wives, my father loved my mother, Bibi jan (literally translated as "beautiful dear"), the most. But in my parents' mountain village culture, love and marriage seldom meant the same thing. Marriage was for family, tradition and culture, and obedience to all those things was deemed more important than individual happiness. Love was something no one was expected to feel or need. It only caused trouble. People believed that happiness lay in doing one's duty without question. And my father genuinely believed that a man of his standing and position had a duty to marry more than one woman.

My mother had stood on the large stone terrace, safely behind the gates of the *hooli*, as the party of a dozen or so men on horseback ambled its way down the hillside, my father dressed in his finest white *shalwar kameez* (a long tunic and trousers), brown waistcoat and lambskin hat. Beside his white horse, which had bright pink, green and red wool tassels dangling from its decorated bridle, were a series of smaller horses carrying the bride and her female relatives, all wearing white burkas, accompanying her to her new home, the home she would share with my mother and the other women who also called my father husband. My father, a short man with close-set eyes and a neatly trimmed beard, smiled graciously and shook hands with the villagers who came out to greet him and witness the spectacle. They called to each other, "Wakil Abdul Rahman is here," and "Wakil Abdul Rahman is home with his very beautiful new wife." His public loved him and they expected no less.

My father, Wakil (Representative) Abdul Rahman, was a member of the Afghan parliament, representing the people of Badakhshan, just as I do today. Before my father and I became members of parliament, my father's father, Azamshah, was a community leader and tribal elder. For as long as my family can remember, local politics and public service have been our tradition and our honour. It can be said that politics runs through my veins as strongly as the rivers that flow across the mountains and valleys of Badakhshan.

The Badakhshani districts of Koof and Darwaz, from where my family and my surname originate, are so remote and mountainous that even today it can take up to three days in a four-wheel drive to reach them from the provincial capital of Faizabad. And that is in good weather. In the winter, the small mountain passes are completely closed.

My grandfather's job was to help people with their social and practical problems, connecting them with the central government offices based in Faizabad and working with the provincial district manager's office to provide services. The only way he could go to speak to the government authorities in Faizabad from his home in the mountainous Darwaz district was by horse or donkey, a journey that often took him a week to ten days. In his lifetime, he never once flew in a plane or drove in a car.

Of course, my grandfather was not the only one who travelled in this rudimentary way. The only way any of the villagers could connect with the bigger towns was on horseback or on foot; that was how farmers bought seed or took cattle to market, how the sick got to a hospital and how family members separated by marriage visited each other. Travel was possible only in the warm spring and summer months, and even then it was dangerous.

The greatest risk of all was the Atanga crossing. Atanga is a large mountain bordering the Amu Darya River. This clear green waterway is all that separates Afghanistan from Tajikistan, and it was as dangerous as it was beautiful; in spring, as the snow melted and the rains came, its banks swelled, creating a series of deadly, fast-flowing currents. The Atanga crossing was a series of rough wooden stairs fastened to either side of the mountain for people to climb up and then down the other side.

The steps were tiny, rickety and slippery. One small stumble and a person would fall down straight into the river and be swept away to certain death. Imagine returning from Faizabad with the goods you had just purchased, perhaps a seven-kilo bag of rice, salt or oil—precious cargo that had to last your family all winter—already exhausted after a week of walking, and then having to risk your life negotiating a treacherous pass that had probably caused the deaths of many of your friends and relatives.

My grandfather could not bear to see his people being killed in this way year after year, and he did all he could to force the government to build a proper road and a safer crossing. However, although he might have been richer than most people in Badakhshan, he was still just a local official living in a remote village. Travelling to Faizabad was as much as he could do. He did not have the means or the power to travel to Kabul, where the king and the central government were based.

Knowing change would not come in his lifetime, my grandfather decided his youngest son would take over his campaigning role. My father was just a little boy when my grandfather began grooming him for a future in politics. One day years later, after months of solid lobbying, one of my father's biggest successes in parliament would be the realization of my grandfather's dream to get a road built over the Atanga Pass.

There is a famous story about the road and my father's audience with Zahir Shah to discuss the project. He stood in front of the king and said, "Shah sahib, construction of this road has been planned for years, but there is no action—you and your government plan and talk but do not keep your promises." Although the parliament at that time was made up of elected representatives, the king and his courtiers still ran the country. Direct criticism of the king was rare, and only a brave or foolhardy man would attempt it. The king took off his glasses and looked long and hard at my father before stating severely, "Wakil sahib, you would do well to remember you are in my palace."

My father panicked, thinking he had gone too far. He hurriedly left the palace, fearing that he would be arrested on the way out. But a month later, the king sent his minister of public works to Badakhshan to meet my father and make plans for the construction of the road. The minister arrived, took one look at the mountain and declared the job impossible. There was no more to be said; he would return home at once. My father nodded sagely and asked him to go for a short horse ride with him first. The man agreed, and they rode together to the top of the pass. As they dismounted, my father grabbed the man's horse and raced back down, leading it behind him, leaving the minister alone on the mountain all night long to give him a taste of what it was like for villagers who got trapped on the passes.

The next morning my father returned to pick up the minister. He was furious, half bitten to death by mosquitoes, and he had lain awake all night terrified that he would be eaten by wild dogs or wolves. But now he had some direct understanding of how harsh life was for the local people. He agreed to bring engineers and dynamite so the pass could be created. My father's pass at Atanga is still there, and this feat of engineering has saved thousands of Badakhshani lives over the years.

But long before the pass was built and my father became an MP, my grandfather had appointed the little Abdul Rahman an *arbab*, a community leader. This effectively gave the boy the powers of a tribal elder at the age of twelve. He was asked to settle the villagers' land, family and marriage disputes. Families who wanted to arrange good matches for their daughters' weddings would come to him for advice in choosing a suitable husband. Before long, he was negotiating health and education projects, raising funds and meeting with the provincial officials in Faizabad. Although he was barely more than a child, these officials knew that under our *arbab* system he had the support of local people and they were prepared to deal with him.

These early years gave my father such a solid grounding in the issues facing our community that by the time he grew into adulthood he was ready to lead. The timing was perfect, for at that time real democracy was beginning in Afghanistan. In 1965, the king decided to establish a democratic parliament, giving people a role in decision-making by allowing them to vote for their local members.

The people of Badakhshan felt they had suffered years of neglect by the central government and were excited that their voices would finally be heard. In the election, my father was voted into the new assembly as the first-ever member of parliament for Darwaz, representing people who were not only among the poorest in Afghanistan, but also among the poorest in the world.

Despite their poverty, Badakhshanis are also people with pride, people who stick to their values. They can be as wild and angry as the ever-changing mountain climate but also as tender and tenacious as the delicate wild flowers that grow on the granite river banks.

Abdul Rahman was one of them and knew their qualities better than anyone. He took on his new role with nothing short of total dedication.

In those days, the only contact Badakhshanis had with the outside world was through radio. My father had inherited from my grandfather the only radio in our village, a chunky wooden Russian wireless with brass controls. On the day of my father's first address to the parliament in Kabul, all the villagers gathered at our house in Koof to listen to the broadcast.

No one except my elder brother Jamalshah knew how to turn on the radio or even increase the volume. Bursting with pride that her husband was a member of parliament, my mother threw open the gates of the *hooli* to allow the public in to hear the speech and called for Jamalshah to turn on the radio for her.

My brother, however, was not at home. In panic, she ran through the village calling him, but he was nowhere to be found. The speech was about to start, and back at the *hooli* a crowd was gathering: cousins, village elders, women, children. Some had never heard a radio before, and all wanted to hear their new representative address parliament. She could not let my father down but had not the faintest idea how the contraption worked.

She went up to the radio and tried all the knobs, to no avail. As the crowd watched her in anticipation, she felt a wave of rising panic and fear and started to cry. Her husband was going to be humiliated, and it would be her fault. If only Jamalshah were there. Where was the boy? In frustration, she brought her fist down hard on the top of the radio—and, amazingly, the thing spluttered and crackled into life.

She couldn't quite believe her luck, but still no one could hear it, as the volume was too low. She didn't have a clue what to do. One friend, my father's fourth wife, suggested bringing the loudspeaker. The women had no idea what it did or how it worked but had seen the men use it before. They carried it over and placed it next to the radio, doing what they could to connect it. It worked. The entire village heard my father's speech in the live parliamentary proceedings. My mother beamed with joy and satisfaction. She was a woman who lived through her husband, and she later described this to me as one of the happiest days of her life.

My father soon gained a reputation as one of the hardest-working members in the king's parliament. Although Badakhshan remained desperately poor, these were good days for Afghanistan overall; national security, the economy and society were generally stable. This, however, was not a state of affairs that our neighbours could easily accept. There is a saying in Afghanistan that our location and geography—between the great powers of Europe, China, Iran and Russia—is bad for Afghanistan but good for the world. It is true. Ask anyone who plays Risk, the board game in which players aim to take over the world, and he or she will tell you that if you win Afghanistan, you win a gateway to the rest of the globe. This has always been true. Back then it was the height of the Cold War, and my country's strategic and geographical importance was already shaping the tragic fate that would later befall it.

My father was outspoken, straightforward and hard-working, respected not only in Badakhshan but throughout the country for his generosity, honesty, faith and fierce belief in traditional Islamic values. He was also unpopular with some in the king's court for his refusal to kowtow to the elite or to play the political power games beloved by so many of his peers. Above all else, he was an old-fashioned politician who believed in the nobility of public service and in helping the poor.

He spent long months in Kabul advocating for roads, hospitals and schools and was successful in getting funds to complete some projects, though not all. The Kabul-based rulers did not see our province as particularly important, and it was hard for him to get central funding. This constantly angered him.

My mother recalled how she would start getting ready for his arrival a month before the annual parliamentary recess—preparing different kinds of sweetmeats and dried fruits for him, cleaning the house and sending the servants to the mountains to collect wood for all the cooking his arrival would inevitably involve. In the evenings, a long queue of donkeys loaded with wood would enter the *hooli* gates, and my mother would direct them into the wood store in the corner of the garden. In her own way, she worked as hard as my father did, never accepting second best and always seeking perfection. But my father barely thanked her for it. At home he could be a terrifying tyrant; my mother's bruises were testament to that.

Six out of my father's seven wives were political matches. By marrying the favoured daughter of a nearby tribal leader or powerful elder, he strategically consolidated and secured the power base of his own local empire. My mother's father was an important elder from the next district, a district that had previously fought with my father's village. In marrying my mother, he essentially secured a peace treaty.

A few of his wives he loved; two he divorced; most he ignored. Over his lifetime, he took a total of seven wives. My mother was without doubt his favourite. She was petite, with a pretty, oval-shaped face, pale skin, big brown eyes, long shiny black hair and neat eyebrows.

It was she he trusted the most and she who kept the keys to the safe and the food stores. He entrusted her with the coordination of the cooking for his huge political dinners. It was she who took charge of the servants and other wives as they cooked endless supplies of scented *pilau* rice, *gosht* and fresh hot *naan* bread in the *hooli* kitchen.

A row of servants and brothers would pass the piping-hot pots along from the kitchen to the entrance of the guest house next door, where my father entertained visitors. Women were not allowed to enter these exclusively male areas. In our culture, a married woman should not be seen by a man who is not her relative, so on these occasions my brothers, who would never otherwise be expected to do any housework, had to help.

At such dinners, my father required everything to be perfect. The rice had to be fluffy, and each grain had to separate perfectly. If it met his standards, he would smile with satisfaction at his good fortune and his most excellent choice of wife. If he found a few grains stuck together, his face would darken and he would politely excuse himself from his guests, walk into the kitchen and, without saying a word, grab my mother by the hair, wrench the metal ladle from her hands and beat her across the head with it. Her hands—already scarred and misshapen from previous beatings—would fly to her head in an attempt to protect herself. Sometimes she would be knocked unconscious, only to get up again and, ignoring the servants' frightened stares, rub hot ash into her scalp to stop the bleeding before again taking charge and ensuring that the grains fell apart perfectly in the next batch of rice.

She endured this because, in her world, beatings meant love. "If a man does not beat his wife then he does not love her," she explained to me. "He has expectations from me and he beats me only when I fail him." This may sound strange to modern ears, but it was what she truly believed. And this belief sustained her.

She was determined to carry out my father's wishes not only out of a sense of duty or fear but also out of love. She truly and utterly adored him.

So it was with sadness that my mother watched the wedding procession winding its way through the village on the day that wife number seven came home. She was standing on the terrace next to a servant woman who was grinding flour with a pestle in a giant stone mortar. Fighting back tears, my mother grabbed the pestle and ground it into the mortar stone furiously, even though, as the lady of the house, she would not normally take on this task.

But self-pity, even on this day, was not a luxury she was allowed. She was responsible for cooking the feast and had to ensure that the first meal his new bride took in Abdul Rahman's home would include the finest delicacies and treats befitting his status. If she didn't prepare a delicious banquet for her new love rival, he would be angry.

One part of the ceremony, however, was just for her. As head wife, she was to greet the party and place her fist firmly on top of the new bride's head to denote her own superiority and the latter's submission to her as a wife lower down the scale. She looked on as three women—the bride, her mother and her sister—were helped to dismount, once they were safely inside the *hooli* gates. They removed their burkas, and the beauty of the two young women was revealed for all to see. Both had long raven-black hair down to their waists. One stared directly at my mother with confident green eyes and pouty lips. My mother put her fist down firmly and calmly on the woman's head. The woman looked aghast, my father coughed and laughed and the other girl turned scarlet with embarrassment. My mother had picked the wrong woman, placing her fist on the sister's head. Her hands flew to her mouth in consternation, but it was too late; the wedding party had moved inside to begin the feast. Her one chance to show this young woman publicly just who was in charge of managing the house had passed.

Now, thirteen months later, my mother was giving birth in a remote mountain shack. Bereft at the loss of favour of the man she loved, she was alone and wretched. Three months earlier, the young wife had given birth to a son, a bouncing rosy-cheeked baby named Ennayat who had beautiful eyes as large as chocolate saucers. My mother hadn't wanted any more children and knew this one would be her last. For the entire pregnancy, she was sick, pale and exhausted, her body simply giving in to the strain of having borne so many children. Ennayat's mother, meanwhile, was more beautiful than ever, glowing with the joy of a first pregnancy, her breasts firm and her cheeks flushed.

Six months pregnant herself, my mother helped deliver Ennayat into the world. As his lungs filled with his first breath and he screamed his arrival into the world, Bibi jan held her hands to her stomach and prayed silently that she too would give birth to a boy, thus giving her a chance of winning back my father's favour. Girl children in our village culture were considered worthless. Even today, women pray for sons because only a son gives them status and keeps their husbands happy.

For thirty hours, my mother writhed in agony during my birth; semi-conscious by the time I was delivered, she had barely enough energy to express her dismay at the news I was a girl. When I was shown to her, she turned away, refusing to hold me. I was mottled blue and tiny—I could not have been more different from Ennayat, the bundle of health. My mother was on the verge of death after my birth. No one cared if the new girl child lived or died, so while they focused on saving my mother's life I was wrapped in cotton muslin swaddling cloth and placed outside in the baking sun.

I lay there for almost a day, screaming my little lungs out. No one came. They fully expected that nature would take its course and I would die. My tiny face was so badly burned by the sun that in adolescence I still bore the scars on my cheeks.

By the time they took pity on me and brought me back inside, my mother was feeling much better. Amazed that I had lived and horrified at the state of my burnt face, she gasped in horror as her initial coldness melted into maternal instinct. She took me in her arms and held me. When I finally stopped crying she began to weep silently, promising herself that no harm would ever come to me again. She knew that for some reason God had wanted me to live and that she should love me.

I don't know why God spared me that day. Or why he has spared me on the several occasions I could have died since then. But I do know he has a purpose for me. I also know he truly blessed me by making me Bibi jan's favourite child from that moment on, forging a permanently unbreakable bond between mother and daughter.

Dear Shuhra and Shaharzad,

Early in my life, I learned how difficult it is to be a girl child in Afghanistan. The first words a newborn daughter often hears are the commiserations given to her mother. "It's just a girl, a poor girl." That is not much of a welcome to the world.

Then, when a girl reaches school age, she does not know whether she will get permission to go to school. Will her family be brave or rich enough to send her? When a brother grows up, he will represent the family and his salary will help feed them, so everyone wants sons to be educated, but usually the only future for girls in our society is marriage. They make no financial contribution to the family, and so in many people's eyes there is little point in educating them.

When a girl reaches the age of twelve, relatives and neighbours may start to gossip about why she isn't married yet. "Has someone asked her for her hand?" "Is anyone ready to marry her?" If no proposals are in the offing, gossipmongers will mutter that it is because she is a bad girl.

If family members ignore this chatter and let the girl reach sixteen, the legal age for marriage, before finding a partner for her and if they allow her to marry someone of her choice or at the very least allow her to disagree with her parents' choice, then she stands a chance of experiencing some happiness in her life. If, however, the family is under financial pressure or swayed by gossip, they will marry off their daughter before she reaches the age of fifteen. The little girl who heard "just a girl" at her birth will become a mother herself; if she delivers a girl child, the first words her baby will hear will also be "just a girl." And so it goes on, generation after generation.

This was my beginning. "Just a girl" born of an illiterate woman.

"Just a girl" would have been my life story, and probably yours too. But the bravery of my mother, your grandmother, changed our path. She is the heroine of my dreams.

With love,
Your mother

TWO

Stories of Old

{ *1977* }

THE EARLY PART of my childhood was as golden as the mountain dawn—the light that tumbled directly from the sun across the Pamir mountain range and down through the valley onto the roofs of the mud houses in our village. My memories of that time are hazy, like images from a film. They are bathed in the colours of orange summer sun and white winter snow and suffused with the smells of the apple and plum trees outside our house and the scent of my mother's long, dark plaited hair, all lit brighter by her radiant smiles.

The Koof Valley, where we lived, is known as the Switzerland of Afghanistan. It is lush and fertile, banked with trees of rich greens and yellows—colours I have never seen anywhere else. Our house looked out onto a sparkling blue river, and pine and elm trees grew tall along the grassy banks that rose steeply into the mountains.

The noises I recall from my early childhood are of a donkey braying, the sound of hay swishing as it was cut, the trickling of river water and the peals of children laughing. Even today, my village sounds just the same. Koof remains the only place in the world where I can close my eyes and fall into blissful, peaceful sleep within seconds.

In front of our house was a garden, organized with great efficiency by my mother. We grew everything we needed: fruits of all kinds, peppers, olives, mulberries, peaches, apricots, apples and huge yellow pumpkins. We even cultivated silk for weaving carpets. My father took great delight in importing trees and seeds from abroad, and our garden housed one of the few black cherry trees in all of Afghanistan. I remember the day it arrived and the sense of importance and occasion as the seedling was planted.

During the warmer months, the women would come and sit among the mulberry trees for half an hour or so in the late afternoon—the only time of day they could relax. Each would bring a small dish of something to eat, and they would sit gossiping and chatting while the children played around them.

In those days, many villagers used to wear wooden shoes, because getting to Faizabad to buy conventional shoes was so difficult. An old man in the village used to make them; they looked like carved Venetian gondolas and were very strong. He would hammer nails into the base of the shoe so it would stick to the ice when the women went outside to fetch water in winter. My greatest dream was to own a pair of these shoes, though they were tough to wear and not made for children. When women came to visit, leaving their shoes at the door, I would put them on and go out to play. Once, I was wearing a beautiful embroidered dress a friend of my mother's had made for me. I wasn't supposed to go out in it, but I didn't want to take it off, so I put on some wooden shoes and went to play with my friends near the spring. Inevitably, I fell over in my big shoes, ripping the dress.

But my world began with the *hooli* kitchen, a mud-plastered room with three large wood-fired ovens at one end, a deep bread oven called a *tanur* in the centre and a tiny high window at the other end.

LIKE MOST Afghan village women of her generation, my mother spent more than half her life in the kitchen, sleeping, cooking and taking care of the little children. In this room, she reigned supreme.

The women baked bread three times a day, sometimes making as many as fifty or sixty loaves, and the room was always full of smoke

from the fires. Between batches, they had to prepare lunch and dinner. If my father had guests, the heat from the wood burning in all
four ovens became unbearable. On those occasions, we would all
feel excited, and I would boost my popularity by bringing friends
into the kitchen to eat the leftovers. Most of the villagers were much
poorer than our family, and the chance to taste strange delicacies
was too good to pass up. We children were never allowed anywhere
near the guest house, and if we ever thought to risk a peep inside,
a mere glance from one of my father's security men guarding the
doorway was enough to send us scattering for cover.

Away from the eyes of the men of the house, the kitchen was a
place of laughter and women's chatter, where children were guar-
anteed treats from the many pots of dried fruit and sweets lining the
shelves. On cold winter nights, after the bread was baked, we would
sit with our feet beside the dying embers of the *tanur,* a carpet over
our legs to keep us warm.

At night, we would unroll our mattresses onto the kitchen floor
and sleep there. The wives and daughters did not have their own
bedrooms, only their own mattresses. When the boy children were
smaller, they would also live and sleep in this female world. As they
grew older, the boys went on to share a bedroom. Mother would tell
us stories. First, she would recount tales close to home. She talked
to us openly about her marriage, how she had felt when she first met
my father and how hard it was for her to leave her childhood behind
to become a wife, with all the duties that entailed. Then she would
regale us with stories of faraway queens, kings and castles and warriors who gave everything for honour. She told us love stories and
tales about big wolves that made us scream in terror. I would listen
and look out the window at the moon and stars. I was certain I could
see the entire sky.

I had no idea the rest of the world lay beyond the big mountain
at the end of the valley and I didn't care. My mother loved me and I
loved her; we were inseparable. It was as if she somehow gathered up
all the love she had lost from my father in those later years and gave
it to me twice over. She had recovered from her initial disappointment at my being a girl after hearing a story recounted by my aunt

Gada, my father's eldest sister. Informing him of my birth upon his return to the village, my aunt had declared, "Abdul Rahman, your wife has given birth to a mouse, a tiny red mouse." He laughed and demanded to see me, the first time he'd ever asked to see a newborn girl child. Looking at my scarred face and the third-degree burns caused by the sun, he threw his head back and laughed uncharacteristically. "Don't worry, my sister," he told my aunt. "Her mother has good genes. And I know one day this little mouse will grow to be as beautiful as her mother."

When my mother heard this story, she cried tears of joy. To her, it was my father's way of telling her he still loved her and of reassuring her that she should not feel like a failure for providing him with a last daughter instead of a son. She told that story often. I must have heard it hundreds of times.

But by then my father was a distant man. In those days, politics in Afghanistan was becoming a very dangerous game. The regime had recently changed. Mohammed Dawoud Khan had removed Zahir Shah in a peaceful coup d'état while the king was abroad in 1973, declaring himself the first president of Afghanistan. He suspended the constitution and abolished the parliament.

Soon afterwards, my father was imprisoned for disobeying the president. He was vocal in his criticisms of the new regime, putting pressure on Dawoud to restore the previous constitution and parliament. Rumblings of political discontent were heard across the country. Unemployment was rising, social problems were on the increase and Afghanistan's neighbours, particularly Pakistan and the USSR, were once more beginning to play out their political strategies on our soil.

My father was mostly away in Kabul and was rarely home. When he was absent, our house was relaxed and children's laughter rang throughout the rooms. But when he was home, the women of our household hurried nervously along corridors, feverishly preparing meals for his guests and trying to keep the children silent so as not to disturb him.

My friends and I were generally happy when my father was home because we could be as naughty as we liked, filching chocolate from the kitchen stores safe in the knowledge that my mother was too preoccupied with him to stop us.

I have few real memories of my father. I remember him walking around, wearing a white *shalwar kameez* with a smart brown wool waistcoat on top and a sheepskin hat, his hands clasped firmly behind his back. The *hooli* had a long, flat roof, and in those days he would walk on it for hours on end. He would start pacing restlessly back and forth in the afternoon and carry on until evening without stopping—just walking and thinking, always in the same position with his hands behind his back.

I had a sense even then that my father was a great man. That whatever the stresses and troubles he brought home to us and however frightening the beatings, they were all due in part to the multiple pressures he was under: the pressure of maintaining a home and extended family as large as ours, the pressure of political life, the pressure of representing some of the poorest people in Afghanistan. He barely had any time to himself. When he was home, our guest house, a single-storey dwelling at the back of the *hooli*, was always full of visitors: some sought his advice or wisdom; others wanted him to resolve a family dispute; still others brought news of errant tribes or violence in the mountains; and some were simply needy and desperate for his help. His door was closed to none, and he had no time for light relief or relaxation. How, then, could he be blamed for demanding great things from his family?

Of course, I don't condone my father for beating my mother, but in those times it was the norm. In other ways, he was a good husband to her, as far as tradition would allow. Perhaps today I understand him more than I ever have because I understand his workload. I understand the pressure of political life, the feeling of never having any time alone, free from duty and the burden of responsibility. I think my mother understood too, and that was why she endured so much.

Under the sharia law system my father espoused, a man is supposed to treat all his wives equally, sharing himself without favour among them. I too believe in sharia justice. In theory, and in its purest form, it is a fair system based on Islamic ethical values. But affairs of the human heart do not follow theoretical principles, and in polygamous marriages such equality cannot exist. How could a man help it if his heart preferred some wives over others?

My father's suite of rooms was called the Paris suite and was decorated with hand-painted murals by an artist who had been brought especially from Kabul. The room had two windows looking out over an apricot garden, and in summertime a fresh apricot-scented breeze wafted into it. No modern air conditioning could ever compete with that delicate scent.

When he was home, a different wife would share his bed each night. The exception was his first wife, the Khalifa. In order to take more wives than the sharia-allowed maximum of four, my father had divorced two of his original wives and made his first wife what is known as a Khalifa. Under this agreement, a woman retains the title of wife and is cared for financially but loses the intimacy that comes with marriage and never sleeps with her husband again. I remember the sadness in this woman's eyes, the power and status that should have come from being first wife totally destroyed by her forced sexless status. Instead, my mother, the second wife, became head wife. The Khalifa never showed my mother any anger or disrespect, but I wonder if she too had felt devastated and hurt when my father first brought my mother home or when she was given the head wife status. How was it for the poor Khalifa to be usurped by a teenage girl?

I like to think my father looked forward most to the nights he spent with my mother. She recalled how after the necessary marital intimacies, they would lie there together until the early hours just talking. He would tell her stories of his work, sharing with her the strains of his political life in Kabul, and give instructions on how she was to handle the land, the latest wheat harvest or the sale of some cattle in his absence. She was so authoritative when he wasn't there that she earned the local nickname of Deputy Wakil sahib, or deputy representative boss.

The harder things were for him politically, the more he relied on my mother. As long as his home was harmonious and ran like clockwork, he could deal with all the machinations of parliament. It was she who ran the farms and business, who kept order in the house when he was away and who solved disputes between the wives. She needed a large amount of her own political skill to negotiate such matters.

Certain wives, particularly the third one, Niaz bibi, resented my mother's status and tried to turn my father against her. This woman was intelligent and frustrated by her life of drudgery, so it is easy to understand why she would be jealous of the few freedoms and small powers my mother enjoyed. But her attempts to win my father's favour in this way always failed, not only because my father didn't like to believe ill of my mother, but also because my mother could foresee a difficult situation arising and take evasive action.

Her strategy was kindness. She could have beaten the younger wives and made them do the hardest work, but instead she tried to create a happy house in which all the children were loved equally and where wives could work together as sisters and friends. When one of the younger wives was caught stealing from the household food store, a large locked cellar at the back of the kitchen, my mother didn't tell my father, knowing that he would give the miscreant a vicious beating. Instead she dealt with the matter in secret. This strategy slowly earned her the others' gratitude and loyalty.

Only one wife, number six, was chosen not for her political usefulness but for her practical homemaking skills. She was a stunningly beautiful Mongolian woman selected for her ability to weave the most beautiful rugs and carpets. She taught my mother this art, and I would watch as they sat together in comfortable silence for hours, their hands rhythmically spinning and threading the richly coloured yarn.

But my mother's best friend was wife number four, Khal bibi. She called my mother Apa, elder sister. Once, my mother became sick with a serious eye infection, and in the absence of doctors in the village a female elder suggested that if someone were to put their tongue on the eye and lick it clean each morning, the natural antibiotic in the saliva would heal it. Such was their closeness that Khal bibi volunteered without hesitation. Each day for eight weeks, she licked my mother's swollen, pus-filled eye until, just as the elderly lady had promised, it healed.

My mother did not have such a relationship with wife number three, Niaz bibi, with whom she could never get along. One day, as the women sat on the floor eating *naan* for breakfast, the two began quarrelling. Although I was only about eighteen months old, I somehow sensed the enmity between them. I toddled over to Niaz bibi and yanked down hard on her braids. She gasped with shock and began laughing, taking me in her arms and cuddling me. She and my mother forgot their quarrel and both laughed out loud. "This one is a very clever girl, Bibi jan, just like her mother," laughed her enemy, showering my face with kisses.

Even at that early age, I had a sense of injustice about the position of women in our culture. I remember the quiet despair of the wives who weren't loved or noticed by my father and the trials of those who were. I recall watching in horror once as my father chased my mother along the corridor and began beating her. I flew at him, kicking him and trying to protect her. He flung me aside with one arm.

Once, my father viciously tore out a chunk of her hair during a beating. Her brother visited a week later and, as was the custom, he spent time with the men of the family so my mother was unable to talk privately to him about what had happened. Before he left, my mother prepared his lunch for his long journey home across the mountains on horseback. She cleverly hid the locks of her torn hair in the wrapping. After a full morning's riding, he stopped in a clearing for lunch, unwrapped his food and found his sister's hair. He understood the message immediately, mounted his horse and galloped straight back to our house, challenging my father and telling my mother her family would ensure she would be granted a divorce if she wanted it.

This family support was unusual. Most women were encouraged not to complain about beatings and to endure them in silence. Girls who fled to a family home to escape a violent marriage would often be returned by their father to the very husband who had brutalized them. Beating was a normal part of marriage. Girls grew up knowing it had happened to their mothers and grandmothers and expecting it to happen to them.

But Bibi jan was close with her parents, whom she visited every year, and her brothers loved her. Her brother sat with her in the *hooli* garden and told her she was free to leave with him, that he would take her home right there and then if that was what she wanted. She was at a point of despair, constantly depressed and suffering splitting headaches and crippled hands from the beatings with the metal ladle. She was also tired of the humiliation that came with each new wife. She had had enough and seriously considered divorce.

But she knew that leaving my father would also mean losing her beloved children. In Afghanistan, as in most Islamic cultures, after divorce children stay with their fathers rather than their mothers. She asked to see her children and looked into their eyes and faces. She said nothing at the time but told me years later that she could see herself reflected in her children's eyes. She couldn't leave them. Giving up her children was too great a price to pay for bringing an end to her own sufferings.

So she told her brother that she would stay with her husband and children and that he should go home alone. Reluctantly, he got back onto his horse and left. I have no idea how my father reacted after the brother left. Did he beat my mother again for her insolence? Or was he tender, kind and regretful, realizing just how close he had come to losing the woman he needed? Probably both.

I REMEMBER my sisters being married off one by one. The first sister to be married had a trousseau brought especially from Saudi Arabia. Caskets of fine cloth and gold jewels befitting the wedding of a daughter of Abdul Rahman were brought to the *hooli* and unpacked with care as we all oohed and aahed. On that day, she became an important commodity, a jewel to be traded. It would be the only time in her life she was treated with such importance.

I also recall the day my sister-in-law arrived. She had been married to my elder brother at the age of twelve—the age my daughter Shaharzad is today. He was seventeen, and they were expected to begin a full sexual relationship immediately. It is unthinkable to me that my daughter should suffer a forced physical relationship at such a tender age. My sister-in-law was still such a child that my mother had to help her bathe and dress in the mornings. I wonder what my mother felt on seeing the injuries inflicted on this poor girl by her own son. Did she recoil in horror at the injustice of it all? Yet this was the life and the fate of women. A girl grew up expecting to get married as soon as a suitable suitor came along; not doing so brought shame on the entire family. So perhaps all my mother could do was try to comfort the girl, give her the lighter chores and know that just as the elder women had done, the girl would grow to accept her fate without complaint. It was a cultural conspiracy that bound them all together in silence and acquiescence. None of them could challenge or change it.

Yet without even being aware I was doing so, I broke boundaries and challenged these norms. This was partly because of my close friendship with Ennayat, the son of the seventh wife, who was born just a few months before me. Despite the initial rivalries surrounding our births, he and I were instant best friends, enjoying a special sibling love that has lasted to this day. He was naughty and mischievous, and I even more so. Knowing that as a girl I was more restricted, I was always challenging him into ever-greater naughtiness on our joint behalf. We were joined in our mischief by Muqim, my mother's son who had been born three years before me. We were the three little musketeers.

I was forever getting Ennayat into trouble. We would sneak into orchards and steal apples, or I would make him steal from my father's stores and distribute the stolen goods to my friends. I remember filling our shirts full of dried apricots from the kitchen one day, Ennayat encouraging me to get as many as possible. I tied my belt under the stash to hold it in. As we sneaked back across the garden in front of the wives who were preparing food on the terrace, the apricots began to drop out one by one. I was walking with my back to the wall, helplessly hoping they wouldn't see, when a large pile of apricots fell out onto the floor. I was mortified, and Ennayat was furious with me for failing in our mission. The women, however, just laughed at us both indulgently. Another of our favourite games was stealing cake and eating holes in it from the bottom up, then replacing it on the shelf so no one would notice—until, of course, it came to be eaten.

Recently, I asked Ennayat to recall what I was like at that age. He replied in a dryly humorous style typical of big brothers the world over, "You were ugly and very, very annoying."

Today, Ennayat and my other brothers are the most wonderful any girl could wish for. They support my political life, campaigning for me and protecting me when they can. But growing up, we all knew that they were boys and I was a girl. In our family, as in every other family in Koof, boys were the ones who really mattered. A boy's birthday was celebrated, but a girl's never was, and none of my sisters ever went to school. Girls were second best, and our fate was to stay at home until we married and left to join our husband's family.

Boy children also had power within the family hierarchy, and a brother's word or order was often more powerful than the word of a mother. When my mother went to the cellar stores, my brother Muqim would follow her and ask for sweets. She wouldn't give him many because such delicacies were usually reserved for guests. He'd get angry, stomp his feet and leave the room, but then my mother would take hold of my hand and, without looking at me, silently put some chocolates in my hand. If Muqim saw, he would be furious and tell my mother that if I ate them he would stop me from going out. As a boy, he had the power and authority to control what I did or did not do, despite whatever my mother said to the contrary. I hated the idea of not playing outside with my friends, so I would begrudgingly give him the sweets and run out to play.

I heard the word *dukhtarak* often and early in my life. It's a common derogatory term for a girl that roughly translates as "less than a girl." Instinctively, I never liked it. Once, when I was no more than five years old, one of my older cousins called me *dukhtarak* and ordered me to make him a cup of tea. I stood up in a room full of people, my hand on my hip, and replied, "Cousin, I will make your tea, but you will never call me that name again." Everyone in the room laughed uproariously.

I also heard it the only time my father ever spoke directly to me. He had organized a political rally in our garden and wanted to share some news reports with the gathering. He had placed large speakers in the trees, and he spoke into a microphone; it was the first time we small children had ever heard stereo sound. Curious, we sneaked up as close as we could without being seen so that we could listen. But I soon became bored and started to make noise. My father was talking when suddenly my squeals disturbed his flow. He stopped and turned directly towards us. He stared at me, and I froze for what felt like minutes. Then he shouted, "*Dukhtarak!* Girls! Go away, you girls!"

We ran as fast as our legs could carry us. I was so terrified of him after that, I didn't ever want to see my father again, petrified even weeks later that if he saw me he would be so angry that he would kill me.

In my childhood fantasies, little could I have imagined that it was he who would soon be killed and that my golden existence was about to come to a brutal end.

Dear Shuhra and Shaharzad,

I grew up in the 1970s and '80s. I know that seems a very long time ago to you. It was a time of great political change around the world and a time when the people of Afghanistan suffered from the Soviets and from the lawless commanders of the Mujahideen.

Those years were the beginning of disaster for the people of Afghanistan and for my childhood. When the Communist revolution started, I was three years old, an age when a child needs love, security and the warm bosom of home. But at that time, most of my friends' parents were talking about immigration to Pakistan and Iran, preparing for lives as refugees. Children listened as their parents whispered about things people had never seen before, equipment called tanks and helicopters.

We overheard terms like "invasion," "war" and "Mujahideen," but they were meaningless to us. Yet although children did not understand, they sensed something was wrong from the way their mothers clutched them close at night.

I am happy you have never experienced the uncertainty and fear of a time like this. No child should ever have to.

With love,
Your mother

THREE

A Terrible Loss

{ *1978* }

THE YEAR WAS 1978, and both the Mujahideen and the Russians were beginning to make their presence felt in Afghanistan. We were still in the Cold War, and the Soviet Union was keen to show its strength. It had an expansionist agenda at that time; Afghanistan lay between Moscow and the warm-water ports of Pakistan, where the USSR wanted to place its naval fleet. It therefore needed control of Afghanistan and was beginning to exert its influence to achieve that end. Eventually, it would invade the country.

In later years, Afghan fighters known as the Mujahideen would defeat the Russians and become heroes of the people. But for now, the Afghan public knew of the Mujahideen only as anti-government rebels who first made their presence felt in northern Badakhshan.

The regime in Kabul changed again. President Dawoud, who had taken power from the king and forced him into exile, did not last long. He and his entire family were assassinated in his palace, and Communist sympathizers Nur Muhammad Taraki and Hafizullah Amin took control, Taraki becoming the first Communist-backed president. However, just a few months later, he was killed by Amin on the orders of the Moscow government.

Amin took over the presidency. He is remembered as one of the cruellest presidents Afghanistan ever had, heading a terrifying Soviet-backed regime in which torture and arrests were commonplace. He attempted to do away with anyone—intellectuals, teachers and religious leaders—who opposed the government or dared say a word against it; they would be dragged from the house at night and either taken to the Puli Charkhi, Kabul's largest jail, where they faced interrogation and torture, or simply thrown into the river. In those days, Afghanistan's rivers swelled with the corpses of thousands of people, all murdered without reason or trial.

During this time, my father continued his work, trying to remain focused on helping Badakhshan even through these days of terror. He was still outspoken, despite the risk of torture or imprisonment. Perhaps the regime knew he was more useful to them alive than dead, and he was eventually ordered by the government to return to his province with the instruction to settle and silence the Mujahideen. Government officials made it clear that the penalty for failure would be his death.

A man of peace, my father was certain he could reason with the Mujahideen—who after all were fellow Afghans. He understood the political uncertainties of the time and the calls for social justice. These were men from his own province, Badakhshan, and he was convinced that he could calm their fears, listen to their complaints and offer to help them in exchange for their co-operation with the government.

But the Afghanistan my father thought he knew, and the values of patriotism, Islamic tradition and natural justice that he believed in so strongly, had already begun to disappear.

It was with a heavy heart that he arrived in Badakhshan on his mission. He had no love for the Amin regime and in truth did not know what was best for the people of Afghanistan. He gathered his provincial elders together in a *jirga*, a meeting of tribal leaders and elders, and told them what he had seen in Kabul: a government that killed with impunity, that prevented young people from being educated for fear they would turn into dissidents and that had created a system in which teachers and intellectuals lived in fear. Political opponents were simply crushed. After the promise of the heady years of Zahir Shah's reign—when Afghanistan had been seen as one of the world's fastest-developing countries, a thriving tourist destination with bustling ski resorts, a modern electric bus system and a business-led burgeoning democracy—it was devastating to witness the reality of Communist rule.

Some of the Afghans who had gone to the mountains to support the Mujahideen truly believed they were fighting for the future of Afghanistan. My father might have been a government servant, but he understood and respected the Mujahideen for their efforts. He asked the elders for their advice.

The *jirga* debated for hours. Some wanted to join the rebels, whereas others wanted government rule, for better or worse. In the end, local imperatives won the day. A man stood up to address the assembly in a clear voice. "Sir," he said, "we are already very poor and we cannot bear the burden of fighting. We should talk to the Mujahideen and bring them down from the mountains."

The group eventually agreed to go and talk to the rebels. My father's determination to bring fundamental changes to the lives of those he represented and his refusal to accept no for an answer were qualities that had endeared him to his supporters. So on this day when he asked hundreds of local elders from all over the province to go with him to talk to the Mujahideen on behalf of a new government regime no one respected, not one of them refused. They all went gladly.

This large group of elders led by my father set off on horseback to go to the rebels' camp. The beautiful Pamir mountain range is as high as it is treacherous. Fertile, lush valleys soon give way to rocks of different colours—blues, greens and orange ochres that change with the light—then to towering snow-covered peaks and plateaus. Even today there are few roads in Badakhshan, but then there were only donkey and horse tracks, some so narrow and steep that the only way to pass was to get off and walk behind your mount, hold onto its tail, close your eyes and pray the sure-footed beast didn't slip. To fall was certain death—you would plunge down the mountainside into the icy river below and be swept away by the rapids.

After a day and a half of solid riding, the men reached the highest point of the Pamir, which gives way to a wonderful natural plain—almost as high as the heavens. In winter, men from all over the province gather here to play *buzkashi*, the original form of the western game of polo. It is a game that tests the skills of both rider and horse, in which the players race to pick up a heavy cow carcass and place it into a goal area marked with a circle at the end of the pitch. In ancient times, the carcass was a dead prisoner. Games are fast and exciting, sometimes involving hundreds of riders and lasting for several days. It is a game as wild, dangerous and clever as the men who play it and it expresses the true essence of the Afghan warrior.

As my father rode, however, thoughts of the pleasures of a *buzkashi* game were far from his mind. He remained calm and composed, wearing his lambskin hat as always, mounted on his white horse at the head of the group. And then, all of a sudden, three men appeared in the middle of the road, aiming rifles at them.

One of them shouted, "So it is you, Wakil Abdul Rahman. I have waited a long time for this chance to kill you."

My father shouted back in a cool voice, "Please listen to me. The government of Afghanistan is strong. You cannot defeat it. I come here to ask you to work with it, to stand together and to co-operate with us. I will listen to your needs and I will take them to parliament." The man simply laughed and fired a shot. Other shots rang out from behind the mountains. Pandemonium ensued. The village men, who were mostly unarmed, ran for their lives.

My father's horse was hit. As the animal reared up in pain, my father lost his stirrup footing and was dragged along as his mount galloped away. The wounded horse headed for a small river that ran along the edge of the *buzkashi* pitch. Some of the younger men tried to follow my father, but he shouted at them to flee and save themselves. "I'm an elder," he yelled as he was pulled along the ground. "They will talk to me, but they will kill you. Just go."

The Mujahideen gave chase and caught up with my father. They captured him and held him hostage for two days. I don't know if they gave him an opportunity to talk, listened to his reasoning and considered his offers or if they beat and humiliated him. All I know is that two days later they executed him with a bullet straight through the head.

News of his death reached the village quickly. Despite the remoteness of the region, news has always travelled fast in a well-developed system of urgent messages being relayed from hamlet to hamlet along the way. Some of the men who had accompanied my father had already arrived home and reported the shooting of his horse. In Islamic rite, a body must be buried within twenty-four hours, facing Mecca. My family could not bear the idea of my father's body being left alone on the mountainside without proper burial. He had to be brought back. But the Mujahideen sent word to warn us that they would kill anyone who attempted to retrieve the body. No man wanted to be shot and killed himself while bringing home a dead body.

So it fell to a woman to show bravery. My aunt Gada gathered her long skirts and put on her burka, announcing to the shocked male gathering that she would go to retrieve the body of Wakil Abdul Rahman. As she strode out of the room and straight up the path to the mountains, her husband and one of my father's cousins had little choice but to follow her.

After walking for thirteen hours, they found him; his body had been dumped halfway between the village and the rebel camp.

I was three and a half years old. I remember clearly the sadness of the day he was shot, hearing both men and women weeping and feeling alarmed by the fear and confusion in the village. I lay awake that night listening, until at around 2 A.M. I heard my aunt's voice ringing out loud and clear as she approached the village. She was carrying my father's wooden staff and tapping it on the ground.

"Wakil Abdul Rahman is here. Get out of your beds. Come to greet him. He is here. We have brought him. Wakil Abdul Rahman is here."

I leapt out of bed thinking, "He's alive, my father's alive."

Everything was going to be all right. Father was here. He would know what to do. He would restore order and stop everyone's tears.

I ran into the street barefoot and stopped dead in my tracks at the sight of my mother weeping and clutching at her clothes in horror. I darted past her and saw my father's dead body. The top part of his skull, where he had been shot, was missing.

I began to cry. I didn't yet fully understand the enormity of what had happened, but I understood enough to know that our life would never be the same.

The body was brought into the *hooli* and laid out in the Paris suite before burial. My mother went to see the body and prepare it for the funeral the next day. Of all the wives, only she went into that room to say her final farewell to him. In the room where I and her other children were conceived and where husband and wife had, in all too rare moments, lain and talked, creating their own private world together, she endured this task, as she had endured all the other tasks in her harsh life, with dignity and duty. She did not scream or wail but quietly washed and prepared the body in accordance with God's wishes. In his death, just as in his life, she did not fail my father.

In the morning, thousands of local people poured into Koof to say their last goodbyes to him. Their sadness and fear for their own futures created an atmosphere so heavy it felt like the very sky was falling down on our heads.

Grey-haired old men with beards, white turbans and green coats sat in the garden crying like babies. My father was buried on a peak behind the *hooli*, facing Mecca and the valley of Koof he so loved.

For the villagers, the loss of the man who had championed their causes and supported their needs was a turning point in their lives. It also marked the beginning of the political upheaval that was about to become a full-blown war in Afghanistan.

For my family, the loss of my father meant the loss of everything: our life, our wealth, our figurehead, our entire reason for being.

Dear Shuhra and Shaharzad,

When I was a little child, I didn't know the words "war," "rocket," "wounded," "killing," "rape." Words that sadly all Afghan children are familiar with today.

Until the age of four, I knew only happy words.

I long for those summer nights when we would all sleep on the big flat roof of my uncle's house. His house was just next door to the hooli, and its roof had the best view of the valley so the whole family liked to gather there. My mother, my uncle's wives and the woman I called "my little mother"—my father's fourth wife and my mother's best friend—would sit and tell well-worn tales until late into the night.

We children would sit quietly enchanted under the blue sky or the bright yellow moon listening to these sweet stories. We never closed the door at night, and there were no security men with guns like there are today. There were no thieves or other dangers to worry about.

In those happy times and with everyone's love surrounding me, I little realized that my life had begun with my mother's degradation and sorrow at my birth and that I had been put out in the blazing sun to die.

I never felt that my birth had been a mistake. I felt only that I was loved.

But this happy life did not last for long. I had to grow up fast. My father's murder was just the first of many tragedies and deaths that would befall our family. My childhood ended when we were forced to leave those beautiful gardens of Koof, with their cold spring water and shady trees, to become homeless refugees in our own country.

   The only thing that did not change was the constant smile of my mother, your grandmother.

With love,
Your mother

FOUR

A New Start

{ *1979–1990* }

ALTHOUGH SHE GRIEVED deeply for the man she loved, my father's death was in many ways the making of my mother.

In those first few months, her natural leadership ability came to the fore. It was she who took control of the family, organizing resources and deciding the fate of children. Her years as my father's right hand, her efficient home management and her ability to foster peace within our extended family enabled her to lead our family out of this dark period. Her priorities were keeping the children together and safe. She received many offers of marriage, but for the same reason she had once refused to divorce my father she rejected all suitors. She would not risk losing her children.

In our culture, a stepfather is not obliged to take on children from a previous marriage, as the tragic experience of Ennayat's mother demonstrated. Still young and somewhat flighty after my father's death, she married a handsome young man who had worked for my father as a shepherd guarding the family cattle. He had recently returned from Iran, where he had gone to find work, bringing back exciting consumer goods that could not be found in our remote village, such as a tape recorder. He wooed her with his tales of sophisticated life in Iran and with his newfangled machinery.

Aside from Ennayat, my father's seventh wife had borne him three other children: a girl, Nazi, and two boys, Hedayat and Safiullah. She insisted on taking the children with her to her new home, but the new husband refused to feed or clothe them. When my mother, who was sympathetic to her, visited a few weeks later, she found Ennayat, Nazi and Hedayat crying outside in the yard. They were not allowed into the warmth of the house and were hungry and dirty. She immediately took them home with her.

But the young woman refused to give up her baby, Safiullah, and my mother left without him, something she regretted forever because a few days later he became feverish and was left to die without food or comfort. We heard that he cried alone for hours, his little face covered with flies, while this man would not allow his mother to even pick him up. He died a lonely, horrible death. Ennayat has never gotten over it and named his first-born son Safiullah in his brother's memory.

Khal bibi, who had been so dear to my mother, was luckier. She married a local leader, a kindly man who had no children of his own. Almost unheard of in our culture, he raised her two sons as though they were his, even leaving them his property when he died.

Niaz bibi, the wife who didn't get on with my mother, married a teacher and remained in Koof. Despite the disagreements between Niaz bibi and my mother, years later when I was campaigning for parliament this man helped me enormously, arranging my transport and accompanying me on the campaign trail. The extended family structure is hard for people in the western world to understand, but in my view it is a wonderful thing. Such ties transcend generations, petty arguments and geography. Family is family.

Zulmaishah, the Khalifa's child and my father's eldest son, inherited the *hooli*. He was later killed, and the second-eldest son, Nadir, the son of my fifth mother—one of the wives my father divorced—inherited it. He still lives in it to this day.

WE DID not have much time to grieve in the first days and weeks after my father was killed. The world beyond the mountains was looming ever closer, and the rapidly disintegrating political situation was about to come crashing down on us.

A few days after his death, the commanders who had killed my father came looking for us. We ran up to the fields where our cattle were kept and hid behind a large rock ledge, watching as they looted the house, stealing all they could carry: the radio, the furniture, the pots and pans.

A few weeks later, we were all sleeping on the roof of my uncle's house when they came back in the middle of the night. They woke us up with blows from their rifles, yelling and screaming, demanding to know where Abdul Rahman's sons were. My brother Muqim was just seven years old, but we knew that they would kill him if they found him. Somehow my mother managed to pass him to a cousin on the next roof, who hid him underneath her skirt. Unlike other women in some parts of Afghanistan where the *shalwar kameez* is the norm, village women in Badakhshan traditionally wear loose pantaloons covered by a long, full skirt. That skirt saved my brother's life that night.

The Mujahideen grabbed my elder sister Maryam and my sister-in-law, my elder brother's wife. Both girls had just turned sixteen. The rebels started to beat them. My uncle tried to stop them but was beaten back. They took the girls off the roof and down towards the *hooli,* my uncles and male cousins screaming at them that this was against Islam. It was *haram,* forbidden, for any Muslim to touch a woman who is not his blood relative or his wife.

We were forced to watch from the roof as they beat the girls all night long, pistol whipping them and hitting them with rifle butts, demanding again and again to be shown where the weapons were hidden. No one claimed to know. My mother was grim-faced and white as a sheet, but she said nothing. We all watched as they put the bayonet of the gun to my sister's chest and pressed it in until she began to bleed. We had a guard dog called Chamber who was chained near the gate of the *hooli.* Desperate to protect his family, he tugged at his chains until they broke and rushed towards the men, barking and snarling. They simply turned and shot the poor dog dead.

The men beat the two girls until dawn, when the call to prayer reverberated over the mountain. They left then—presumably to go and pray.

Two days later, they came again and threatened to kill us all. This time they forced Nadir, then a teenager, to show them where the guns were. My mother had known all along and had watched silently as her daughter and daughter-in-law were beaten without betraying the whereabouts of the weapons. She knew that with the guns gone, we would have no means to protect ourselves. They had taken everything we had, and the next time they came they would murder us.

The men of the village were so horrified by what had happened to our girls that they sent word to the Mujahideen that if they came back the villagers would take up shovels, pickaxes, sticks, whatever they had, to protect their women. The Mujahideen agreed not to terrorize the village, but they wanted the family of Abdul Rahman dead. Their commander gave permission for his men to execute us. For the second time in my short life, I would stare death in the face and win.

They came early the following morning. By now, the Khalifa and her children had moved to Khawhan, another village where my father owned a big house and more land that needed guarding, so my mother was the only wife left in the *hooli*. Fortunately, my brothers Ennayat and Muqim were out playing and were able to hide in neighbouring houses. My mother grabbed me, and the two of us ran into the cattle barn. Our neighbours frantically started to pile up pieces of dung on top of us to give us cover. I remember the smell and the choking, bitter taste of the dung. It felt like I was being buried alive. I clung tightly to my mother's hand, too afraid to cough for fear of being heard. We remained like that for hours, silent and terrified, the only comfort coming from the sensation of my mother's fingers wrapped around mine. We could hear them searching for us, and at one point they came right up to our hiding place. If they had prodded the dung pile, it would have tumbled down to reveal us. For reasons only God knows, they did not.

After they finally left, we came out of our hiding place to find the world had turned to terror. My mother didn't waste time collecting our clothes; she grabbed me, my two brothers and my elder sister, and we ran—through the garden, into the hay fields and onto the river banks. We were leaving all we had behind and we didn't dare even to glance back.

It was as though my mother's life was disintegrating with each step she took. All the beatings, all the pain, all the years of drudgery and work had been to build a home and a life. A life that ended as we ran for our very survival along the river bank.

As we expected, the men had returned to search again and saw us running away. They started to give chase. They were stronger and faster than we were. I was getting tired and began to stumble, slowing the others down. My sister started to scream at my mother to throw me into the river to save the others: "If you don't throw her they'll catch us and we'll all die. Just throw her in."

She almost did. My mother picked me up and lifted me into the air as if to throw me but then looked into my eyes and recalled her promise at my birth that no more harm would ever come to me. From somewhere deep inside, she gathered reserves of strength, and instead of throwing me to my death she put me on her back, where I clung on as she ran with me. We were behind the others, and I could hear the men's footsteps getting closer. I thought that at any second they would be upon us, tear me from my mother's back and kill me. If I shut my eyes, I can still feel the clammy, cold, terrible fear of that moment.

Then suddenly, we saw a Russian soldier.

We had reached the other side of the valley, which was government-controlled land. Our would-be assassins turned and ran back, and we collapsed with exhaustion and relief. My mother started to weep.

That Russian was the first of many I would see in the following years. They were foreign invaders on Afghan land, and although they would bring education and development in some areas they would also commit many atrocities against innocent Afghans. This man, though, was kind to me. Tall and blond, handsome in his uniform, he called me over to him. Hesitantly, I walked towards him. He handed me a bag of sugar, and I ran to give it to my mother. That was the first time my mother had ever taken charity from a stranger, but it was not to be the last.

At first, the five of us stayed near the river in the home of a teacher named Rahmullah. He was one of the kindest people I had ever met, with warm eyes that crinkled when he smiled and a neat grey beard. His family was poor and couldn't really afford the extra mouths to feed, but as one of my father's political supporters he felt honoured to give the Wakil's family the hospitality of his simple two-room home.

His garden backed directly onto the river, and I remember splashing about happily with his daughters. The relationship with his family would endure. Years later, Rahmullah came to me for support when his daughter needed help escaping a forced marriage. The family had arranged the match when she was a child, but the man in question had grown up to be notoriously violent and the girl wanted to refuse him. The man's family insisted that the match go ahead, but Rahmullah supported his daughter's right to refuse. I negotiated with the two families, eventually getting the other side to agree to break the engagement. The girl was then free to follow her dream and train to be a teacher like her father. In gratitude, Rahmullah gave me all the help he could in my political campaigns. When I visit the area today, I love nothing more than to share a simple lunch of rice and chicken by the river with this warm and loving family.

After staying with them for two weeks, my mother was restless, confused about what to do and where to go. We heard that our house had been burned and my sister and sister-in-law killed. Thankfully, the news was not accurate; the girls had survived.

My two elder brothers, Jamalshah, a student, and Mirshakay, a police chief, had moved to the provincial capital of Faizabad before the attacks began. When news of what had happened to us finally reached the town, they chartered a flight to pick us all up.

My mother sobbed with relief as the helicopter landed. It was the first time I had ever flown, and I remember running ahead of the two boys and my big sister. Inside the helicopter were two large wooden chairs. I snuggled up in one and my mother and sister sat in the other. I remember smiling smugly at Ennayat and Muqim because I had a chair and they did not.

Mirshakay had rented a house for us in Faizabad. He couldn't afford much on his policeman's salary; it was a two-room mud shack. Local people gave my mother basic kitchen equipment. The fancy imported china on which she had served meals in the *hooli* was a thing of the past. She joked that we were living in a doll's house because it was so tiny, but she did her best to turn it into a home for us by putting hangings and tapestries on the wall to brighten it up.

By now I was seven. I still looked like a typical village girl, dirty hair and face, baggy *kameez* trousers, a long scarf that trailed in the mud and a pair of red wellington boots. I was out of place in the big town.

From the doll's house, I watched young girls go to school. They looked so smart and bright, and I yearned to be like them. No girl child in my family had ever been educated, because my father had not seen the need. But he was no longer here. So I asked my mother if I could go to school. She looked at me for what felt like hours before finally beaming a big smile at me. "Yes, Fawzia jan, you can."

Everyone else was against it, particularly my elder brothers. But my mother stood her ground. I was to go with Muqim to the school the next day and ask permission to join. We entered the headmaster's office. It was smart and clean with padded chairs, and I felt tiny and very grubby, my nose running and my face covered with dirty marks. Suddenly embarrassed, I took my scarf and wiped a large trail of snot from my nose with it.

The headmaster frowned and peered at me. How was a dirty little village girl here in Faizabad asking to be educated? "Who are your people?" he asked me. When I answered haughtily that I was the daughter of Wakil Abdul Rahman, his eyebrows shot up in surprise. How our family had tumbled down the social scale since my father's death! The kindly man said that I was admitted to the school and could start the next day. I remember running home to tell my mother, my scarf trailing in the mud and tripping me up. My little heart was so full of excitement that I forgot my father's death, the loss of our home and our life of poverty. I, Fawzia Koofi, was going to school!

I WAS so determined to make the most of every moment at Kockcha school that it didn't take me long to catch up with the other girls; soon I was regularly achieving second or first position in class. Our education was fairly basic: we had general studies for half the day and then studied the Holy Koran at the local mosque with the Mullah Imam for the other half. My mother, who was totally illiterate, was very interested in Koranic studies.

At night I slept with my brother Muqim in our mother's bed. Our routine was always the same. She would ask us what we had studied, and we had to tell her what we could remember and recite the Koran to her while she made verbal corrections. It was her way of being involved in our education and she was passionate about it.

By the time I got to Pamir high school, the first high school in Faizabad, I was a confident child. I cut my hair short to look like the other girls. My brothers were furious, but again my mother calmed them down and encouraged me in my newfound confidence and progress.

Sometimes we had access to television, and I learned about Margaret Thatcher in the U.K. and Indira Gandhi in India; both women remain political heroines of mine to this day. I would watch them with my mouth open and think to myself: how is it possible for a woman to stand in front of all those people, and where does she find the power to speak to them? How can a simple woman lead a nation?

Sometimes my friends and I would go up onto the roof of our school and play. Slowly, my horizons were broadening. Just as I used to stand in the kitchen of the *hooli* when I was a toddler, looking up at the sky and thinking my whole existence was contained there, I now stared down at the city streets surrounding the school. I had moved on to believe that the whole sky stood on the mountains around Faizabad and that all the world, my world, consisted of that city and the surrounding areas.

I was extremely happy there, but when I was eleven my brother Jamalshah was promoted and posted to Kabul. We were to go with him. I think the day we moved was one of the most exciting days of my life. Not only was I thrilled to be moving to the exciting capital city, a place I had only seen pictures of on TV, but I was also transferring to a big high school there. I was so excited as we drove through the city streets for the first time that I thought my heart might burst with joy.

Kabul was exactly as I had dreamed it would be: exciting and loud. I marvelled at the yellow taxicabs with black stripes down the sides and gazed in wonder at the blue Millie buses with female drivers in their smart blue miniskirt uniforms. (In those days Kabul had the world's only electric bus system, called the Millie bus; the glamorous female drivers were nicknamed Millies.) I loved the glitzy shops with all the latest fashions on display in the windows and the smell of delicious barbecued meat floating from the hundreds of restaurants. The city entranced me and embraced me, and I loved it back with all my heart. I still love it today as much as I did then.

Those three years we stayed in Kabul were some of the happiest of my childhood. My mother loved the city too. To her, shopping in the big bazaars was a wonderful, exciting adventure. It may not sound like much, but this was an independence she could never have dreamed of when she was married to my father. I too enjoyed undreamed-of liberty. I experimented with fashion and talked about poetry and literature with my friends. We would walk home from school along tree-lined boulevards, carrying our school books with pride.

These new school friends seemed to me extremely sophisticated and glamorous. Their families had houses with swimming pools, their mothers were chic with bobbed hairstyles and their fathers were indulgent and kind, trailing the faint scent of aftershave and Scotch whisky behind them. Some of the girls even wore makeup and nail varnish. My brothers banned me from using cosmetics, but one day I put some on at a friend's house, also borrowing some long socks and a short skirt. My friend and I were casually sauntering along the road, delighted with our sophisticated appearance, when Jamalshah drove past. He saw me and slowed down, staring out of the open window. With no time to hide, I turned and faced the wall. My thinking was, ostrich-like, that if I couldn't see him, he couldn't see me. But of course he did. And he was waiting for me when I got home. When he made as if to beat me, I ran away to hide. I heard him bellowing with laughter, calling my mother to tell her the tale. She laughed too, and shamefaced I quietly sneaked back in for dinner.

Those days in Kabul were carefree and light. Once again, however, the wider world was about to collide violently with my safe little world.

Dear Shuhra and Shaharzad,

When I was young, I felt like my life changed all the time. Each time we found a safe place to live or a moment of calm, the war forced change back upon us.

I hated change in those days. All I wanted was to stay in one place, in one home, and to go to school. I had big dreams, but I also wanted a contented life. I want the same for you. I want you to fly free and find your dreams, but I also want you to have a happy home, a husband who loves you and one day the joy of having children of your own.

In your short lives, you've had to experience more changes than I would have wished for you. Tolerating a bad situation is often easier than having changes forced upon us. But sometimes I worry that I have asked you to tolerate too much: my long absences, your fears that I will be killed and that you will be left motherless.

Sometimes tolerating something is the wrong approach. All great leaders have shared the ability to adapt and start anew. Change isn't always our enemy, and you must learn to accept it as a necessary part of life. If we make a friend of change and welcome it in, then it may choose to treat us less painfully the next time it comes to call.

With love,
Your mother

· · FIVE · ·

A Village Girl Again

{ *1991–1992* }

IT WAS THE beginning of the 1990s. Apartheid in South Africa had ended, the Berlin Wall had come down and the great Soviet Empire was dismantling. The Cold War was reaching its final years.

The Mujahideen fighters were seasoned veterans by now. They had fought a war of attrition against the Russian invaders, and in 1989 they succeeded in sending the Soviet army back to Moscow. Crowds cheered and clapped as the Red Army was forced to make a humiliating retreat. The rebels' morale had never been higher, and many people saw them as heroes. The most popular of them all was Ahmad Shah Massoud, the man known as the "lion of the Panjshir." He was seen as the most brilliant of all the Mujahideen leaders and the strategist behind the Russian defeat. His image is still found on posters all over Afghanistan.

Now, with the Red Army gone, the fighters were eager to seize the full power of government. They sent their armies sweeping towards Kabul. The Mujahideen resented what they saw as a Communist puppet government, which still had very close links to Moscow even though there was no longer a Russian military presence. The government at the time was headed by President Najibullah, a leader who did bring some economic progress and development but who would always be unpopular for having allowed the Russian military on Afghan soil. For three years, the Afghan army remained under his control and fought to keep the Mujahideen at bay, but eventually it was overwhelmed and Najibullah's government collapsed.

People hoped this would bring stability and with it a new, purely Afghan government. But almost immediately after defeating the government, the Mujahideen began to fight among themselves. With the common enemy defeated, simmering ethnic tensions rose to the surface. Although they were all Afghans, these generals spoke different languages and had different cultural beliefs depending on what part of Afghanistan they came from. They could not agree on how to share power. These battles and power struggles between different commanders would eventually turn into the Afghan civil war, a bloody, brutal war that lasted well over a decade.

I WAS sixteen years old when I heard on the radio that President Najibullah had been arrested as he tried to flee Afghanistan. We were all shocked by what was happening and very worried for our country.

We were still living in Kabul, where I went to high school, but the week it happened we had been visiting our home province of Badakhshan, staying with relatives in Faizabad on an extended holiday.

The day after the report of the president's arrest, we heard shooting coming from the mountains above Faizabad. The Afghan army had set up positions on one side of the mountains that encircled the city, while the Mujahideen had dug in on the other. The two sides exchanged fire with rifles and machine guns and occasionally artillery. It seemed to me that the Mujahideen were firing a lot more than the army, which didn't have as many guns or as much ammunition as its enemy.

The army soldiers appeared to be only defending their positions and weren't offering much resistance. Large numbers of Afghan soldiers had already deserted. Many were unwilling to fight their countrymen, and the soldiers knew exactly what the Mujahideen were capable of doing to any Russian soldiers they had caught during earlier battles: torturing and killing them. The torture became more gruesomely creative as time went on. Sometimes they burned people alive. Other times they would ask a prisoner his age and then nail that number of nails into his skull. Still other times they would cut a prisoner's head off and pour boiling oil into the corpse. When the hot oil encountered the nerve endings, the decapitated body moved around for a few seconds as if it were dancing. This form of torture was aptly called the "dead man's dance."

The Afghan army knew that it was the new enemy and couldn't expect any more mercy than the Russians had. Many soldiers simply slipped off their uniforms and returned to normal civilian life.

After two days of fighting, the Mujahideen were declared the new government. Peace talks for the surrender and handover of power had already started at a conference in Geneva two years earlier, in 1989. So when the government in Kabul collapsed, few were surprised. Suddenly Faizabad was full of Mujahideen fighters who had come down from their mountain positions. I remember watching them, thinking how interesting and grizzled their faces looked. These were men who had been living in mountain camps, subsisting on scarce rations and fighting almost daily battles for several years. In my mind, soldiers wore smart uniforms, so it was very strange to see these casually dressed men in jeans and sneakers.

I wondered how some of them could ever readapt to civilian and civilized life. And I was not alone in that thought. The government offices were suddenly full of these men, and they terrified the locals; many schools shut their doors because parents refused to send their daughters, fearing they might be raped by these ex-fighters who now stalked the city streets.

But overall, most people in Afghanistan were happy that the Russians were gone and still hoped that the Mujahideen would settle their disputes and form a decent government.

These political changes marked a very depressing period in my life. I was just a teenager; if I wanted to travel around the city, I had to wear a burka for the first time in my life. The Mujahideen were not religious fundamentalists and did not impose the wearing of the burka, but wearing it was more a question of safety. With so many male ex-fighters around, men who might not have seen a woman for years, it just was not a good idea for a young girl to show off her beauty in public.

In the old days, wearing a burka was a sign of nobility, but it also had a practical use. It was designed to protect a woman from the harsh elements, the burning sun, dusty sand and fierce winds.

I know that many people in the West today see the burka as a sign of female oppression and religious fundamentalism. But I don't see it that way.

I want the right to wear what I think is best, but within the confines of Islam. Covering the hair with a head scarf and wearing a long loose tunic that covers one's arms, chest and bottom is enough to satisfy the Islamic rule of being modest before God. Anyone who says a woman must cover her entire face to be truly Islamic is wrong. A burka is definitely not an Islamic requirement but is usually worn because of cultural or societal reasons.

I am also aware that in some western countries, wearing a face-covering burka has become a political issue, with certain politicians and leaders wanting to ban it by law. While I believe that all governments have a right to determine the laws and culture of their own countries, I also believe in freedom of choice, and I think western governments should let Muslim women wear what they want.

One day my mother, sister and I got dressed up in our nicest clothes for a party at my aunt's house. I was wearing makeup and was very pleased with how I looked, and, unusually for me, I even felt rather beautiful. Before the arrival of the Mujahideen, I would have just put a head scarf on to cover my hair before stepping outside. But now my mother insisted that I wear a burka that she had borrowed for me from a neighbour. I was furious. I had never worn a burka in my life, and here I was in my nicest clothes, with my hair and makeup done for a party, and she wanted me to cover myself in a heavy blue sack.

I refused, and we got into a terrible argument. My mother pleaded, cajoled and threatened me, insisting that it was for my own protection. She argued that the soldiers could not be trusted if they saw me uncovered and that I should hide myself to avoid unwanted trouble. I was crying, which only made me angrier because it ruined my makeup. In a moment of teenage rebellion, I decided that if I had to wear a burka, I wouldn't go to my aunt's at all. I sat on the floor with my arms folded, refusing to budge. Eventually, my mother talked me round. I did want to go to the party, and since I had spent so long getting ready it would be a shame not to. And so I begrudgingly pulled the burka over my head and reluctantly took my first steps onto the streets of Faizabad and this strange new world.

Peering through the tiny blue mesh eye slot, I felt as though everything was closing in on me. The mountains seemed to be perched on my shoulders, as if the world had somehow grown both much larger and much smaller at the same time. My breathing was loud and hot inside the hood, and I felt claustrophobic, like I was being buried alive—smothered beneath the heavy nylon cloth. In that moment, I felt something less than human. My confidence evaporated. I became tiny and insignificant and helpless, as if the simple act of donning the burka had shut all the doors in my life I had worked so hard to open. School, pretty clothes, makeup, parties—all of these things meant nothing to me now.

I'd grown up seeing my mother wear the burka, but I felt as though it was merely something that belonged to her generation, a cultural tradition that was slowly dying out. I had never felt any need nor had I been asked by my family to conform to it. I saw myself as part of a new generation of Afghan women, and the traditions of the burka did not represent my ambitions for myself or for my country. Unlike my mother, I had an education, and I was eager to expand upon it. I had opportunities and freedoms. One of them was the freedom to choose whether or not to wear a burka—and I chose not to.

It wasn't that I had, or have, a particular problem with burkas. They are traditional and can offer women some degree of protection in our society. Women all over the world must occasionally deal with unwanted attention from men, and for some women wearing a burka can be a way of avoiding that. What I object to is people imposing their decisions about what a woman should wear. I hated it when the Taliban government made the wearing of the burka law. How would women in the West react to a government policy that forced them to wear miniskirts from the onset of puberty? Islamic and cultural ideals of modesty are strong in Afghan society, but they are not so strong that a woman must, by virtue of her gender, be hidden beneath a nylon sack.

When we got to my aunt's house, I was relieved to get the burka off. The experience had left me feeling shocked and scared about what my life and my country were turning into. I couldn't enjoy the party and instead kept to myself, reliving the horrible experience of the walk, suffocating beneath the tiny walls of my portable cell. All the while, I plotted how best to get home—how I would dash back hoping to avoid anybody I knew. I wasn't ready to admit to myself, let alone anybody else, that a burka had become part of my life.

I MISSED Kabul and my school and friends there. But Kabul airport had now been closed by the Mujahideen. Our sense of isolation from the capital started to become very real. I was extremely worried about what was happening there. Although they were now the legitimate government, the Mujahideen were fighting each other; various generals had taken control of different ministries, and although it wasn't yet all-out civil war the news from Kabul was that things were quickly descending into chaos. I was particularly concerned that my school, if it hadn't already been destroyed in the fighting, might be closed and I would never be able to return to my studies.

We listened closely to the radio for any scrap of news. It was hard to know what to believe. The Mujahideen government had been smart enough to seize the radio and television stations. The announcers assured us that all was well and calm, but we knew we were watching and listening to propaganda. My mother and I listened as a radio announcer told us the schools were open and girls were able to attend. But in reality, parents were reluctant to send their daughters to class because they didn't think it was safe.

And I could see the changes on television. The beautiful, intelligent female news presenters suddenly disappeared from the screens.

In their places, dowdy old women in scarves stumbled their way through the news.

Afghanistan had had some highly respected women presenting the evening news. They were smart and glamorous and executed their jobs with utter professionalism. They were important role models for me and girls like me. I loved following their changing hairstyles as much as I loved listening to them report the international news. They were living proof that Afghan women could be attractive, educated and successful. But their sudden disappearance from the screens made me very worried.

I went to my mother in tears one day, upset, scared and frustrated by all that was happening. She just listened to me as I poured my heart out. When I finished, she announced that we would find temporary admission to a school in Faizabad.

I missed Kabul and the heady glamour of my friends' houses terribly. But I was pleased to be back at school, even though the school in Faizabad—which had once seemed so large and overwhelming— now seemed tiny and parochial.

I was stuck with the burka, though. I began to get used to the feeling of being enclosed, but I couldn't get used to the heat. There was no bus service in Faizabad, so I would walk to school in the sun, the sweat running down my body. I sweated so badly that my skin developed black spots from the perspiration and lack of air.

Despite my discomfort, I made lots of friends. I was enjoying being back in the classroom and the opportunities that came with it. My teachers invited me to take part in some gardening classes after school, where we could learn about plants, propagation and soil care. This was Badakhshan, where despite the farming culture even today the understanding of biology and farming science is very basic. This class interested me, but my mother wouldn't let me continue with it. Even with my burka, she was scared that her teenage daughter might attract the roaming eye of a Mujahideen fighter. Every minute I was outside the house was another minute that might lead to an unwelcome marriage proposal—and a Mujahideen marriage proposal is not one you turn down without serious consequences. To do so would almost certainly invite them to take what they wanted by force. As far as my mother was concerned, going to school was an essential risk she would allow me to take; learning about plants after school hours was a luxury her beautiful daughter could live without.

The arrival of the Mujahideen had changed many aspects of my world outside the house. But it also changed my home life in unexpected ways. I had been back at school for a month when my half brother Nadir appeared at our door one day. I hadn't seen him for fifteen years, since he had disappeared as a boy to fight the Russians. The man who stood in our living room was now a Mujahideen commander. He and his men were responsible for the supply routes into Koof, ensuring that the fighters there had enough arms and ammunition. It was a very important role for a Mujahideen fighter and not one the generals handed out often.

My mother was glad to see her stepson, of course, but she wasn't shy about venting her displeasure at his job and at his apparent lack of support for the family at a time of crisis. My brother would have been, at least as far as the Mujahideen were concerned, within his rights to beat her or maybe even kill her for such insolence. But he didn't. So great was the respect my mother commanded within our family that he apologized to her. He was a man now, he said, and he knew right from wrong. His priority was no longer fighting. It was now doing what was best for the family.

He wanted to take me to his village, where he could protect me from the other Mujahideen. His rank within the fighters would be enough to guarantee my security there. But he was clear that while I remained with my mother in Faizabad, not even his influence was sufficient to prevent local gunmen from forcibly marrying me should such a scheme occur to them.

This was my mother's greatest fear, and so it was decided that I would go with Nadir to the village where he lived in Yaftal district. The only way to get there was on horseback. Later that day, he arrived at the door with two white horses fitted with a type of bridle decorated with wool tassels, common in Badakhshan. I hadn't ridden a horse since I was a little girl. And, as ever, my burka conspired to make my life difficult. Trying to even sit on a horse while wearing a burka is a challenge, let alone riding an animal through busy traffic. It startled at every blaring horn and strange noise. In the end, my brother had to take the reins and lead the horse through the city, while I did my best just to stay on. Every time the horse kicked or bucked, he would rein it in, just as I thought I was about to fall onto the road.

I had never felt more backward than I did that day. Here I was, dressed in a burka while being led on a horse. I felt like I had regressed to my mother's or grandmother's generation. At that moment, it seemed like neither my country nor my life was ever going to move forward.

We rode out of Faizabad and on towards my brother's village house. We had two days of solid riding ahead of us, and the roads were very poor, barely even dirt tracks. I had taken control of the horse, so I was pleased with myself. The burka still made it difficult for me to ride, especially when I had to steer the horse around corners. With my restricted vision, I was very disoriented. And if the horse stumbled in a hole, it was very hard to retain my balance.

As night fell, we came to a village where we could rest. Although we had been travelling only a day, already I could see the differences in the people. The village women were very welcoming and eager to talk to the new arrivals. As we spoke, I noticed how filthy their hands were, black with dirt from long, hard days working in the fields and infrequent bathing. Their clothes were those of simple rural peasants, which I suppose shouldn't have surprised me, but I just couldn't shake the feeling that somehow I had gone back in time. First the burka, then the horse and now the dirty village women who lived their lives in much the same way as their grandmothers and their grandmothers' grandmothers had—it was like watching my country's future unravel before my eyes.

When I woke I found I was very stiff and sore. Horse riding can create aches in places you never thought possible. But I was still pleased with myself for riding unassisted through such tough terrain after a long time out of the saddle. You need to be skilled to ride in this part of Afghanistan. Sometimes your life depends on it.

I HAD been living with Nadir and his family for two weeks when we went to visit an uncle and some of my other distant family in a nearby village. I was sitting with a woman who knew my mother when she asked me if I had been in Kabul when my brother Muqim was killed. I was completely shocked. I hadn't heard anything about this. Everybody in the room could see the look of horror on my face and realized I didn't know. My uncle was first to react. His instinct was to deflect the subject and he tried to suggest the woman was talking about one of my half brothers, Mamorshah, who had been killed by the Mujahideen fifteen years previously.

That brother had been among a group of village men who helped fight off the Mujahideen when they attacked the town of Khawhan. He spent all night firing out of a small bathroom window in his house armed with just a pistol. In order for him to reach the high window, his poor wife had to crouch on all fours as he stood on her back. Both he and his wife survived that battle, but after that he was a marked man. He fled to Tajikistan for a while, but eventually he tried to sneak back into Afghanistan. That was when they caught him. In another sign of the strength of the extended family, my mother spent the night going from local commander to local commander begging for his release. He wasn't her blood son, but she loved him as her own, just like she loved all the other wives' children. But she failed. Like my father he was executed with a bullet to the head at dawn.

But I knew all about this story. And I was only a little girl when it had happened. So why would she ask me if I was there? Despite what the family said to the contrary, I was sick with worry that they were really talking about Muqim. He lived in Kabul and I feared it was he who had been killed. I was in shock. I didn't want to eat anything. My heart was palpitating and I felt sick. I wanted to sprout wings and fly to Kabul to check if he was all right.

On the way back to his house, Nadir continued to insist that the lady had made a mistake. I knew in my heart he was trying to protect me, but I chose to believe the lie rather than accept the terrible truth.

Perhaps it was the uncertainty over whether Muqim was dead or not, but I found life in the village really difficult after that. I was beginning to miss my family very much, especially my mother. I was having trouble adjusting to life in the country too and longed to be back among the bustle and energy of the city, preferably Kabul. Everything was just so unfamiliar. I even found the basic village food of boiled meat and *naan* unusual and inedible. I began losing weight. Most of all, I was missing my classes.

There was no television or radio, so once the evening meal had been eaten and tidied away the family simply went to bed—normally by 7 o'clock each night. It was far too early for me. To occupy myself on those quiet evenings as I lay in bed, I would go over different math problems and formulas for chemistry and physics. It kept my mind occupied and helped me feel at least some connection with the lessons I missed so much. And as I remembered the numbers and symbols, part of me hoped I could soon return to Kabul and find it as it was when I had left it more than a year ago.

It wasn't long afterwards that I asked Nadir to let me return to Faizabad. I missed my mother so much and really needed to be near her. I started discussing this with my family, but it was decided that instead of my returning to Faizabad, my mother, sister, brother-in-law and I would all move back to Kabul together. Mirshakay, my mother's second son, was now a police general in the capital, and he had decreed that Kabul was currently safe enough for us to return. Nadir and I took the horse ride back to Faizabad, and from there we all took a flight to the city of Kunduz.

I was so happy to be back with my family, especially my mother. I did not tell her what I had been told about Muqim's death, because I still couldn't bring myself to fully believe it was true. When I felt the nagging, sickening waves of unease wash over me, I simply shut it out of my mind. My mother was very pleased to have me back too, and although neither of us knew what to expect in Kabul we were both very excited to be returning.

From Kunduz we had to take a three-hundred-kilometre bus journey. That July was very hot, even compared with the usual summer temperatures of Afghanistan. The sun scorched the mountains, and the rocks became so hot around midday that you could not touch them or you risked burning your hand. The wind whipped up the dust so that it swirled around in mini tornadoes, which got into houses, inside cars and machinery and constantly in your eyes. I was becoming used to my burka, but of course I still resented it. The dust had no respect for women's modesty and it would find its way inside the blue cloth and stick to my sweating skin, making me itch and wriggle even more than usual.

At least on the horse ride to and from my brother's house I had been in the breeze, but now I was crammed into a stifling bus with my family and dozens of other people trying to get to Kabul, and the temperature inside my burka was unbearable. The road from Kunduz to Kabul is one of the most dangerous in Afghanistan. It has improved over the years, but even now it can be a nerve-racking journey. The road's narrow rutted surface spirals around the jagged mountains, which on one side pierce the turquoise sky and on the other plunge hundreds of feet down to the jagged rocks of the gorge below. Many unfortunate people have met their deaths down there. There aren't any safety barriers, and when trucks and larger vehicles, such as our bus, meet going in opposite directions, they squeeze past each other a few centimetres at a time while wheels teeter along the crumbling lip of the cliff.

I sat in my bouncing, swaying seat listening to the roar of the bus's engine, as the driver worked his way furiously up and down the gears, occasionally tooting his horn to remonstrate with passing motorists. Fortunately, I had my physics calculations and formulas to distract me and happily drifted off in a trail of numbers. Anything to keep my mind from the rivers of sweat that ran down my back and matted my hair inside the hood of my burka.

As the heat of the day began to wear off, the mountains turned lilac. The landscape softened, and now and then we passed a shepherd squatting near his flock as it grazed on the sweetest grass around the riverbeds and shadier spots. Donkeys snuffled among the wild poppies, and every few miles the burned and abandoned remains of a Soviet tank or truck littered the side of the road.

When we approached the outskirts of Kabul, tired, damp with sweat and irritated by the layer of dust that tickled our noses and made our skin itch, our bus slowed to a crawl in a long line of traffic that stretched out in front of us. Hundreds of cars, packed bumper to bumper, blocked the road. We waited, uncertain of what was happening. Without air flowing through the windows, it became unbearably hot once again. Many of the children were crying, pleading with their mothers to give them water.

A man with an AK-47 rifle approached the bus, sticking his bushy black beard and brown *paqul* hat through the door. His *shalwar kameez* was sweat-stained and dirty. The passengers strained their ears to hear the conversation. The delay, the gunman told the driver, was because a Mujahideen commander, Abdul Sabur Farid Kohistani, was being appointed prime minister of the new government and the roads in the capital had been closed as a security precaution to let his convoy through. I took it as a bad omen of what was to come. Not even the Russians had needed to bring an entire city to a halt to move dignitaries around. Afghanistan was in the control of the Mujahideen, who were veteran fighters, not politicians or civil servants. Yes, they had bravely relieved our country of the Russian invaders, and for this I respected and admired them. But I wondered how men with zero political experience could run the country efficiently.

When the roads were eventually reopened, we made our way through the city. There were signs of recent fighting—destroyed buildings and burned-out vehicles. Mujahideen fighters stood at checkpoints, guns at the ready. We went to my brother Mirshakay's apartment in an area called Makrorian, a series of Russian-built apartment blocks. He lived on the fifth floor.

Mirshakay had been given a very senior job at the Ministry of the Interior, where he was helping run the police force. When we entered the apartment, the living room was full of guests, mostly men, waiting to speak to him. Some were there on official police business, some to plead the case of jailed friends or relatives who were in jail and others, many from Badakhshan, to make a social visit. It was a chaotic scene.

My brother came to meet us on the third floor, and I burst into tears. The city had changed so much since the last time I was there. I was really afraid of what it meant for my family and my country. But I was most concerned that Muqim wasn't there to greet us too. His absence confirmed my worst fears, yet nobody seemed prepared to acknowledge the fact of his death. When I asked where he was, I was told he had gone to Pakistan and planned to go to Europe. "When?" I asked. About forty days ago, I was told. But I knew I was being lied to. Then I saw his photograph on a shelf in the living room. The frame had been decorated with silk flowers. It was an ominous sign, the first outward confirmation of Muqim's fate.

"Why did you decorate the photo frame with flowers?" I asked my sister-in-law. She squirmed uncomfortably. "Because, you know, since Muqim went to Pakistan, I just miss him so much," she replied. I knew she was lying. In Afghanistan, we decorate a photograph with flowers as a sign of mourning, as a tribute to the dead. My family was trying to protect me. But I didn't need protecting—I needed the truth. My mother, who had absolutely no idea of the truth yet, believed the story about his going to Pakistan.

Later that evening, I was casually exploring the apartment, picking up the books and photographs that lined my brother's living room. I found a diary and opened it out of bored curiosity rather than genuine suspicion. Inside was a poem. It laid out the terrible truth in verse. Written by a man called Amin, who had been my brother's best friend, it was a poem of lament, describing how Muqim had been killed. I had read only the first three lines before a scream exploded from my lips. It was more a wail of anguish than rage. Here was eloquent proof of Muqim's murder. My mother and brother rushed into the living room to see what was the matter. I was crying uncontrollably and barely able to talk. I just stood there, holding the journal in my hand, waving it at my mother. She took it from me with trembling hands. My brother looked horrified, as my mother stared uncomprehendingly down at the poem. The time for lies, no matter how well intentioned they were, was over. When my mother finally heard the truth, her scream was heartbreaking.

Its piercing crescendo echoed off the concrete walls, drilling down into our brains. The irrefutable evidence of my brother's death had struck me like a hammer blow. For my mother, it was almost too much. My family gathered in the room, the secret of Muqim's fate now in the open.

That evening, our grief bonded us—I, my mother, my sister, my brother and his two wives plus my three aunts wept and asked why such a good, healthy young man had been taken so unjustly from us. Why? Another of our family's brightest shining stars had gone.

Dear Shuhra and Shaharzad,

Family... It's a simple word but possibly one of the most impor-
tant a child will ever learn. Family is the home that a child is born
into, the place where it should be kept safe, warm and protected.
Whether hail or rain or even rockets and bullets pierce the night
air, a family should be there to protect a child. Safe in the house,
a child should sleep soundly in its mother's arms with a father
standing by.

Sadly, many children, you included, don't have two parents.
But at least you have a mother who loves you and tries to make up
for the loss of a father in your lives. Some children don't even have
that. So many poor Afghan children lost everyone in the war and
have no one left to care for them. Siblings are also such an impor-
tant part of family. I had so many brothers and sisters I almost lost
count. Our extended family had rivalries and jealousies, espe-
cially among my father's wives. But never were the children made
to feel unloved. Each mother loved all the children equally, and it
was a wonderful thing to know I was loved by so many mothers.
When my father, your grandfather, died, my mother took responsi-
bility for trying to keep all the children together so that we stayed
a proper family.

My siblings and I fought and argued and sometimes we would
kick, punch and tear each other's hair, but we never stopped lov-
ing each other. Or looking out for each other. I battled hard against
my brothers to remain in school and be independent, and even
though they didn't like it they loved me and let me do it. Of course
now they are so very proud of their little sister the politician. They

are also proud of themselves for having been open-minded enough to help me achieve my dreams. By doing so, we have helped to keep our family status and our political honour.

I wish I had given you a brother. A fine, decent young man who would have loved his two sisters so much. I am sure you would have squabbled and fought with him too. But I know you'd have loved him. I would have named him after the brother I lost.

Muqim.

With love,
Your mother

SIX

When Justice Dies

{ *May 1992* }

A SHORT STORY for Shuhra and Shaharzad

The wind and the rain lashed down from the Hindu Kush mountains onto Kabul that Friday night. The dusty roads quickly turned to mud, thick and slippery underfoot. Open sewers filled with brown water and burst their filthy banks, forming ever-growing stinking ponds. The streets were deserted, except for a barely discernible movement in the shadows. A man breathed heavily in the dark, the rain catching in his beard and forming rivulets that cascaded into the ankle-deep puddle he was standing in. He loosened his grip on the AK-47 assault rifle. The Russian-made gun was heavy and slippery. He made his way slowly, deliberately, through the black quagmire, placing each foot carefully, testing the ground before trusting it with his full weight.

Then he turned to face the six-foot-high compound wall and delicately lifted his gun onto the top. Even on a night like this, the clatter of a badly controlled weapon could carry a long way. Steadying himself, he paused, arms held up at shoulder height, before springing like a cat, grasping the top of the wall cleanly with both hands. He dug his toes into the bricks, searching for purchase on the wet surface. The muscles in his arms and back strained as he fought to control his weight. Throwing his right elbow onto the top of the wall, he pressed his face into the rough cold cement, swinging his left leg in an arc to catch the high edge. Heaving the rest of his torso onto the top of the wall, he panted silently, scanning the dark compound for any sign of guards. Seeing none, he dropped to the ground, his feet splashing noisily as they made contact. He pushed the safety lever on his AK-47 down with his thumb, clicking it into the firing position.

Crouching low, he used the cover of the shadows of the fruit trees to move towards the main house. Inside, everything was dark. The rain obscured his vision, and he fumbled at the brass door handle. It turned with a scrape of the bolt. He held his breath now, easing the door open a crack, slowly widening it as his eyes adjusted to the dark room. It was quiet inside. The sound of the rain was muffled against the heavy roof tiles, but he was aware that he was dripping loudly on the tiled floor. He moved across the living room in his crouch, gun poised. The tap-tap, tap-tap of his sandals on the floor was amplified against the close brick walls of the hall. He found the bedroom door and paused. He readied the gun, holding it pistol style in his right hand, and with his left he tested the knob. It gave and opened a crack.

And then, the man murdered my brother in cold blood.

The assassin had emptied his gun into Muqim as he lay sleeping in bed. A Kalashnikov's magazine holds thirty bullets. The gunman held the trigger down until the gun was empty. Then he fled.

My sister-in-law woke to the sound of gunfire. She and my brother were asleep upstairs on the other side of the house. My brother tried to calm his wife, assuring her that the firing was probably just someone shooting in the air to celebrate a wedding or the victory over the Russians. Then a terrified neighbour started shouting from outside the yard that Muqim had been shot.

He was only twenty-three when he died. Tall, handsome and clever, a law student with a black belt in karate—very unusual at that time, even in Kabul—he was one of my favourite brothers. We had grown up playing and fighting and loving and falling out. A kind word from him would make me smile for hours; a harsh one would bring tears to my eyes in an instant. He, Ennayat and I had been playmates our entire lives. Muqim had narrowly survived being murdered as a little boy when he was hidden from would-be assassins under a woman's skirt. This time, there was no one to hide or protect him.

It was such a devastating blow. I felt like a part of me had been killed. After my father's death, all my brothers had taken on a much greater role in my life. Muqim relished his new patriarchal powers and would order me about, telling me to wash my socks or brush my clothes. I was his adoring little sister and I didn't mind his bossiness. All I wanted was his approval and attention.

Most of the time, he encouraged my education and would say to me, "Fawzia, I want you to become a doctor." Knowing that he had such belief in me always made me feel very special. But sometimes, if he was upset or frustrated, he would forbid me from going to school the next day, wagging his finger at me sternly and declaring, "Tomorrow you stay at home. You are a girl. For girls, home is enough."

So he could be very traditional in his outlook—but I always forgave him for it because it seemed to be his way of dealing with stress. He was a bit like my father that way. Usually the day after he'd banned me from going to school he would come home with a gift—perhaps a new school bag or pencil case. Then he would ask me to go back to school and remind me of how smart he thought I was and what great things I was going to do with my life. If one of my other brothers said I couldn't go to school, they really meant it. But with Muqim, I knew it was just talk.

From the clothes he wore to the food he ate, Muqim was always very particular about what he wanted. So when he told me he was in love with a girl he had met at university, I knew he was serious. He was in his first year of law school, and she was starting her medical training. When he told me she was very beautiful, I didn't doubt that either. He used to point to my prettiest doll and say, "This girl is as beautiful as that doll. Except she has blue eyes."

He had loved her for four years, but in all that time he had never been able to tell her how he felt. He used to spend hours hanging around outside her house, hoping for the merest glimpse of her. Muqim had sent her letters declaring his love, but she sent them back unopened. She was a very traditional girl, and a traditional girl doesn't open letters from unsanctioned suitors. But he was hoping to change that. He was looking forward to my mother's return to Kabul because she was going to visit the girl's family and propose the match. If my father had been alive he would have done it, but instead it fell to my mother in her role as matriarch. But he was killed before the proper, decent approach could be taken.

It is always hard to come to terms with the death of a loved one. The sense of loss is enormous, and the hole the person's absence leaves feels like it will never be filled. The ache of knowing you will never see that person again throbs like a bad tooth. Except there's no painkiller you can take to relieve the pain.

The fighting between the Mujahideen forces and the government meant the police were unable to mount much of an investigation. Even my elder brother's status as a senior police commander could do little to bring Muqim's killer to justice. The only evidence the killer left was a sandal dropped by the wall as he fled. But it was the type of sandal worn by men all over Afghanistan, and this was long before the days of DNA testing and forensic evidence. Afghanistan was in a state of war, and during wars people die. The fact that Muqim's death was murder meant little under the circumstances. Hundreds of people were being murdered every day, women were being raped and homes were being looted and destroyed. Food and water was scarce. Justice was in even shorter supply.

Mirshakay blamed himself for Muqim's death. Not only had he failed him as a policeman by not capturing his killers, but he also felt personally responsible. As a police general, he had a team of bodyguards. They would travel with him everywhere, and at night their job was to guard the house as he and his family slept inside. Because it was a Friday, the day of prayer and observance, and such a horrible, wet night, my brother had felt sorry for his bodyguards and dismissed them early, telling them to go home to be with their families. Muqim got home from the gym at around 10 P.M. He was soaked to the skin in the rain and complaining about an eye infection. My sister-in-law fetched her kohl from her makeup bag. In Badakhshan, women often use a type of kohl eyeliner made from herbs found in the mountains that are said to be very good for treating eye infections. She put some on his eye, then he went to bed. That was the last time anyone saw Muqim alive. If the bodyguards had been on duty, there's no way the gunman could have entered the house and Muqim would still be alive. Mirshakay was torn apart with fury at himself that he had let the guards go home early.

One of the great questions we ask ourselves in life is why. Why do things happen? As a Muslim, I have my beliefs. I believe them to be true, and they are a large part of me. I believe God alone decides our fate. He chooses when we live and when we die. But even that certainty doesn't make the painful events and losses of my life easier to bear.

With Muqim's death, we simply didn't have any answers to the question of why. Why would somebody kill such a kind, intelligent, gentle young man? He was a brilliant student trying to make a life for himself. He wanted a career and a wife and a family. He wasn't a threat to anybody. But his life was taken away in an instant. In Islam, a dying person is supposed to recite the name of Allah three times before passing away. Poor Muqim didn't have time to do that.

Not having time to say goodbye to someone I loved was something I was becoming used to. But there was no point in asking why that was either. It was just how our life was in those days.

Dear Shuhra and Shaharzad,

As you grow older, you will learn about loyalty. Loyalty to your faith, to family, to friends, to your neighbours and to your country. In times of war, our loyalty can be sorely tested.

You must be loyal to the true and good nature of your Islamic faith, helping and loving those around you even when you might feel you cannot. It is important to be loyal to your family, both the living and the dead. Our family bonds do not cease at the grave, but we must also be careful not to remember the dead at the expense of the living. You must be loyal to your friends, because that is the action of a true friend. And if they are true friends themselves, then they will also be loyal to you and be ready to act when you need their help.

You must be loyal to your fellow Afghans. Not all Afghans are the same; we speak many different languages and live in many different ways. But you must be able to see past those ethnic and cultural differences and remember the thing that unites us—Afghanistan. You must be loyal to your country. Without loyalty to our country, we have nothing as a nation. We must work hard to improve our country for your children and their children.

Loyalty can be a hard lesson to learn sometimes, but there are few lessons more valuable.

With love,
Your mother

SEVEN

The War Within

{ *1992–1993* }

I **WAS GLAD** to be back in Kabul and was eager to resume my old life—
or what little of it remained in what was now becoming a full-blown
civil war.

We were still living in my brother's apartment in Makrorian, a
word that roughly translates as "living space." The apartments had
been built by the Russians using the latest technology, such as a
communal hot water system that served over ten apartment blocks,
each block housing fifty apartments. It is a testament to the quality
of Soviet-era construction that many of the Makrorian blocks have
survived even today despite being shelled countless times; even
the hot water system still works. Today it remains a sought-after
neighbourhood.

I was able to resume my English language lessons in Kabul. They
were too important to me to give up, even though they meant regular journeys through the streets, which had become the battle-
ground where the Mujahideen commanders and their men played
out their deadly power struggles.

Kabul was divided into different sectors. The central parts, Khair
Khana, Makrorian and around the King's Palace, were controlled
by the Mujahideen government, which was by then headed by

President Burhanuddin Rabbani, a former general from Badakhshan and a man my family knew well—hence my brother's senior position at the Interior Ministry. The famous "lion of the Panjshir," Ahmad Shah Massoud, was his minister of defence.

The west of Kabul was controlled by a man named Mazary, the leader of an ethnic group called the Hazaras. (Said to be the direct descendants of Genghis Khan, the Hazaras are identifiable by their classic Mongol looks, round faces and large almond-shaped eyes. They are unusual in being Shia Muslims; the majority of Muslim ethnic groups in the country are Sunni.) An area on the outskirts of Kabul, Paghman, was controlled by a man named Sayyaf and his people. Yet another area was controlled by the fearsome Abdul Rashid Dostum, the leader of the ethnic Uzbeks. Just outside the city walls, towards the south, was Gulbuddin Hekmatyar, the leader of a group called Hizbi Islami; a second Hizbi Islami leader, Abdul Sabur Farid Kohistani, was the prime minister.

Essentially, despite having a shared government and having been allies when fighting the Russians—when they were given the name of the Northern Alliance, as most of them originated from the north of Afghanistan—these commanders were now fighting each other for power. As the civil war grew more brutal, short-term allegiances shifted and changed with the weather.

The fiercest opponent of the Mujahideen government was Hekmatyar, who was unhappy with his role in the government and wanted more power and seniority. Every day, his men fired scores of rockets into Kabul from their base in the higher ground at the edge of the city. The rockets exploded in marketplaces, schools, hospitals and gardens, and scores of people were being killed or injured. Sometimes the situation changed overnight. A group that had previously supported the government might suddenly turn against it and start fighting. A few days later, with hundreds of civilians dead, the group might use the national TV station to announce it had all been a misunderstanding and it was now supporting the shared government again. The public had no idea what would happen from one day to the next. Probably our leaders didn't either.

The journey from home to my English class was once a simple short taxi ride, but the route took me through some of the areas of fiercest fighting. Some neighbourhoods and streets could be avoided, but others I had no choice but to cross, whatever the risk. I would take a convoluted route that changed depending on what political group currently held the upper hand. Gathering intelligence from people on the street was essential to successfully navigating the route, as was the taxi driver's constant search for the scarce supplies of petrol.

Packs of gunmen would roam the streets, and the danger of snipers was constant, their choice of target indiscriminate. A crack from a rifle accompanied by the dull thump of the bullet would often send some poor soul toppling to the ground, another desperate search for food, water or medicine brought to a premature end. Machine gunners set up in the damaged homes around key intersections, their positions carefully chosen to both conceal themselves and give the maximum field of fire—all the better to catch your enemy in the open. Often all that could be glimpsed of them was the tops of their heads in the gloom of their cover among the rubble, but everyone knew they were peering over their steel gunsights for any sign of movement. Vehicles often drew the deadliest attention, but overall they were still the fastest and safest way to travel. On more than one occasion, my taxi was targeted by artillery rockets.

Some roads were targeted by the artillery commanders. When their spotters signalled an approaching car, all they needed to do was open fire and chances were the car, truck or possibly tank would be blown off the road. I remember gasping once as rockets came rushing down a street towards me. But over our heads, the boughs of trees stuck upwards like fingers waiting to catch the projectiles. The rockets hit the branches and exploded, filling the street with shrapnel and shards of splintered wood as we sped along the road and out of range. If it were not for the trees, the rockets would have ripped the flimsy car apart, and both me and the driver with it.

Few taxi drivers would risk going out among the fighting for the meagre payment of a fare. Those brave enough to do so were motivated by the threat of starvation. Not driving meant that they and their families would not eat, spelling a death even more certain than the bullets that hummed through the air. So it was often impossible to find a taxi to take me to class, and on those days I would have to walk, darting from cover to cover, trying to avoid the areas where I knew the gunmen were and praying I didn't stumble across the path of others I didn't know about.

I would have to walk back again after class, sneaking along alone in the dark. Sometimes it took me as long as two hours to get home. It was very dangerous for anybody to be on the streets at night, but especially a young girl by herself. Aside from bullets and rockets, I ran the additional risk of being raped. When night fell, the shooting became more unpredictable. Nervous in the dark, the gunmen would curl their fingers a little tighter around their triggers and nothing more than a loud footstep or the tumble of rubble could attract a burst of bullets.

Often, my mother would nervously keep watch for me at the bottom of our apartment building dressed in her burka, peering out into the night and scanning the shadows. The occasional clatter of gunfire echoing across the sky would send her heart jumping into her mouth. Her imagination must have tormented her as she waited for her daughter to reappear from her journey through the war zone. Her relief at my return was obvious, but she never showed it by hugging me. Instead she would be quick to scold me, putting her hand into my back as she pushed me firmly up the stairs and through the safety of the front door, all the while tutting and clucking at me: "Even if these English classes make you president of this country, I don't care. I don't want you to be president. I want you to be alive." My brothers and sisters also didn't like me taking such great risk to go to the class, but they would never tell me this directly. Instead, they would nag my mother and ask her to stop me from going. They could not understand why she willingly let me risk my life like this, night after night.

But my mother would probably have thrown herself head first into machine gun fire if it meant I could still go to school. She was illiterate but fiercely intelligent. By seeing me get educated, she was somehow educating herself too. She took genuine delight in talking to me about my classes, and her commitment to me never wavered. She just ignored my siblings' pleas and nagging, placating them with her winning smile.

Looking back on those times, however, I too am staggered that she allowed it. I feel guilty when I think about the fear I must have caused her every time I disappeared into the bullet-riddled night. A fear that must have been made all the more acute by the recent loss of Muqim. His death affected the whole family, but none more so than my mother. Every morning, she would visit his grave and put fresh flowers on it. But this simple loving act of a bereaved mother soon gave way to more erratic and, for the family, very worrying behaviour.

BY NOW the city was turning into a killing zone. From the neighbourhoods where the fighting was worst, we heard reports of hundreds of civilians dying each night. We could hear the crackle of gunfire ripple across the city. On still nights, it would echo off the hills and mountains that surround Kabul, haunting the whole city with the terrible events it was witnessing.

Rocket fire was most common. The rockets were indiscriminate and would land without warning, sometimes destroying a family home, leaving its residents buried beneath the earth walls, sometimes a shop or a school or a group of women buying vegetables for the evening meal at a market stand. All you would hear was a whizzing sound as the rocket flew through the air; then the whiz would suddenly stop, and seconds later the weapon would fall and detonate. You never knew where or on whom it would land.

For Afghan women, the constant fear of death was made worse by the twin threat of sexual violence. The tragic story of my friend Nahid illustrates this. Nahid was just eighteen and lived in an apartment near ours. One night some gunmen burst into her house, apparently to rape or kidnap her. Rather than face this fate, she threw herself from a fifth-floor window. She died instantly.

In other stories, we heard how women had been found with their bodies mutilated or their breasts cut off. In a country where morality is everything, it was hard to believe we had descended into such evils.

One evening, at around 7 o'clock, I was cooking the family meal of rice and meat when I realized my mother wasn't home. Normally she would be in the kitchen or organizing other aspects of household life. I had an unpleasant feeling that I knew where she had gone and I had to go in search of her. I was still in my mourning period for Muqim, so I put on my black head scarf and slipped out the door. When a guard near our apartment building told me which direction she had gone in, I knew my worst suspicions were right. She was on her way to visit my brother's grave.

There weren't any taxis about and buses weren't running at all, so I set off on foot towards the centre of the city. At first, the streets were eerily quiet. The Kabul I had known before the war was bustling at night with cars and motorbikes and people walking to visit friends. Now the streets were all but deserted, cleared by the rattle of gunfire that lay between me and my brother's grave.

I kept walking nervously, aware that my mother was somewhere ahead. I began to see bodies in the street, freshly shot or torn to pieces by explosions, their corpses not yet beginning to bloat. I was terrified. But I wasn't afraid so much of dying as of the fact that these dead bodies were people's family members. And that tomorrow, it could be my family lying here.

When I got to an area called Deh Mazang, I came across a taxi. The driver had removed the back seat. He was piling the car with bodies. He was covered in blood, his white shirt now streaked crimson, with darker flecks congealing around the pockets and buttons. His car looked like a slaughterhouse; the victims of the fighting, men and women with twisted limbs and shattered heads and torsos, oozed blood into the footwell, forming thick pools that dribbled through the rusted holes in the floor and onto the dusty road beneath. The driver, clearly in shock, was lathered in sweat as he tried to stuff another corpse into his car. In Islam, a swift burial is very important, and it may not even have occurred to him that his life was in danger. He simply worked at his grim task as though he was loading sacks of rice.

I just stood and stared at the strange sight for a moment. He and

I were the only people on the street that warm summer night. The only sound was the crackle of gunfire, and the grunts of a brave middle-aged taxi driver risking his life to ensure a group of people he'd never met got a decent burial.

When he was satisfied that he could fit no more bodies in his car, he started up the engine with a cloud of blue exhaust smoke and drove towards the hospital, the back doors still open, the passengers' dead limbs dancing as the suspension sagged over every bump and pothole. The sight of the dead and dying made me think of my family, and I had to battle with my mind as it transposed their faces onto these nameless victims. I wasn't far from the graveyard now, and I knew I had to keep going to find my mother.

It was getting dark, and I was walking past Kabul University when a group of uniformed men shouted at me. They wanted to know where I was going.

I didn't answer but just lowered my head and walked faster. One of the men raised his gun and asked me again, "Where are you going?" I stopped and turned, looking into the gun.

"I'm looking for my brother. Somebody said they had seen his body just around the corner. I need to go and check," I lied. He thought for a moment before lowering his gun. "Okay, go," he said. I hurried off, my heart pounding. For a moment, I had thought they were going to do something worse than shoot me.

The cemetery was a dusty spread of earth the size of several football fields. Years of war and fighting had pre-empted life's inevitable consequence, and the newest graves were cramped together, oblong piles of small rocks with roughly hewn gravestones pushed into the ground for support. On the higher ground, where the more prestigious plots lay, graves were often fenced with iron palings, now silently rusting in this lonely place. Tattered green flags, a sign of mourning, flew over them.

My mother was hunched over the grave. I could see her quietly organizing the bright bunches of yellow silk roses on Muqim's grave. Immersed in her thoughts, she didn't hear my footsteps as I approached. She was shaking as she cried and caressing a photograph of my brother. He looked so young and handsome in it. She turned and looked at me. I stood there crying tears of both relief at having found her and sadness at the scene.

Feeling overwhelmed, I knelt beside her. For a long time we held each other and cried. Then we talked about my brother and how much we missed him. I asked her why she had risked her life coming out here at night. Had she not seen all the dead people and the men with guns and did she not realize how worried I was? She just gave me a sad, tear-stained look as if to say, "You know why," before turning back to the photograph.

We sat there so long I didn't realize how dark it was getting. There were few working street lights because of the war. I started to get very scared. We couldn't risk going back the same way we'd come; it was too far and too dangerous even to attempt. So we resolved to wait another hour until it was completely dark, and then crept out of the graveyard. We made for a shortcut we knew well to a different house that had belonged to my father when he was a member of parliament. It was on the edge of the city, in an area called Bagh-e-bala, opposite the famous landmark of the Intercontinental Hotel, home to affluent Kabulis, many of them former politicians. Some of my father's relatives had been living there to keep the house safe for us. We wouldn't be able to get home tonight, but at least we would be out of danger if we could get there. My mother and I crept through the tiny alleyways that separated the houses. Any noise or panicky movement could draw attention in the form of bullets, and so we inched our way forward, up the hill and towards safety.

The house was built in traditional Kabuli style, made from large grey-brown bricks and very square, with small windows to keep the heat out in summer and the warmth in during the freezing winters. A sloping roof of curved tiles ran parallel to the hill. At the back was a small courtyard with fruit trees and flowers. As we hammered on the door, I wondered if the trees were still there. My relatives answered, visibly scared. They thought it was the Mujahideen coming to rob or kill them. When they realized who it was, they dragged us inside and shut the door. I was so relieved to be safe, but I felt very sad to be back in this house so unexpectedly. This was actually the house my brother Muqim was living in when he was murdered. My mother knew this too, and she started crying again. We were both so physically and emotionally exhausted it was all we could do.

My relatives brought us tea and some food, but neither of us could eat anything. We tried to force down a little tea at their pleading. Blankets were fetched and we went to bed, on my mother's insistence, in Muqim's room. Neither of us slept that night. I lay wrapped in a blanket thinking about my brother and the terrible things I had seen that day. How it felt to watch my country implode. How a taxi driver loading dead bodies into his car was the most civilized and humane thing I had seen all day; how a woman will walk through rocket fire to mourn a beloved son; and why men with guns who fought with such bravery to free Afghanistan from the Soviets were now destroying this country to satisfy their personal lust for power.

My mother wept all night, her knees pulled to her chest, lamenting her loss. That night seemed to drag on forever. In some ways I wish it had. By dawn, there was enough light in the room to see the bullet holes from the rounds that had sprayed from the gunman's Kalashnikov and killed Muqim. That terrible sight only seemed to strengthen my mother's resolve. Her determination and pragmatism were returning. That morning, she made hot green tea for me, then staunchly announced we would be moving out of the apartment at Makrorian, and moving here, closer to the cemetery. My mother's logic was impeccable as always—if you must walk in a war zone, better make it a short walk.

But the real reason was that she wanted to live here in this room with its physical memories of Muqim. There was the small single bed, the cover riddled with bullet holes. The wardrobe with his suits and other clothes still hanging inside. A small shelf holding his books and karate trophies. And, nailed to the wall above the shelf, his karate belts of yellow, brown and black. As upsetting as all these reminders of him were, they gave my mother comfort and helped her feel close to him.

This house had spectacular views of the city. But now, instead of enjoying a stunning cityscape that stretched out towards the mountains, we were forced to witness the fighting that raged beneath us like a horror movie. Machine guns spluttered and rockets hissed and roared as they exploded into buildings. From our high lookout, we could see the two sides exchange fire, tracers from the explosives lighting up the darkness. I watched the fighters as they organized themselves and directed fresh attacks on enemy positions.

Some of the homes in the city had been built using coloured plaster. I was watching the battle one day when an artillery rocket landed directly on top of a pretty pink house. The blast made the earth tremble and sent chunks of masonry flying more than a hundred metres into the air. The place where a house had stood just a few seconds previously was now a mist-like cloud of pink dust settling over the surrounding buildings. I saw the same thing happen to a blue house—there was nothing left when it exploded like a ghastly firework, fading out with a trail of blue fog rolling through the streets. The tragic inhabitants inside had been blown to smithereens.

For me, one of the saddest moments was when the polytechnic, a good institution built by the Soviets, got hit in the fighting. During their time in Afghanistan, the Russians had built many educational institutions. All Afghans wanted the Russian invaders gone, but at the same time they were thankful for some of their infrastructure and buildings. A lot of young high school graduates studied at the polytechnic, which remained open after the Russians had left, graduating in vocational skills such as computer science, architecture and engineering. Even the great Ahmad Shah Massoud had studied there.

As a little girl, I had longed to go there one day. That dream ended the day the polytechnic library was destroyed. It was late in the day, and the fighting was beginning to die down. I don't know if whoever fired the rocket intended to hit the polytechnic, if he wanted to destroy it and all it represented. Neither side was using it as a base, so perhaps it was an accident. Either way, the result was the same. When the rocket exploded in the side of the library, I gave a little gasp of shock. Then, in the way you watch a scary movie, not wanting to see the horror but unable to turn away, I looked on, feeling more and more sickened as the smoke gave way to flames, licking at the gaping wound. Inside were thousands of books that had helped educate many young Afghans. Books that were now fuelling an ever-growing fire. There was no fire brigade, of course. Nobody rushed to save all this knowledge that could help improve our country and educate our people. Nobody except me even seemed to notice. I watched it burn until it was time to go to sleep. I went to bed numb with the idea that so many words, so much literature and learning, had perished. But I also felt guilty for caring about books when people were burning too.

My mother quickly settled into her routine in that house. Every morning, she would wake, eat a simple breakfast of *naan* bread and green tea and make the dangerous journey to my brother's grave. She would take the shortcut down the hill, weaving through the alleys and rocky tracks that ran over the hillside before creeping across the open ground to the cemetery. She would return a little later, puffy around the eyes from crying.

This routine upset her, but it also seemed to strengthen and galvanize her despite the risks, and her return to the house was usually marked by a flurry of domestic activity. My relatives had been living there and guarding the property, but they hadn't turned it into a home. My mother set about this job, organizing, rearranging and decorating. Furniture was cleaned and aired, rugs beaten, pots and pans scoured and buffed until they gleamed black or copper. The yard was emptied of rubbish and swept.

Sometimes she would go sit in my brother's room wailing in grief. But she never cleaned it. It was left as we found it, broken and bullet-marked. It was simply understood that for however long we were living here, the bedroom was to stay untouched, at least until my mother decided otherwise. My brother was to be remembered in death as he was in life: bright and beautiful like the silk flowers on his grave—not for the violence of his last living moments.

My brother Mirshakay tried to visit us every day. He wasn't very happy, to put it mildly, about my mother's decision to stay at the house. But he understood her reasons and was prepared to let us remain there for the moment. Sometimes he would also bring my sisters or his wife, and on those nights we would sit down and have the kind of meal we might have had in more peaceful times. We would gossip and laugh, but despite the banter there was no escaping the underlying fear we all shared about our future.

IT SEEMED to be a turning point for the city's middle class. Until now, most had been prepared to sit out the fighting and see what happened. Leaving prematurely meant leaving your house open to looting. But with the civil war showing no signs of ending, many intellectuals and professionals fled to Pakistan. They would load the essentials for an uncertain life—mostly clothes, documents and jewellery—into their cars, try to secure their homes and then slip out of the city during a lull in the fighting. Most Afghans live with their extended family, so usually it was the father and his wife or wives, plus the children, who drove to Pakistan. Elderly or more distant relatives were left behind to guard the house and scratch out an existence as best they could.

Nobody condemned those who left for their decision. Many who stayed behind would have gone too if they'd had the chance. And when the fighting intensified, the choice to leave seemed the right one. One morning, a man I knew to be a friend of my brother Mirshakay appeared at the door. He was visibly frightened, having driven through some of the areas of intense fighting. He insisted we come with him immediately. My brother had sent him to take my mother and me back to the apartment at Makrorian. My mother refused to leave, and she and the man argued for a while as he pleaded with her to follow my brother's wishes. But my mother was adamant that she would not leave her son's grave unattended, and nothing this bedraggled messenger could say or do would make her change her mind. My mother was an immovable force, and she was determined that we would remain in the house, whatever the risks.

Or so she said at the time. But the news we received just a few hours later instantly changed her mind. My mother had been out trying to buy food when she heard the story. The night before, a group of Mujahideen had smashed their way into a house a few doors away and raped all the women and girls inside. My mother showed little concern for her own safety, but the virginity and sanctity of her daughter were paramount.

In Afghan culture, rape is despised, but it is an all-too-common crime in times of war. While the rapist can be put to death, the woman must endure a much longer punishment, becoming a social pariah even in her own family. The victims of rape are often cast out like harlots, as if they had done something to provoke the attack or inflame the loins of the man who was driven mad by lust and unable to control himself. No Afghan man would marry a woman who had been raped. Any suitor would want to be certain his bride is pure, no matter how violent or unjust the circumstances of her deflowering.

My mother had changed from determined to stay to determined to leave. She didn't give me the full details of the attack but ordered me to collect my things before she set about doing the same. I was really scared, but I also knew better than to debate the subject with her. We were leaving. Now.

My brother's messenger had already left in his car, so the only way back to the apartment was on foot. The memories of my first journey through the city still haunted me, and the thought of doing it again made me feel sick. We'd have to run down boulevards of sniper fire, go through checkpoints, risk seeing dead bodies left from the previous night's shelling.

My mother left our relatives with instructions to keep guarding and maintaining the house, before we nervously stepped onto the street. We started running. We both knew we had a long way to go, and I think we just wanted to get it over with. We ran from house to house, careful not to linger out in the open, scanning doorways and darkened windows for any signs of movement, listening for gunfire that might signal the presence of a machine gun or sniper up ahead.

We hadn't gone far when a woman came running towards us. She stood immobile in front of us, screaming hysterically, "My daughter, my daughter." I could hear from her accent that she was Hazara.

I was too scared to open my mouth, but my mother asked her what had happened. The woman's head was shaking with uncontrollable emotion, the blue hood on her burka wobbling with every convulsion of grief. Her tears formed little beads on the mesh, embroidered and glistening in the sunlight. The woman's house had been destroyed days earlier in the fighting. She and her daughter had no alternative but to flee. They took shelter in a Shia mosque, where around 150 other women, their husbands dead or caught up in the fighting, were taking shelter.

The woman told us how the mosque had been hit by rocket fire and set ablaze, and I remembered then that I had seen the building burning in the distance as I stared in silence through the window of my father's house. The mosque had burned very quickly. Those who survived the explosion rushed for the exit, but in the smoke, dust and screaming, dozens must have been trampled or overcome by the smoke and flames. The woman told us how she and her daughter were near the explosion when it hit, knocking them off their feet in a blast of concrete and roof tiles. When they came to, the building was already burning. Women and children were screaming and crying and running in panic. The only light came from the flames that leapt higher by the second. Some women dragged their children to safety by stepping on other children, while the screams of countless mothers trying to locate their youngsters separated from them in the dark were deafening, adding to the panic.

The woman's daughter had spotted a hole in the wall caused by the explosion, and the pair of them had crawled through and wriggled to safety. They had hidden all night and then in the early morning, exhausted, dehydrated and starving, they had approached a Mujahideen checkpoint, begging to be given safe passage. She told us how the Mujahideen commander had agreed to allow her through so they could escape. The woman was cautious and had told her daughter to stay hidden while she approached the checkpoint alone. But once the soldier told her she could pass freely, she called out to her daughter to come forward too. The girl came out of her hiding place.

This was the moment the men had been waiting for. They grabbed the girl. The commander dragged her into a steel shipping container that served as his field office. Then he held her down on the table and raped her in front of her mother. The daughter screamed for her mother's help as the men violated her, while others held the woman back, forcing her to watch.

Some Mujahideen soldiers were raping women with impunity—it was every woman's greatest fear. But the soldiers might have had an additional reason in this case. There were some instances in which Hazara women were targeted for rape or had their breasts cut off. Sunni Islam is the dominant form of the religion for the world's 1.5 billion Muslims. The key difference between Sunni Muslims and other Islamic sects relates to a historical debate about the true successor of the Prophet Mohammed. The Sunni believe that the first four caliphs, or spiritual leaders, are the true successors, whereas the Shia believe the Prophet's cousin and son-in-law, Ali ibn Abi Talib, is the rightful successor. It is a division almost as old as Islam itself and over the course of history has proven to be as bitter and bloody as any seen in world religion. During the civil war, Hazaras were often massacred just for this reason, and in later years they were also targeted by the Taliban, who saw them as infidels. Today, many Hazaras still feel that other ethnic groups regard them as having lower status.

When the girl's ordeal had ended, the commander had simply taken out his gun and shot her, as if disposing of something distasteful. Then he let the poor mother go.

After she had told us her story, there was little my mother could say. She just clutched the poor woman's hand, and taking mine in her other hand she started running. The three of us ran hand in hand through the battle-scarred streets, over the bodies, around the burned-out cars and through shattered buildings.

We just ran and ran, terrified of what we might run into, but more fearful of what we were trying to leave behind. When we rounded a corner, we saw the most wonderful sight we could have hoped for—a taxi.

My mother begged the Hazara woman to come and stay with us at the apartment, but the woman declined, saying she was going to try to find some relatives who lived farther out of the city. They argued some more over it, but the lady was very determined. Eventually, the taxi driver told us to hurry up. We got in and drove home to the apartment in Makrorian. My brother didn't know whether to shout or laugh with joy when he saw us. He was furious at my mother's refusal to come sooner in his messenger's car. When he found out that we'd walked alone and heard the story of the poor Hazara lady, he shot a filthy look at my mother for having risked the same thing happening to me. But he let it go. We were home and safe for now.

But something had changed for my mother. In the weeks and months that followed, she grew weaker and weaker. She began to have difficulty breathing. She had suffered allergies all her life, but they started to get worse; the slightest thing—cheap perfume, the smell of fried food or even a dusty wind—would now set them off and affect her breathing. She tried to convince us she was well and not to worry, but we could see her fading before our eyes. Yet still she fussed over me, cooking for me when I was studying, insisting I go to my English class and waiting for me when I got home.

As summer turned into winter that year, I felt as though the rest of the world was starting to lose interest in Afghanistan. The West seemed pleased that the Soviets had been defeated and gone home, and that was all they needed to know about Afghanistan. For Pakistan and Iran, neighbouring countries with keen interest in what happened across the border, the various Mujahideen commanders had become proxies, used to fight out their own battles on neutral soil. But even as the Mujahideen fought for power, settled old scores and struck deals with neighbouring governments, a new power was growing elsewhere in Afghanistan. A movement was growing in the *madrassas*—religious schools—in the south of the country. A movement by the name of Taliban, which would one day shake not only Afghanistan but the whole world.

Dear Shuhra and Shaharzad,

Life is a miracle given to us by God. At times, life can feel like both a blessing and a curse. Sometimes it gets almost too much to cope with, but we do cope because humans have a great capacity to endure suffering.

But we human beings aren't great. Only God is great. Humans are like tiny little insects in the wider universe. Our problems, which sometimes seem so big and insurmountable to us, are really not.

Even if we live a long time, our time on earth is still very short. What matters is how we spend our time here and the legacy we leave behind to those left on earth. Your grandmother left a far bigger legacy to all of us than she ever knew or could have understood when she was alive.

With love,
Your mother

EIGHT

Losing Her

{ *November 1993* }

THE FIRST TIME I saw the man I would marry, my mother was dying.

In the previous three months, she had gotten progressively worse and now she was barely able to breathe and too weak to move. She had been admitted to hospital, but everyone could see she didn't have long to live.

I had heard rumours that a man called Hamid from a district called Khawhan, which is near to our home village in Badakhshan, wanted to send a marriage proposal to me. I had never met him and knew little about him, except that he was an intellectual type and a teacher.

One night, I was sitting by my mother's bed when several Badakhshani men came to pay their respects to her. Hamid was among them. I was embarrassed, because it is not culturally allowed for a woman to meet a man who is interested in marrying her until an engagement has been agreed. And I was still only seventeen. I wasn't sure I even wanted to get married.

There was a group of ten men, and although I'd never seen him before I knew instantly which one was Hamid. He was young, with a lean body and a face that was both handsome and intelligent. Not bookish, but with an expression of curiosity and empathy. He was someone you instantly warmed to.

I was secretly pleased that my suitor was physically attractive. I tried very hard not to look at him directly; that would have been very bad. But in the close confines of the hospital, I couldn't avoid glancing at him.

My mother was sitting in a wheelchair, so weak she could barely speak. But she still tried to play the gracious hostess, the role that came so naturally to her, fussing over her guests and asking if they were comfortable. The sight of her broke my heart. At one point she asked me to remove the blanket covering her knees and to wheel her into the sunlight. Hamid leapt up and leaned over to help remove the blanket. He was so gentle with her, rearranging a pillow behind her head with such tenderness and care that I was taken aback. In a flash, I realized this was a rare Afghan man and a man who might treat me with tenderness too.

My mother must have had the same thought, because when the men left she took my hand in hers and looked into my eyes. "Fawzia jan. I want you to be happy in your marriage. I like this man. I think he is enough for us. When I recover we will both go to live with him."

Her eyes searched mine for a reaction, and when I smiled and nodded she beamed, her spirit and strength still shining strong through her watery pale eyes. I turned away, biting back tears. I wanted so much for my mother to come and live with me and this kind man, and for me to be able to look after her as she had looked after me. But she was growing frailer by the minute.

I was sleeping at the hospital, refusing to leave my mother's side, and the next day I heard that Hamid had sent a proposal. In the traditional manner of asking for a lady's hand, male members of his family came to our house to speak with my brother. But my brother was also at the hospital with us that night. A proposal can be made only in person, so it wasn't to be.

The following morning, the hospital doctor, a warm lady with grey hair and green eyes, asked to speak to me in private. She wanted to impart the news she had already told my brother the night before.

"Fawzia," she said gently, "all trees blossom and all trees wither. It's the nature of life. It is time to take your mother home."

I understood what she meant. My mother was dying; there was no hope. I screamed and pleaded and begged for her to stay in the hospital. They could try new medicine, there must be hope, something they could do . . . The doctor hugged me and shook her head silently. It was over.

We took her home and tried to make her as comfortable as possible. Typically, she refused to rest or sit still and insisted on attempting to carry out chores. Once, my brother told her, with tongue in cheek, that if she didn't rest, he would have to physically restrain her. For a while, I lay on the bed with her. I stroked her hair and told her stories about my life at school just as I had always done. She told me how proud she was of me, about her amazement that the daughter of an illiterate woman like her had become educated. And she jokingly reminded me that I might still one day be president.

Normally, I loved it when she talked like this, buoyed by her dreams and her belief in me. But on that day, I couldn't see anything but a gaping black hole, the emptiness of the inevitable fate that was about to come. I fell asleep. At about 2 A.M. I heard her calling for me. I found her outside the bathroom, where she'd collapsed. She hadn't wanted to wake anyone and had attempted to go to the bathroom herself. I half picked her up, half dragged her back to bed in the living room. She felt like a tiny bird in my arms. That sight of her is a memory seared in pain across my brain. It was terrible to see a woman like that, a woman of such strength and dignity, who had endured so much in her life—beatings, death, tragedy, the loss of her husband and son—too weak to even take herself to the bathroom.

As she lay back to sleep, her breath started to rattle a little. Then I took her to her bedroom and placed her on the mattress on the floor. Unlike in the days of her marriage when she was expected to either share her husband's bed or sleep on the kitchen floor, she now had a bed of her own. But she was too weak to climb in and out of it, so she slept on the mattress. I also think she secretly preferred the floor, having grown so accustomed to it over the years.

Usually when she slept there, she liked to have one of her grand-children, my brother's children, with her. That night, she had my six-month-old niece, Katayoun, sleeping next to her. I smiled when I saw the baby's little fingers curled around my mother's hair. I had also done that as a child. I waited until I was sure she was asleep, then I crawled into her proper bed and went to sleep.

That night, I had a very unusual dream in which I saw nothing but fear and a blackness. I was trying to run away from it. I woke up with a start.

I looked over at my mother on the mattress and realized that her blanket was not shaking. There was no sign of breathing.

I lifted up the blanket and could see she was almost gone, her breathing so weak it was imperceptible. My screams woke up the rest of the family. My brother had been about to start his morning prayers. He ran into the room clutching his Koran so he could read her some verses as a last goodbye. I screamed at him to stop. I didn't want to believe my mother was taking her last breaths.

I shouted at my family to bring a doctor. Someone ran next door to a neighbouring house where we knew a doctor lived. They were back within minutes, but the doctor simply repeated what every-one knew. She was passing out of this life, and there was nothing we could do. I heard his words but I couldn't take them in. "I'm sorry," he kept saying. "I'm sorry. She's almost gone."

I felt like throwing myself out of the fifth-floor window. The lights had gone out. The stars had fallen out of the sky, and I wanted to follow them. I did not see how I could live without her.

For forty days after her death, I slipped in and out of conscious-ness. The shock and trauma had sent my body into almost total shut-down. I was really not in a fit mental state for at least six months after that. I didn't want to talk to anybody or go anywhere, and no one could get through to me. I am not even sure I wanted to live. My family was incredibly supportive. No one forced me to try to move faster; they let me take my grief at my own pace. They were grieving too, but they all knew my mother and I had had a special bond.

All my life, I had shared a bedroom with my mother. I couldn't sleep unless she was lying next to me, my fingers curled in her hair. I lay awake at night and tried to imagine her there. I cried and cried for her. I wailed for my mother as if I were a newborn baby.

After six months of watching me grieve like this, my family feared I'd never improve. They had a family conference and decided the only thing that might help me was a return to education. Mother had died in the autumn, and now it was spring again. A new term was beginning, and my brother suggested I go back to study English and also take a computer class. By now, even those brothers opposed to my education knew it was the only thing I might choose to live for.

At the time my mother had fallen sick, I had been due to take my high school leaving exams. I'd been too upset to take them, but the teachers arranged for me to take them now. If I didn't do so, I'd automatically fail. So I had to go. And of course it helped. Slowly, I entered the world again.

My nineteenth birthday was approaching. I admitted myself to the university exam preparation classes; I had decided I wanted to study medicine and become a doctor. Hamid knew that I was in this class. Sometimes, even though he wasn't supposed to, he would drive his car over and park it at the end of the street. He thought I couldn't see him, but I recognized the car and the man inside. I never approached him or waved. To do so would have been culturally indecent of me.

After a couple of weeks of this, he grew braver and would walk over to greet me as I left class. It was very formal, and we never discussed anything personal or our feelings for one another. He'd ask how my family was, I would reply politely and that was that. In Afghan culture, there can be no courtship or dating. We were not even allowed to speak on the telephone. There were no cellphones in those days, and the land lines were not working as all the power lines had been damaged by the fighting. We obeyed the cultural rules, which we both respected. But these little moments with him were enough for me: even if he spoke only three words to me, I would live off the memory all week and replay it over and over in my head. Hamid's smile eased some of the grief for my mother. I would remember her words: "This man is enough for us, Fawzia jan."

By now, the fighting was beginning to calm down. The different Mujahideen factions had begun to broker agreements with each other. Kabul was still a divided city, with the various factions in control of different areas, but they had started negotiations with each other and begun drafting a new government constitution. Most people saw this as a sign that the war was behind us. Soldiers no longer patrolled the streets, and it was safe not to wear a burka. I always covered my head with a scarf, of course, but I also proudly wore jeans and fashionable long embroidered tunics in bright colours.

The sense of relief on the streets was palpable. Cinemas that had closed because of the fighting sprang back into life, showing the latest Indian films, and children returned to play in parks that had formerly been home to snipers. The bustling streets around the centre of Kabul once more smelled of *kabab* as street vendors and their customers felt safe to be out. The indomitable spirit of Kabul city surged back once more.

My life was also beginning to take on a regular pattern again. But I was still deeply traumatized. One of my favourite possessions was a beautiful doll, who sat in a cart and carried a stuffed dog with her. I was too old to be playing with dolls, but I needed security and comfort, and the doll seemed to give me that. I would spend hours brushing her hair and putting nice clothes on her, obsessively arranging a vase of flowers next to her cart.

Hamid wasn't the only person trying to propose to me at this time. Various Mujahideen commanders also came to see my brothers to ask for my hand. Fortunately, my brothers would never have forced me to marry against my will. I had to agree to the match. The more I compared these men with Hamid, the more I knew it was him I wanted to marry. I didn't want to be the wife of a soldier; I wanted to be the wife of the intellectual with kind eyes.

Hamid was a trained engineer but he ran a small finance company, a kind of money exchange. He also taught chemistry part-time at the university. The idea of being married to a lecturer with his own business was a far more romantic notion to me than being married to someone who carried a gun for a living.

His family came several times to talk to my brothers and send the proposal, but each time my family said no. My brothers' biggest fear was that Hamid's family were not as rich as we were and that there would be too great a difference in our lifestyles. Hamid relied on his salary to make ends meet and had no other sources of income. My brothers also wanted me to continue the family tradition of expanding our political networks by marrying someone from a politically useful family. Hamid's family was not that.

My brother Mirshakay discussed it with me honestly. He told me he knew I liked this man but that he was trying to protect me by opposing the match. "Fawzia jan, how will you cope if he loses his job? You've grown up in a family where no one had to rely on a monthly salary to live. Imagine the stress each month of having to pay for rent and food and not knowing where the money will come from."

But my brother's concerns didn't worry me. I had always wanted to work too. My education had given me career prospects. We would both work and contribute to the household. We would be a team, real partners. I wanted a life in which I could make the decisions along with my husband. Unfortunately, this was not something I could explain to my brother. Culturally, I could not tell him I liked Hamid or how we spoke to each other outside the university. That would never have been allowed. But my silence and the clear expression of pain on my face when my brother spoke negatively about him probably told him all he needed to know.

I tried to get the support of my sisters, thinking they could help win my brother over, but they too were opposed to my marrying Hamid. They all wanted the best for me—and in their eyes, a life of wealth and status was best. They told me stories of wedding parties they had attended with thousands of guests where the bride was given her weight in gold jewellery. They tried to enthuse me about the kind of wedding I might have if I married one of my richer suitors. But it meant nothing to me. What use was gold? I wanted the gift of freedom. In the life they wanted for me, I would have felt like a bird trapped in a gilded cage.

I came from a family in which polygamy was the norm, but I knew I didn't want it for myself. My father had seven wives, and my two elder brothers each had two, so I had seen too much of the pain and jealousy the women suffered. Many of the suitors who came for me were already married, and I'd have been wife number two or three. I didn't want to destroy another woman's life in the same way I had seen my father's later wives destroy my mother. And I would never have coped with the lack of independence that came with that situation. I think I might even have killed myself after a week of a life like that.

The next winter came. By now, I had a diploma in English and had started volunteering as an English teacher, teaching women of all ages. It was an amazing experience for me, watching the light go on in my pupils' faces when they understood something. I loved it.

I didn't ask for a salary, but one day the head of the course gave me about two thousand afghanis, the equivalent of forty dollars. They were my first-ever earnings. I was so proud I almost cried. I didn't spend the money but kept it in my purse and just kept looking at it. I wanted to keep it there forever.

As the snow started to fall, I was finally feeling happy. I passed my university entrance exam and got a place in the medical school. I was teaching, and I had some independence. The raw, angry hole in my heart that was my mother's absence was still there, but the pain had dulled to a manageable level.

The fighting was becoming more and more sporadic. Rabbani's government had finally achieved a degree of calm. In the summer of 1995, a peace agreement was brokered. Hekmatyar agreed to lay down his arms in return for the position of prime minister within the Rabbani government. The motive behind the peace agreement was the growing influence of the Taliban in the south.

No one knew much about the Taliban, other than that they were religious students who had studied at the *madrassas* in the border regions between Afghanistan and Pakistan. Stories abounded about how these young men wore white clothes and called themselves the "angels of rescue." Villagers living in the south, like people throughout Afghanistan, had grown tired of the civil war, the lack of rule of law and the weak central government. As the fighting raged in Kabul, people living in quieter provinces had felt ignored and neglected. Their overwhelming poverty had not disappeared but had only worsened in the chaos, and they were desperate for a proper government that could help them.

These men who called themselves angels arrived in villages on the back of pickups and set about restoring order and security at the community level. They were almost like self-styled vigilantes, but for people who had been too scared to open their shops for fear of looting or to send their children to school these vigilantes started to make individual neighbourhoods safe. That was enough to foster confidence in them.

Ironically, the latest Mujahideen peace treaty allowed the Rabbani government to function effectively for the first time. The civil war was over, and the Mujahideen government was finally sharing power peacefully and doing a decent job of running the country. But it was all too little, too late to placate a desperate population. Calm had descended, but calm in Afghanistan is as fleeting and fragile as the life of a butterfly. The Afghan people were already looking for new heroes to believe in. The Taliban were on the ascent.

PART TWO

My dear mother,

I still wait and hope that you will come back. Even now, my breath catches in my throat when I remember that you are no longer in this world with me. I'm a politician now. But sometimes I'm just a silly girl who makes mistakes. When I do, I imagine you'll be there gently chiding me and correcting me. If I arrive home later than usual, I still expect you to be waiting in the yard for me in your burka, prodding me in the back until I reach the front door.

I still wish I could sleep curled next to you, as I did until the last days of your life. I want to lie next to you with my fingers in your hair and listen as you tell me stories about your life. Stories about your good times, your bad times, your sufferings, your patience and your hopefulness.

Mother, your stories taught me how to live.

Those stories taught me that as a woman I should learn to suffer and be patient. I remember as a child when I was not happy during the day—when one of my brothers would tell me not to go to school, or my mind couldn't concentrate properly in the class, or I saw my classmate's father coming to pick up my friend from school with his nice car, or when my girlfriend Nooria talked about her father. At those times, I would feel very sad about the loss of my own father, and a great sorrow would take over my heart. At those times, I thought that I was the weakest and poorest girl in the world—but whenever I remembered your stories, I grew stronger. How could I be weak when you told me how you had married when you were sixteen years old? How so often you endured a new woman marrying my father and how, despite your pain, you stayed with my father and his other wives so that your children could have a good future?

It was important for you that my father should be the best man in the world; that is why you always tried to make the best food for his guests and why you always kept the yard tidy. That is why you would always be nice to the other women of the family so they didn't become jealous and create problems for him. I think of how you used all your natural intelligence to try to solve people's problems when my father was not around, and how after my father was martyred you realized how important it was that his children—both girls and boys—go to school and live with you in the same house so that you would know their problems and be there for them. It was important for you that my brothers should grow to be men of good character and become people who could do something for their country. You suffered and starved yourself so my brothers could study and go to university.

When I remember all this, I still feel amazed that through all these problems and heavy responsibilities you laughed. You laughed all the time.

I wish I was able to face my problems laughing like you.

Mother, my entire world was in these stories.

The interesting thing was the older I became, the more I wanted to hear these nighttime tales; they would make me feel calm and safe in bed. Maybe I was trying to escape from the war all around us.

You were the refuge from my surroundings. The best moments in my life were after you had finished the stories and would turn your attention to me. Promising me I'd become someone important. Telling me my father's words after I was born, that I would grow to be like you. Beautiful, clever, wise and warm. They were small words, but they became my inspiration to struggle and strive for a better life.

When I asked you what I would become, you'd smile and reply, "Maybe, Fawzia jan, you will be a teacher or a doctor. You will have your own clinic and will treat the poor patients who come from the provinces for free. You will be a kind, good doctor." Then I would laugh and say: "No, Mother, maybe I will be a president." I said this because once I heard you telling a neighbour, "My daughter tries so hard at school. I am sure she will become president."

I learned so many life lessons from those stories.

And I have never felt so calm and safe with anybody else as I did with you. Mother, I learned from you what self-sacrifice really means. I learned from you that literacy alone is not enough to bring up good children but that intelligence, patience, planning and self-sacrifice are what really count. This is the example of Afghan women, women like you who would walk miles with an empty stomach to make sure your children got to school.

I learned from you that any human, even a "poor girl," can change everything if she has a positive and strong attitude.

Mother, you were among the bravest of the bravest Afghan women. I am glad you were not here to witness the horrors that came next in our lives—the Taliban years.

Your daughter,
Fawzia

NINE

One Ordinary Thursday

{ *1996* }

I WILL NEVER forget the day the Taliban came to Kabul. It was a
Thursday in September. I had stayed home from university that day
to study. My sister Shahjan needed to buy bread, and I needed a new
pair of shoes, so in the afternoon we walked to the bazaar together.

I was wearing one of my favourite brightly coloured head scarves
and a tunic. My sister told me a joke, and I giggled. A shopkeeper
smiled at us and said, "You ladies will not be able to come here
dressed like that tomorrow. The Taliban will be here and this will
be your last day of pleasure in the market, so be sure to enjoy your-
selves." He was laughing as he said it, his green eyes smiling and the
lines around them crinkled. I thought he was joking, but his remark
still made me angry. I stared at him furiously and told him this was
a wish he'd be taking to the grave because it would never come true.

I only vaguely knew who the Taliban were—religious students
who had formed a political movement—and we still didn't know
what they stood for. During the years we were fighting the Russians,
the Afghan Mujahideen had been joined by thousands of Arab, Pakistani and Chechen fighters. They had been funded by other countries, such as the USA, Pakistan and Saudi Arabia, to help fight the

Soviets. Each of those countries had its own vested interests and political reasons for helping us. While their help in our battle was initially welcomed, these foreign Mujahideen fighters brought with them a fundamentalist version of Islam, Wahhabism, which was new to Afghanistan. The Wahhabis originated in Saudi Arabia and form a particularly conservative branch of Sunni Islam. *Madrassas* in the border regions between Pakistan and Afghanistan promoted this type of Islam to young Afghan men, many of them barely children and many of them vulnerable, traumatized refugees.

But there was a lot of misinformation in those days. Some people in Kabul thought the Taliban were angels, whereas others thought they were Communists coming back in a new guise. But whoever they really were, I could not and would not believe that they, or anyone, had beaten the Mujahideen. The Mujahideen had defeated the mighty Red Army; how could a few students possibly defeat such men? The idea that by the next day they would have taken over the shop in which I was now standing was just ridiculous.

At that stage, I did not see much difference between the Taliban and the Mujahideen. As a child, I had been very much afraid of the Mujahideen. Now, as a university student, I was afraid of the Taliban. In my view, they were all just men with guns. Men who wanted to fight instead of talk. I was sick and tired of all of them.

But that night, we got the shocking news on BBC radio. We listened to it all night long, incredulous at what we were being told. The BBC reported that Ahmad Shah Massoud's men had withdrawn from Kabul and gone back to their stronghold in the Panjshir Valley. I still couldn't accept that it meant defeat. Tactical withdrawal was not an unusual military tactic for Massoud. I truly thought he'd be back to fight before breakfast to restore peace and support the government. Most people in Kabul thought the same.

Suddenly, the front door opened and my brother Mirshakay, the senior police chief, came in looking terrified. He spoke rapidly, saying he didn't have much time. He had asked his wife to pack his bag. He, like many senior government officials, was leaving to join Massoud in Panjshir.

I had so many unanswered questions about the future. I started to argue with him. His wife began crying. He hissed at us and told us to be quiet in case anyone heard.

Mirshakay had two wives, and it was decided that one would stay in Kabul in the apartment with me, while the other would be taken by her family that same night to Pakistan, where my brother owned a house in the city of Lahore.

It all happened so quickly we could barely believe it was real. As my brother went back out the door, my sister threw a pot of water after him. This is part of our culture: if the water follows the target, it is said he will come back soon.

With Mirshakay gone, we women huddled around the radio. The latest reports stated that President Rabbani and his ministers had also fled. They had gone by plane to Panjshir and from there to Rabbani's home province of Badakhshan. Then it was reported that former president Najibullah, the man who had been regarded as Moscow's puppet and a Communist sympathizer, had been killed. Najibullah had been under United Nations protection. But as the Mujahideen government collapsed, Ahmad Shah Massoud had gone to meet him and offered to take him back to the Panjshir Valley. But Najibullah didn't trust the Mujahideen any more than he did the Taliban and he feared the former were setting a trap to kill him. That was perhaps understandable in his position, but not trusting Massoud at that critical moment was to be his fatal mistake. Within hours of Massoud retreating, Najibullah would be dead.

At 8 o'clock that night, jets flew overhead. My family teased me that "even in war Fawzia keeps her nose in a book." I wasn't particularly fond of the Rabbani government, but at least it was a government. At least there was some kind of system. But now, officials like my brother were leaving their posts and running. I was furious that our leaders were giving up so easily.

We barely slept that night. We just listened to the radio as the country unravelled around us once more. At 6 o'clock in the morning, I looked out the window and saw people wearing little white prayer hats. Suddenly, everyone was wearing them. I quickly closed the curtain and returned to my studies; I wanted to shut out this new world, this latest incarnation of Kabul that I didn't understand.

Then the rumours started. It was a Friday, prayer day. Reports started surfacing that they were beating people to make them go to the mosque. By now we had realized they weren't Communists or angels of rescue. So who were they? Never in the history of Afghanistan had we experienced anything like this. It was clear they were a strange force, not controlled by Afghans. They couldn't be, behaving like that.

We learned that they had forced Najibullah from the United Nations building where he had been staying in sanctuary. The Taliban had stormed the UN compound, dragged him out and executed him. They hung both his body and that of his younger brother at a busy roundabout for everyone to see. For three days, as the bodies slowly turned yellow and bloated, they hung there as a warning. People drove past in scared silence. No one dared take the bodies down.

Then they looted the museum, destroying thousands of artefacts reflecting the history of our land—ancient Buddhist statuettes, Kundan ornaments, eating vessels from the time of Alexander the Great, relics dating from the times of the earliest Islamic kings. In the name of God, these vandals destroyed our history.

The world took notice of this cultural vandalism when they blew up the Buddhas of Bamiyan. These ancient stone statues were regarded as one of the wonders of the world. They were built in the remote region of Bamiyan in the sixth century AD, during the reign of the Kushans, great patrons of art, before Islam was brought to Afghanistan. The giant Buddhas were not only an important piece of Afghan cultural history and a sign of our diverse religious past but also a representation of the livelihood of the Hazara people who live in Bamiyan. The Buddhas had long attracted visitors from all over the world as well as elsewhere in Afghanistan, and a healthy tourist industry had developed in Bamiyan because of them. In an otherwise poor province, this industry represented essential income for the people.

In shocking and tragic TV footage that was broadcast around the world, the Taliban were seen blasting the statues with rocket-propelled grenades and heavy artillery until these great monuments collapsed into smithereens.

Then the Taliban started destroying our minds. They burned the schools and university buildings. They burned books and banned literature. I had only recently started my medical degree course, which I loved. That weekend, I was supposed to have an exam, and I had been studying hard for it. But I was told not to bother going, as my medical faculty had closed. Women were no longer allowed to study medicine at university, let alone be doctors.

In an instant, so much of Kabuli life, the things people took for granted, were gone. Even in the war, small, pleasurable activities, such as meeting friends for a cup of tea in the bazaar or listening to music on the radio, and bigger events, such as a wedding party, had still been possible. But under the Taliban, they disappeared overnight. In our culture, as in most other cultures around the world, a wedding is a rite of passage that involves the whole family and circle of friends. Afghan weddings are traditionally very large; anywhere from five hundred to five thousand people attend. Owning a wedding hall or hotel can be a lucrative business. The best ones can command high prices, and it's not unusual for families to pay the whole bill of twenty or thirty thousand dollars in advance.

During their first weekend in power, the Taliban banned all weddings in public places. Hundreds of couples had to cancel their big days. Not only did they lose their wedding day, the day little girls all over the world dream about, but their families, already struggling because of the war-ravaged economy, lost their money. The Taliban ordered people to have private ceremonies at home with no guests, no music and no fun. The wedding anniversaries of the couples who married that day are a kind of anniversary of Taliban rule. It wasn't the wedding day they expected, but it's something they will certainly remember until the end of their lives.

Of course, many people tried to defy the ban. Proud fathers refused to allow these upstarts to destroy such an important family day and tried to go ahead as planned. Some hotel owners ignored the new rule and carried on business as usual. But the Taliban drove around town in pickup trucks, in their black turbans and carrying guns and whips; when they heard wedding party music, they raided the premises. The so-called angels of rescue had become the harbingers of violence. They burst into the wedding halls shouting and yelling, smashing speakers, ripping tape from video cameras and tearing photographic film. And they beat people senseless. They beat the grooms in front of their brides and knocked elderly grandfathers to the ground in full view of their frightened guests. I kept hearing these stories, but I still could not believe they were true. I think I was in denial.

The next day, my sister, who routinely wore a burka, went to the market to get some vegetables. She came back from the market in a flood of tears. She had seen the Taliban beating all women who weren't in burkas and were wearing only head scarves—women who dressed like me. I listened in shock.

She sobbed as she told me how she watched a man and wife pushing their bicycles along the street laden with shopping bags. The woman wasn't even in modern jeans or a skirt. She was wearing a traditional *shalwar kameez* and had covered her hair with a large scarf. The couple were chatting when the Taliban came from behind and attacked the woman. Three of them set upon her, beating her with wire cable and thumping her around the head so viciously she fell to the ground. When they started to beat the man, he denied she was his wife. To save himself, he denounced his own wife.

The idea that an Afghan man could denounce his wife so easily was horrifying. In traditional Afghan culture, men will fight to the death to protect their wives and families, but the Taliban brought such fear and evil with them that they perverted some of the men of our nation. Not all, but some men—who had previously been good men and kind husbands—were swayed, by fear or the excitement of a mob psychology, into believing this warped ideology.

For the next week, I didn't go anywhere. TV had been banned. The state radio station had been taken over for Taliban propaganda purposes. Woman presenters, even the old, ugly ones with no makeup whom the Mujahideen favoured, had been banned. A popular young male news presenter who had used the wrong word in a report about the death of a Taliban commander was beaten on the soles of his feet and left in a shipping container for three days with no food or water. In his nervousness, he had mistakenly used the word "joyous" instead of "tragic" to describe the death—an understandable slip when you consider that men with whips were standing behind him as he broadcast live. Who wouldn't be nervous?

I couldn't even listen to the propaganda they called news. I wanted real news that would make me feel connected to the outside world. Not having it made me feel like I was in prison. But local grapevine news, delivered from neighbour to neighbour, could not be stopped and each story I heard was more horrible than the one before.

The fighting outside Kabul continued. The Shomali Plain, the area between Massoud's stronghold of Panjshir and the city, became the new front line. Most people were still expecting Massoud's troops to come back. We couldn't believe this Taliban reality was going to be permanent. The only place where I could meet other girls and talk was on the communal balcony of the apartment block when I was cleaning the house. Watching from the balcony, I could see other young girls in the other apartments. Young, beautiful girls were being deprived of their basic rights, of breathing the fresh air and feeling the sun. As soon as these girls heard the sound of Taliban voices they scarpered, running as fast as they could back inside.

I needed to connect with my mother. I missed her badly but was thankful that she didn't have to witness this latest abomination against her country. I wanted to visit her grave but I could not bring myself to put on a burka. I didn't even own one. So I borrowed a black Arab-style *niqab* from my sister. It was like a large cape that also covered the whole face, so I thought I'd be safe wearing it. The streets were deserted, the air so thick with fear you could almost cut it.

Few men and even fewer women dared to go outside; the women who did were dressed in blue shuttlecock burkas, the new uniform of Afghan women. They scurried along silently, doing their shopping as quickly as possible so they could get home to safety. No one talked to anyone. Shopkeepers handed over bags wordlessly; women took them without looking up or making eye contact. Occasionally a Taliban pickup truck would drive by, the men inside glowering menacingly, looking for new victims to beat, as loudspeakers on the top of the truck blasted out religious teachings. I thought that by now I knew fear in all its forms and shapes, but this was a new one. I was cold, clammy and tinged with an icy fury. My fury. After that, I didn't leave the house again for almost two months.

We hadn't heard from my brother Mirshakay since the first Taliban had taken control. Like him, many former Mujahideen and government workers had fled, taking their families with them. The Shomali Plain and the Panjshir Valley—in the province northeast of Kabul—were scenes of fierce fighting but still very much under the control of Ahmad Shah Massoud. But his men weren't the only ones fleeing. Others, former Communists, university professors and doctors, were also fleeing. Grabbing what they could—a few clothes, jewellery, food supplies—they loaded up the car and left town. They left behind everything they had worked for. People who only weeks earlier had congratulated themselves on their good fortune because their houses had survived the civil war intact were now locking the gates of those houses behind them and walking out without a second glance.

Not all of them made it to safety. We heard stories of cars being attacked and looted. People's few possessions were taken from them, gold necklaces ripped from women's necks, earrings torn from their lobes. The looters were criminals taking advantage of the chaos. As people approached the front line—the other side of which promised relative safety—many were killed, their cars hit by rockets or stray gunfire.

I prayed and prayed for Massoud to come back. Each night I went to sleep begging him, willing him, to push back the front line into the city centre. I wanted to wake up and find the Taliban and their twisted ideas gone.

Eventually, we got a letter from my brother saying he had been hiding in his driver's house in Parwan province, just to the north of Kabul—a beautiful area with a river and lush valleys full of trees. In the summer, people have picnics there. Traditional Afghan picnics are a lovely affair—boiled eggs, juice and plump mulberries picked fresh from the trees.

My brother wanted his wife and children to go to him. I decided to travel with them. Even now, despite the dangers, I still could not bring myself to put on a burka, so I wore the black *niqab* instead, making sure my face was fully covered. I also wore a pair of glasses to disguise myself further: even with my face covered, I feared someone would recognize me as the sister of the police officer.

Although Parwan is right next to Kabul and the direct route is only an hour's drive, it was too close to the Mujahideen and Taliban front line to drive directly. We didn't want to risk being hit by a rocket, so we drove south first, from Sarobi to Tagab and then to Nijrab in Kapisa province, which is almost a day's travel on a bumpy road. This was totally the opposite direction of where we needed to go, but the direct route was too dangerous. So we had to loop back, then around, then backwards, then forwards, then backwards again to get to Parwan. Other people fleeing had discovered new tracks over fields, puzzling, circuitous tracks, some leading to nowhere, others to another loop. It was an awful journey. For the twelve hours we drove, I was terrified we'd hit a landmine, be robbed or come under gunfire. We didn't dare risk stopping for a break or for water.

Once again, I felt like I was driving away from my dreams. Every time I tried to start life anew, I was thwarted. This was no life, constantly moving, constantly escaping, living on nerves and ever-dwindling reserves of hope.

I was also driving away from Hamid. I hadn't been able to contact him to tell him I was leaving. And I hadn't seen him since the last day I was at university when he'd walked over to say hello to me. I recalled watching the back of his head as he retreated to the car, loving the way the wind caught his silky hair as it ruffled into little curls. I had spoken hardly more than a few sentences to him, but I truly felt that I was beginning to love him. Now that I was leaving with my family, I had no idea when I might see him again.

And now that the war was officially over, the world also began to move on. The Cold War had ended, and the mighty Soviet Empire was collapsing. The Afghan fight against the Russians was no longer of relevance to the West. It was no longer broadcast internationally on the nightly news. Our civil war was over, and as far as the world understood it the Taliban were now our government. We were yesterday's story. Other tragedies now occupied the front pages.

But our tragedy was not over. In many ways, it was just beginning. And for the next few years, the world forgot us. They were our bleakest years of need.

Dear Shuhra and Shaharzad,

If we Afghans lived in darkness during those years of war, then the days that were about to follow would truly plunge us into the blackest depths of hell. A living hell created by men who called themselves men of God and men of Islam. But these men represented nothing of the Islamic religion according to which I, and millions of other Afghans, live our daily lives. Ours is a peaceful, tolerant and loving faith that accords all human beings rights and equal value.

I want you to understand, as women, that true Islam accords you political and social rights. It offers you dignity, the freedom to be educated, to pursue your dreams and to live your life. It also asks that you behave decently, modestly and with kindness to all. I believe it is a true guide to living correctly in this earthly world, and I am proud to call myself a Muslim. I have brought you up to become good, strong Muslim women.

These men called themselves the Taliban. Their form of Islam was so alien to us it could have come from another planet. Many of their ideas about Islam came from different cultures, mostly from Arab lands. They rode in trucks and carried guns, promising the Afghan people they would keep the streets safe, restore order and promote strong justice and local harmony. In the beginning, many people believed them, but that hope quickly turned to fear and loathing, especially for the women and girls of Afghanistan.

You were lucky not to be young women in those days. Very lucky indeed.

With love,
Your mother

TEN

Retreat to the North

{ *1996* }

IN PARWAN, WE stayed with my brother's driver. The man and his family were not rich but they let us stay in an annex adjoining their house. They refused to allow us to cook, preparing all our food for us. My brother and his family and I were treated like honoured guests, not an unwelcome burden.

Things continued to get worse in Kabul, and my sister and her husband (who was also at risk from the Taliban because he was a police officer) came to join us. It was decided that this pair would move on again to Puli Khumri farther north and find a house, and then we would all go and join them. Although Parwan was still safe for now, it was not far enough from Kabul to remain so for much longer. Importantly for me, no one in the north forced you to wear a burka. For me, that was enough reason to go.

My sister and her husband had been in Puli Khumri, about 250 kilometres away, for almost a week but had not yet managed to arrange a house for us when the Taliban started gaining ground outside of Parwan, edging closer to where we were staying. I was fast asleep when Mirshakay shook me awake, screaming that we needed to get into the car *now*. The Mujahideen had closed the Salang Pass. The second-highest road pass in the world, the pass had been built by the Soviets by blasting a five-kilometre-long tunnel right through the centre of the mountain, an incredible feat of engineering. It was a one-lane pass, accessible only in the drier months. It is also the gateway to northern Afghanistan.

The Mujahideen were worried that thousands of people would now try to flee north, thereby bringing more insecurity and possibly the Taliban with them. So in a brutal but strategic military move, they ordered the pass closed. A move that trapped everyone on one side or the other. And which meant we would be unable to join the others in Puli Khumri.

My brother had managed to get an approval letter from one of the Northern Alliance commanders that allowed us to take two cars through: one for us and one for our security escort. One of the women in our party had neither a *niqab* nor a burka, so I gave her my *niqab*. All I had to wear on my head was a bright red scarf. By now, the fighting was coming so close that if the Taliban reached us and caught us, I would be badly beaten.

The escort car was also red, a Hilux pickup. The irony made me laugh; I wondered how much more visible we, and I in particular, could possibly make ourselves. We drove out of the house into the main street. Everywhere, people were trying to escape. A large coach drove towards us. It was crammed with terrified-looking people, three or four hanging out of each window and more lying on the roof. They looked like bees swarming a hive.

As we left the village for the main road, we joined a convoy of cars. Thousands of people were trying to escape the encroaching Taliban. Their cars were full of clothes, kitchen equipment, blankets and animals. Everything they owned. People were hanging off the sides of cars, anywhere they could.

I saw a man hanging from the door of a taxi. He was Uzbek in appearance, with a round face and almond-shaped eyes. He looked like a Mujahideen fighter. Blood was running down his leg, and he jumped down, obviously unable to hold onto the side of the taxi any longer. He walked over to our car holding a gun; he waved it and ordered us to stop, but the driver ignored him. Then he aimed at the tire and shot. As the tire burst, the car swerved and almost hit the man. I was sitting at the front of the car terrified that he would come and drag me out, but our driver held his nerve and managed to keep going. The man moved on to the cars behind, shooting desperately. I dared not look back to see if he had killed some poor family.

People had no idea where they were heading. They just wanted to get out. It was the beginning of winter, and as we rode up into the mountains towards the Salang Pass the cold began to bite. The altitude made it hard to breathe, and the chill even inside our car bit into toes and fingers. The pass was already closed, and those families without letters of permission had to either stay on the freezing mountain or drive back home and straight into the Taliban front line. Even with the letter, it took several hours to get through. The commanders didn't want to alarm their fighters on the other side of the pass with the sight of refugees fleeing, which would tell them they had lost ground in the battle, so they let only a few cars pass to make it look as normal as possible.

In the queue of cars, my sister-in-law saw her cousin, a young girl who had recently married. She and her husband had their six-week-old baby in the car. They looked terrified; they had no letter of permission. In the freezing cold, the baby would surely die. So we agreed to leave our security car behind and allow their car to take its place. Everything we owned was in the security vehicle: bags, money, jewellery. We were promised it would be allowed through later.

Once safely through the Salang Pass, we needed to take a road that went not over the mountain but around it, our car precariously clinging to the edge. Normally, I am terrified of such heights and flimsy roads but that day I was just relieved that the Taliban had not caught us.

My sister-in-law had managed to arrange a place for us to stay. It had only a few rooms but some sixty people already occupied it. They were my brother's men, former policemen who now had nowhere else to go. That is why we have so many illegal armed groups in Afghanistan. When the system collapsed, they had no option but to join up with whoever had been their officer or leader and form a militia. However, my brother didn't want us to be surrounded by so many men so he asked them to return home to their families.

At midnight, we were told the security vehicle containing all our things had been allowed to pass and was here. I grabbed the bags as they were carried inside. I think I already knew that our jewellery was gone. The people who were supposed to be guaranteeing our safety had taken the lot. These men belonged to another local commander who had done my brother a favour by sending us the escort, so there was little we could do. My sister-in-law went through her luggage again and again, sobbing and almost manically searching through all the pockets for her missing jewellery. I thought she was hysterical. But then she pulled out a handkerchief and blew her nose loudly. I burst out laughing and then she followed suit. What else could we do but laugh? That handkerchief was pretty much all she had left. But at least we were safe again. For now.

Once again, the traumas of my homeland had forced my life to spiral out of my control. My dreams of being a doctor were shattered. By now the Taliban had banned all women from attending school and university. So even if Kabul had been safe enough for us to return, which it clearly wasn't, there was zero hope of my returning to study. Instead, my days were spent in Puli Khumri, cooking, cleaning or drinking *chai* in the garden. It was the life of boring drudgery my mother and sisters had endured, the one I had battled so hard to escape. I was very depressed. Days rolled into dusk, into sleepless nights and reluctant mornings when I would squeeze my eyes shut to block out the sun and the brightly mocking dawn of another new day.

By then so many male students, teachers and professors had fled the country the universities were almost pointless. Taliban rule had transformed Kabul from a war-torn city into a dead city. I honestly couldn't say which was worse.

People were arrested and beaten for the slightest misdemeanour. The Taliban went from door to door asking people to hand over their weapons. They refused to believe that not everyone in Kabul kept guns and wouldn't take no for an answer. If someone refused to hand their gun over or genuinely didn't have one, he was arrested and put in prison. Some families had to go out and buy weapons just to give them to the Taliban in order to release the person who'd been arrested.

One of the worst places someone could be taken was the Department of Vice and Virtue. The mere mention of this name could petrify the hearts of the bravest people. The pretty white stuccoed villa, situated in an area called Share Naw (New Town), had a garden full of lush grapes and scented roses. Here, people who had been accused of crimes against religion or what were called morality crimes were brought to be judged. Men whose beards were not long enough and women caught without burkas were brought here to be beaten on the soles of their feet with wire cable in the rooms inside, while outside Taliban guards sipped tea and told jokes among the roses. Here, terrified Kabuli women who had been accused of immorality were brought to be judged for their "crimes" by bearded mullahs from the conservative countryside villages of southern Afghanistan. Kabul and those villages had always been culturally and socially worlds apart. Women who just a few months earlier had proudly worn the latest fashions and carried books to university were being judged by unwashed men who couldn't read or write.

The Olympic sports stadium, a large round domed building that had once rung with the sounds of applause at cricket or football feats, became home to a new kind of sport—public executions. Adulterers and thieves were stoned to death or had their hands chopped off in front of cheering crowds. In grisly scenes reminiscent of a Roman coliseum, the prisoners were driven into the centre of the stadium in a pickup truck, dragged out and walked around for the crowd's entertainment. Then they were shot in the head or buried up to their waists and stoned to death. It didn't matter to those judging them or to the brutes casting the first stone that the thief may have stolen a loaf of bread to feed his hungry children or that the adulteress had in fact been raped.

All this was supposedly in the name of God. But I do not believe these were the actions of God. I am sure God would have turned away to weep.

Thousands of the Taliban's supporters flocked into Kabul. Ultra-conservative families from the south moved into Kabul, buying houses at rock-bottom prices from those seeking to escape. Wazir Akbar Khan, which had been one of the smartest and most sought-after addresses in Kabul with modern, architect-designed houses, beautiful gardens and swimming pools, became known as the "street of the guests." Favoured Arab and Pakistani fighters who had connections to the Taliban leadership were given houses there. If the house was empty, they just moved in and took over; if it had inhabitants, they were forced out at gunpoint, allowing the "guests" to move in.

Some families have still not regained control of properties they lost during this time. When the Taliban were defeated in 2001 by U.S. and Northern Alliance forces, many people who had been refugees in Europe or America returned to Afghanistan to regain their property. But with no documents and amid postwar chaos and a government rife with corruption, they found this to be a difficult process. I see many people who ask for my help in tracing property ownership. Few succeed. A building boom over the last couple of years has sadly destroyed—often illegally—hundreds of these beautiful, elegant villas with their fruit trees and grape arbours. They have been replaced with so-called "poppy palaces," ugly Pakistani- and Iranian-style buildings with gaudy decorations, smoked glass and lurid patterned tiles—an architecture that owes nothing to Afghan culture and everything to post-conflict profits, all too often gleaned from corruption or the proceeds of the heroin trade.

Today, different types of guests have taken over Wazir Akbar Khan. These houses, which have survived both the war and the developers, have stood the test of time and look just as stylish today as they did when they were built. Now they are inhabited by foreign aid workers and international journalists from global networks such as BBC, CNN and France24. The insecurity they feel in living and working in a capital city with frequent suicide bombings is denoted by the large sections of the neighbourhood that have been barricaded off. In an area known as the "green zone," the streets are blocked with concrete bollards and checkpoints in an attempt to keep suicide bombers out. Those without identification or the correct passes are barred from entering or driving through, a measure that creates traffic chaos and is a constant source of frustration and anger among many Kabulis towards these latest guests.

The British Embassy has recently taken over an entire street of houses for its compound, blocking entrances at both ends. What was once a bustling, rich neighbourhood with children playing ball games on the streets is now a fortress, off limits to most Afghans except those who need to travel there for work.

BACK IN Puli Khumri, we waited for long days. I spent every moment hoping for a return to Kabul. The front line and the areas controlled by the Taliban or Massoud's men kept shifting. But what was becoming sadly clear was that the Taliban were slowly gaining more ground and pushing Massoud farther and farther back.

I had no idea if Hamid was still living in Kabul or if he and his family had also fled. I thought of him constantly, but I also knew there was still a lot of objection from my brothers to our marriage. One day, I was sitting in the yard enjoying the sun on my face and watching snow fall on the mountains beyond. I was yearning for the city and wondering what the weather was like in Kabul when Hamid's sister, her children and one of his uncles arrived at our gate.

It turned out that Hamid had gone to our house and found the curtains drawn and no one there. He had asked around and found out where we had gone. Then he realized that this could work to our advantage. If I was in Mujahideen-controlled land, I was around armed militias and commanders and therefore at higher risk of getting raped. Hamid figured my brother had enough on his plate keeping his own two wives safe without also having to worry about my honour. This might finally make him more open to the idea of our marriage.

So here was his sister at our door with the proposal. She and her uncle, along with her three- and four-year-old children, had come from Kabul to ask Mirshakay once more for my hand. The journey had been a dangerous one. In addition to the fighting, they had gotten stuck when an avalanche narrowly missed their car and blocked the road in front of them; they had spent the night freezing. They could have been killed, and I felt rather angry at Hamid for having put them through all that because of me. Nonetheless, I was secretly thrilled at his newfound determination to make our wedding happen.

As Hamid had thought, my brother no longer had the power he had had in Kabul. He was exhausted and stressed. But he still wasn't quite ready to give in. In our culture, if you want to say no to someone's proposal politely you don't actually say so but rather give the person a list of requests they have no way of meeting. My brother knew Hamid's family had risked their lives to bring this request and he couldn't be so rude as to turn them away with no hope. But he still wasn't prepared to let the union happen. So after we had all finished dinner, he quietly told them the engagement could go ahead only if they paid for a house (which would be in my name) and gave large amounts of gold and jewellery and twenty thousand dollars in cash.

That was a lot of money, especially in wartime and especially for this family, who although not dirt poor were certainly not rich. I was not allowed to be part of the negotiations, of course. Hamid's sister and I were in the next room, and we strained our ears to the wall trying to keep abreast of proceedings. I gasped with horror when I heard my brother's conditions. Amazingly, however, Hamid's uncle agreed. He sounded somewhat shocked and not entirely happy but he did a good job of recovering himself and not appearing flustered. He must have been fuming inside, but he took his turban from his head and placed it in front of my brother as a sign of thanks for accepting the relationship.

Hamid's sister gathered up her children and hugged me goodbye with a warm smile before throwing her burka back over her head. The men put on their turbans before they left. The Taliban had made the wearing of turbans and beards obligatory for all men.

A few days later, my brother was asked to go to the Panjshir Valley, to help plan a new government-led attack on Kabul. After he left, the Salang Pass was closed once again and he was trapped on the other side. We had no news about him for forty days. The tension was unbearable. We had no idea what we would do if he was killed.

Finally, we received news that he had been in Badakhshan. He had been temporarily ordered back there by his commanders to create a new stronghold for the Mujahideen and to help organize a new line of defence. The Taliban were gaining more and more ground, and the commanders feared they were about to take more of the central and northern provinces. Eventually, he was returned to us safely.

The green shoots of spring were already pushing through the snow, but I had started to feel depressed again. Springtime should have meant a new term for me, and I desperately wanted to be back at university.

One day, my sister-in-law asked me to go shopping for the family dinner. For some reason, I kept imagining I was seeing Hamid's face everywhere at the bazaar. Every time I left a shop or turned a corner, I thought I saw him. Then he disappeared. I started to think I might be going mad. When I got home, we had a visitor. He was a teenage boy, one of our distant relatives who was also related to Hamid by marriage. I started to feel depressed again and politely excused myself to go to my room. The boy followed me to say goodbye. As he did so, he thrust a small piece of paper into my hand.

I closed the door of my room and opened the paper. It was a letter. My eyes scanned to the end of the page to see who it was from, but in my heart I already knew. Hamid. He was here in Puli Khumri. I hadn't been going mad at the bazaar. I was really seeing Hamid. He had been following me in secret. The letter told me he was here and that he was going to come the next day to talk to my brother about our marriage. This time, he would ensure that it would really happen.

I barely slept that night. The next day, just as he had promised in the letter, Hamid came to our house and asked to see my brother. Mirshakay was surprised, and possibly a little horrified, when Hamid produced the twenty thousand dollars in hard cash and documents showing proof of a house purchase. Despite all this, Mirshakay still wasn't prepared to give Hamid my hand in marriage.

Even now, he couldn't bring himself to say the final and direct yes that Hamid was waiting for.

Although the family was far from rich, they did own land in Badakhshan and had sold some of it to get the money. It wasn't as if they had nothing, but of course my brother, who owned four houses in Kabul and a house in Lahore, didn't see it that way.

Once again, the negotiations were strictly a male affair and we women sat in a different room. That was a strange feeling for me, sitting quietly and straining my ears to hear my future being argued over like a business transaction. In some ways, it reminded me of my childhood, sneaking up to my father's guest rooms to eavesdrop on the discussions inside. As I listened, I felt an odd mixture of pride, curiosity and powerlessness.

When I heard they had the money, I let out an involuntary squeak. My life had been pretty much dust in Puli Khumri. No university, no stimulation and nothing to do. I had no idea how marriage was going to be, but I figured it had to be less boring than this.

Engagements in Afghanistan are binding and as serious as the marriage contract. Only in exceptional circumstances can they be broken. The enormity of that suddenly hit me. I started to think about all the warnings my brother had given me. His voice kept repeating in my head: "Fawzia jan, do not marry this poor man. You can have any man you want. You will not be able to survive on his monthly salary. Marry a rich man, a powerful man."

I must admit, I started to have second thoughts. It is hard to imagine your life as a newlywed when your country is in ruins. Staying safe and alive took precedence over indulging in dreams. I had no idea what was going to happen, how long the Taliban would be here, whether the fighting would ever end, where we would live, whether I would be able to study again or ever be able to work.

My elder sister saw that I had gone white. She looked at me sternly and said, "Fawzia, you must decide. Now. Right now. If you don't want this to go ahead, this is your last chance to say so. Do you understand?"

A few days earlier, in a last effort to tempt me away from marrying Hamid, Mirshakay had promised me I could go to Pakistan and stay with his second wife in his house in Lahore. He said I could enrol in a Pakistani university. The idea of studying medicine again in a country not blighted by war was a wonderful one. But although I barely knew Hamid, what little I had seen of him convinced me we could make our marriage work. I knew he was an unusual Afghan man, one who would treat me like an equal and genuinely support my desire to work. He was not rich and the future was full of uncertainty, but he still felt like the right choice for me. Because he was *my* choice.

As is so often the case in my family history, it needed a woman to take the decisive action. When my sister Maryam told me to make a decision, I nodded a silent yes. Then she knocked and entered the men's room and asked to speak to my brother. Outside the room, she bravely and sternly told him to stop challenging these poor people. They had the money as promised. It was time for him to make a decision. Yes or no. He pursed his lips and rolled his eyes dramatically, let out a large sigh and then agreed with her, albeit reluctantly.

My sister prepared a bowl of sweets and put some flowers and a handkerchief with a small red flower on it inside the bowl. I still have that handkerchief. The items in the bowl were a sign of our family's final acceptance. The bowl was ceremoniously sent into the room where Hamid was sitting. I wish I could have seen the joy on his face when he saw it and realized his dreams were coming true at last. The sharing of sweets is the traditional Afghan way of formalizing the engagement. The groom's family then put money in the bowl to pay for the wedding. Hamid took a sweet, unwrapped it carefully and ate it, then put another five thousand dollars inside the bowl. He had been prepared for that cost too.

The next day, they came back again for lunch. I was in the kitchen from early morning. As I washed rice and peeled cucumbers, I smiled as I realized how much love I was pouring into the cooking. The simple pleasure of preparing food for those they love is something all women feel at some time. It must be something ancient within us, so much part of our biology and nature. I was reminded of my mother cooking for my father and how she always wanted things to be perfect for him. Here I was doing the same. As I chopped the vegetables, I made sure to cut them just so, into lovely little straight pieces that he would delight in eating.

I was still not allowed to see my husband-to-be. The only glimpse I got of him was as he and his family left. I hid behind a curtain at the window and sneaked a glance at him as he walked to the gate. I think he knew I was going to be watching him, because he stopped and paused, pretending to scratch his head. I think he considered sneaking a glance back at me, but he obviously decided it was too risky in case my brother saw.

As Hamid walked to his car, I felt a surge of excitement. It had been almost four years since his first proposal. He had never given up on his quest to marry me. I was now twenty-one years old, and I was finally going to be a bride.

Dear Shuhra and Shaharzad,

So many times, I and other members of our family survived because of the kindness of other people. People who risked their own lives to help us, offer us shelter or hide us from danger. And we weren't alone. All over our country, ordinary men and women opened their doors to people who needed them. Neighbours turned a blind eye as little girls scurried under cover of darkness to secret girls' schools in underground basements. These schools were run by wonderful, brave Afghan women, who despite the dangers to themselves knew they couldn't let the Taliban destroy the education of a generation of girls.

We had so many war widows in those days, thousands upon thousands of women who had lost husbands and fathers and who were now the main breadwinners in their family and responsible for ensuring their children were fed. But the Taliban denied all women the right to work. So these women, who had already lost so much, were forced to beg and rely on the kindness of strangers. Many didn't survive and many of the widows' children died of disease or starvation. Some did survive, however, because people who saw them begging on the streets did not walk by. Even though they didn't have much themselves, they still gave what little they could. This is what it means to be a true Muslim. To give alms to the poor is one of the main tenets of Islam and the Holy Koran instructs us to do it not only at times of great celebration, such as the start of the Eid festival, but also every other day of our lives.

I know sometimes you get frustrated by the constant queues of people outside the door of our house. These are people who want to talk to me or need my help. Every morning from daybreak, a small queue forms outside our house. Sometimes, before we have even had breakfast, a dozen people are waiting. I know you get upset because these strangers never make appointments and they demand so much of my time, when you too need your mother's time and attention. Especially in the morning, when I am trying to help you pack your school bags and enjoy our few moments together before parliament business takes me away. But girls, as frustrating as it can be, please try to understand that I cannot turn these people away.

This is a lesson I want you to learn. Never turn anyone away from your door because you never know when you might need to throw yourself at the mercy of another.

With love,
Your mother

ELEVEN

Everything Turns White

{ *1997* }

SINCE THEIR INITIAL victory in capturing Kabul, the Taliban had been steadily gaining ground in the north of the country. The Mujahideen were still determined to try to stop them, but areas that had been under the full control of the Mujahideen government began to lose pockets to the Taliban. In the middle of a government-controlled area, a village would suddenly fly the white flag of the Taliban.

Anywhere they had supporters or an ethnic connection among the locals, the flag would appear. In what had previously been government strongholds—Mazar, Baghlan, Kunduz—these white flags kept appearing. As the Taliban gained power in the north, they decimated the culture. They banned women from wearing white trousers or even white socks. They saw the wearing of white as disrespect for the colour of their flag. But in many northern provinces, the common colour for a burka is white. Only in Kabul and in the south was it blue. Most of the women in the north who wore burkas owned them only in white, but the Taliban still beat them for it. They were beaten for not wearing a burka and then they were beaten for wearing a burka in the wrong colour. It was insanity.

By now, the Taliban were moving swiftly across the country. They took full control of Baghlan and Kunduz. Takhar and Badakhshan were the only two provinces in which they couldn't get a foothold. Once they captured a province, they immediately closed the schools and arrested people. It was barbaric. They would torture people without any justice or trial. It seemed they simply made up the rules as they went along. The north, which generally had a more open-minded culture than the south, was in a state of collective shock.

But then some Northern Alliance commanders (the original Mujahideen) started to make deals with the Taliban in order to protect themselves. It was never a meeting of minds because the Taliban were much more fundamentalist in their thinking and their ideas than the Mujahideen ever were. And besides, the Taliban's power sources were based overseas. They didn't really need internal alliances. Even some of the former Communists tried to ally themselves with the Taliban. However, the Taliban usually just used people, then betrayed or assassinated them. As the Taliban saw it, either you were one of them or you weren't.

By this point, our once close-knit family was spread out in little units all over the country. Most of my elder sisters still lived in Badakhshan, having married local village men. I missed them very much. Mirshakay had never been quite the same since Muqim's death and he decided he had had enough of Afghanistan once and for all. His plan was to go to Pakistan to pick up his second wife and from there travel onto Europe.

Before he could start to carry out his plan, Massoud and Rabbani's men sent word that he was needed in Takhar province to help establish a force there to fight against the Taliban. So we followed him there and began yet another temporary life in yet another rented house. A few weeks later, Massoud himself came from Takhar to Panjshir to organize his troops, so my brother took this opportunity to ask for permission and safe passage to take his family to safety to Pakistan via Kabul. Massoud agreed.

Mirshakay took off his uniform and put on civilian clothes, as we women hastily threw what we could into bags. Then, we took a taxi towards Kabul. We reached our old base of Puli Khumri, and because it was late we decided to spend the night there with some of Mirshakay's friends. In the morning, this family decided to return to Kabul with us.

All the women except me wore a burka. I still had the black Arab-style full *niqab*, which covered my face in the same way as a burka did. The women rose early, preparing boiled eggs and potatoes for the journey. The distance wasn't far, but we had no idea how long it would take us because of the fighting.

We set off just before dawn. As the sun rose, we heard the sounds of fighting. We were driving through the front line. The main roads were unsafe because of heavy artillery, so we stuck to the back roads. As dawn broke, we saw a bridge ahead of us connecting two villages on either side of a fast-flowing river, just as the sound of the fighting seemed to get closer. We were almost at the bridge when a mortar hit it and it blew up, exploding into tiny shards of metal and wood.

We had no choice but to get out and walk. My sister-in-law had recently had a baby and carried the newborn with her. She had not expected that we would need to walk, and she had, perhaps not very sensibly, chosen to wear high heels for the journey. We had to walk for most of the day. It wasn't a straight, direct path. We had to climb up a rocky mountain, through gardens of rose and mulberry trees, then down to a path that ran along the side of a river. The main road was too dangerous to walk on because of the heavy artillery shelling coming from either side. That would have made us sitting ducks. At times, so many rockets were whizzing overhead that we had to stop and take cover in bushes. Occasionally, a taxi would take us part of the way—not official taxis but ordinary people charging money to drive people. They risked their lives because they needed the cash.

One car took us right to the front line where the Taliban and Massoud's men were shooting at each other. This was the road over the Shomali Plain crossing Jabul Saraj. We were getting closer to the outskirts of Kabul. Normally, the road would be busy, but no taxis dared drive here now. We joined crowds of people who were also walking. I laughed at the irony: these were the same people we had seen fleeing Kabul the day the Taliban took the city. Now, the once-quieter towns were the scenes of fighting and Kabul was once again the safer option. Hungry wild dogs ran over the plains snarling at people. As I stepped over some grass, I almost trod on a snake. It scared me as much as the rockets.

By now, my sister-in-law had started to cry. She was in her heels and was struggling to carry her heavy baby boy, Irshad. I was wearing flat sandals, so I offered to change my shoes with her. For some reason, I've always been good at walking in high heels, even in the middle of a battlefield. I like to joke that it is one of my more unusual talents.

As we stopped to change footwear, more rockets flew close by so we took cover again. I sat under a tree and was enjoying the few minutes of rest. We had found some apples and were hungrily tucking into them when suddenly my tree started to shake. Then I heard a long whirring sound. A rocket was just above my head. I froze. It exploded just feet away from me, taking the tree and all the leaves with it.

It all happened so quickly. One second I was sitting under the tree and the next second I realized it was not there. Not for the first time in my life, I had narrowly escaped death.

As we walked on, we passed bodies of women and children who hadn't been so lucky when the rockets hit. My brother saw the dead bodies and screamed at us to keep moving. After two more hours walking, we came to what had once been a popular picnic stop by the Sayad River. It was an idyllic place with a fast-flowing stream and trickling waterfalls.

We were exhausted. The high heels were beginning to hurt my feet. A family saw us and came out of their house; they beckoned us inside and offered us tea, bread and mulberries. They even gave me a pair of sandals to wear. I will never forget these little kindnesses from strangers.

Once refreshed, we thanked the family and moved on again. We needed to cross the river now, and the only way over was a hand-made and very shaky-looking footbridge made of planks crudely held together with wire and string. There were big gaps in some

My loving mother, Bibi jan.

My father, Wakil Abdul Rahman.

A happy adolescence
surrounded by family.

My father's house
in the Koof district,
more than one
hundred years old.

I chose a pink dress for *nikah*, the first part of the wedding ceremony with Hamid. It was a vibrant pink that shone a beam of joy amid all the misery of living under the Taliban regime.

Hamid was everything to me, a true and great Afghan man.

My brother Mirshakay was always one of my most loyal supporters.
Here he is surrounded by his children during a birthday.

Pilgrimage to Mecca. My faith has helped me overcome life's most difficult hardships.

I like visiting in the field with the Badakhshani workers.

A speech to a rural Badakhshani community during my electoral campaign in September 2010.

Conversing with a group of illiterate women during my campaign in the rural areas of Badakhshan in September 2010.

Handing out pens to children in 2010.

With Canadian prime minister Stephen Harper. To my right, Sabrina Saqib, the youngest member of parliament.

With American president George Bush and Laura Bush.

To my right, Condoleezza Rice, U.S. secretary of state.

With British prime minister Tony Blair.

My two amazing daughters, Shuhra and Shaharzad, accompany me as often as they can. Here we are in the airplane during my electoral campaign.

A tender moment at home.

By the Koof River in my native village.

These days, I'm seen as a politician first, rather than just a woman. For this, I'm extremely proud.

Traditional Afghan closet!

of the planks, and the whole thing looked like it could collapse at any moment. One of my brother's bodyguards was holding all our passports and documents in his pocket. He stood at the edge of the bridge and began to help us across one by one.

He grabbed my hand and urged me to step onto the first plank. It was evening by now, and the wind was so strong it was hard to even stand properly. Holding the man's hand, I managed to get over, as did my sister-in-law still holding the baby. But as she stepped off, she lost one of the sandals I had given her. She started to cry again. Very loudly. Finally, the bodyguard started to cross the bridge himself. But there was no one to hold his hand as he did so. I watched him as he got to the middle, then a plank beneath his feet gave a little sway and he fell.

As we looked on in horror, a sickening thought went through my mind: if he drowned, all our passports drowned with him. But the poor man suddenly resurfaced with one hand above the water. He was holding the passports aloft. Somehow, he managed to work his way to shore, and my brother dragged him out. He'd kept the passports totally dry. We all fell about laughing, even the bodyguard. My brother hugged and thanked him.

This bodyguard had always been one of my brother's favourite men. He was very loyal. Sadly, after my brother left the country, he joined the Taliban. With no income, he had no choice. Thousands of Afghan men have joined the Taliban for this reason. They might not share the ideology, but if the Taliban are the only people willing to pay the wages they need to feed their families, they join.

After walking another thirty minutes, we reached a Taliban-controlled area and found another taxi. I collapsed into the back seat and fell asleep. When I next woke up, it was dark and the car was driving through the streets of my beloved Kabul. Mirshakay asked the taxi to take us to the apartment in Makrorian. His in-laws had been staying there and looking after it in our absence. The apartment was warm and familiar. I can't describe the relief I felt taking a shower in hot water and eating a proper meal. Even the simplest dish is so much tastier when you have spent the day dodging rockets and bullets in a pair of high-heeled shoes.

Dear Shuhra and Shaharzad,

I love the intimacy we have as mother and daughters.

When I listen to your chatter, it reminds me of how much has changed between my generation and yours. You talk about the wildlife documentaries you've seen on TV and show me Bollywood dances that you've learned from your favourite Indian films. You talk to me about computers and things you've found on the Internet. You have access to the wider world in ways I never did.

I love it when you tell me stories of your friends, even the sad ones. Like the friend of Shuhra's who lives with her father and stepmother. The stepmother treats the little girl badly and Shuhra feels so sad for her friend, she cries.

I love that you have me to share your stories with. I could never talk to anyone about my life because no one was interested. My brothers had no interest in hearing about me and my dreams and the silly little things that had happened to me during the day. Maybe the only time they heard about my school was when I brought my result sheet saying that I had gotten the first or the second position in the class. Then they would show some pride in their clever sister.

Whenever my friends in school talked about their birthday presents or invited me to their parties, I would suffer. I always wished that I could celebrate my birthday as well and then tell my friends about it; sometimes I wanted to lie to my classmates and pretend I'd had a big party with music and dancing. But then I was scared that my classmates would ask me to invite them and I couldn't because it would never happen. Celebrating girls' birthdays was not something that happened in our family.

That is something I wanted to change for you. When it's either of your birthdays we take weeks to plan your party. You have balloons and cake. You even get the privilege of sending the family car to pick up your friends. I love being able to do this for you because I want you to love celebrations. I want you to celebrate the big things and the small things.

Know this: whatever our circumstances there is always something to celebrate about life.

With love,
Your mother

TWELVE

A Taliban Wedding

{ *1997* }

EVERY GIRL DREAMS of her wedding day, and I was no exception.

I always think life is simply a series of important moments. Moments that define us as the individuals we are. And we cherish the best moments all our lives, whether an enjoyable party, the smell of fresh grass after the rain, picnicking by a river, an evening spent laughing and talking with loved ones, the birth of a precious child or graduation from university.

The day a bride goes to choose her wedding dress should be one of those moments. But as I put on my coat to go to the bazaar that morning, I felt like a walking ghost.

Because I was the youngest daughter, my sisters and my mother had always taken great delight in discussing what kind of wedding I would eventually have. Over the years, they had gossiped and giggled about it all, from what I might wear to how my hair would look to what food we'd serve. In those pre-war days, we were a relatively rich family, so the assumption was always that I would have a big wedding, with people coming from far and wide to see me. When I was a little girl, I had never liked this idea, but now that I was finally getting married I so very much wanted that dream day. I wanted to hear my mother talk about her plans again more than anything in the world. The loss of her was still a dull, constant ache.

I had also never imagined that the most important day of my life would take place under the rule of the Taliban. Because of their rules, the wedding would have no music, no video and no dancing. All the restaurants and wedding halls were closed, and joyous ceremonies were now prohibited. I think any woman—wherever she lives in the world—wants her wedding day to be perfect. I know it sounds girlish and silly, but most nights before the wedding I cried myself to sleep. I cried both for my mother and for my lost opportunity to shine as a beautiful bride.

Despite the wearing of the burka now being compulsory by law, I still hadn't been able to bring myself to buy one. When I did have to go outside, I had taken to wearing my mother's old one. Her burka was far more beautiful than the cheap, mass-produced blue nylon ones designed in Pakistan that are so common today. In my mother's era, women saw the burka as a sign of status, and my mother had one befitting her rank as the wife of a powerful, rich man. It was made of dark blue silk with soft folds that rustled gently as she walked, the face covering lightly embroidered with a fine silver mesh over the eye panel. When it got dirty, she took it to a specialist cleaner who steamed and pressed each individual fold into place. For her, it was an object of great pride. For me, wearing it felt shameful. Even after my marriage, I continued to wear my mother's burka: if I had to wear one, then at least it should be one that reminded me of her.

The day we went shopping, my fiancé accompanied us. It was the first time I had seen him in months. The last time I had seen his face properly was my last day at university before the Taliban came to power. The day he came to visit us in Puli Khumri when my brother had finally agreed to our marriage, I had glimpsed only the back of his head as I hid behind the curtain. That day at university, the Mujahideen had been in control and he had sported a neatly trimmed small beard. But under Taliban rule, his hair and beard were longer, and he didn't look nearly as handsome. Through the hated burka, I kept sneaking sideways glances at his beard, thinking how much I disliked the look of it on his face. Once again, I had that overpowering feeling that Afghanistan was slipping back in time. There was no more progress, only the darkness of the uneducated men who now ruled our land.

The Taliban had introduced another new regulation: any woman who went out of the family home, for whatever reason, must have a *muharram*, a male blood relative, with her. This, like so many of the Taliban's rules, was more akin to Arab culture than to our own Afghan culture. In my grandmother's day, women didn't go out alone but with each new generation these things had changed in Afghanistan, as is the natural progression of any culture. Now, the Taliban were plunging us back in time.

If they stopped your car at one of the many Taliban checkpoints that had sprung up all over the city, they would interrogate you, demanding your family name, your father's name and the relative's name, asking endless questions until they were satisfied that the man and woman were blood relatives, not just friends. The Vice and Virtue Department was responsible for enforcing these policies—with a special predilection for beating women. In the wedding bazaar, they were beating women who were, like me, trying to shop for bridal gowns. One poor girl was wearing banned white trousers. Perhaps this girl didn't know about the ban, maybe she was uneducated and poor or maybe she had been too scared to leave the house until today. Whatever the reason, I heard a voice yell at her in Arabic (by now many Arab fighters had come to join the Taliban and live in Kabul). The men took a rubber cable and held her down on the ground while they beat her legs with it. She yelped in pain. I turned away, biting so hard on my lip it bled. I was consumed with anger at the injustice of it and at my failure to stop it.

The sound of the Vice and Virtue car is one I will never forget. It was usually a Hilux pickup truck. It would drive through the streets, always with prayers from the Holy Koran blasting from loudspeakers on the top. When they heard the sound of the car, women caught outside would rush to hide themselves. Even for the tiniest mistake or misdemeanour they would start beating you. Sometimes, they would just look at you and beat you for no reason with the cable. One day, I saw a young girl getting beaten and watched as her mother and sister threw themselves on top of her to try to protect her. The Taliban just continued to beat all three of them. It was truly madness.

On this day, there was a group of us: my sister-in-law, my fiancé and his sister. Fortunately, the Taliban ignored us. We bought the wedding rings, at least creating one small but happy memory from that. I knew Hamid could tell through the mesh of the burka that I was smiling broadly as I watched him pay for the rings. With weddings now under such strict rule, most of the clothing shops in the bazaar hadn't bothered to buy new stock. So little was available that I struggled to find anything I liked. I had always wanted a puff-sleeved wedding dress, but bare arms were now banned.

Afghan brides wear three or four different dresses in succession for their marriage ceremony, each one a different colour and representing something different. For my henna night, I chose a light green shade. For *nikah*, the first part of the ceremony, people often have dark green, but I wanted something unusual. I went for pink. It was a beautiful rosy pink and it felt like a shot of pure joy against all the misery of the Taliban. Just looking at that dress cheered me up. After *nikah*, the bride changes again for the reception party. Normally this is a white wedding dress and veil, similar to the styles worn by brides in the West.

In normal times, my wedding would have been as huge as is customary. Family and friends would have been invited as well as political allies, supporters and villagers from Badakhshan. In our culture, and particularly in a political family like mine, a wedding becomes a big networking affair. But because the wedding halls were closed, we had nowhere to host a large party. In our reduced financial circumstances, I doubt we could have paid for it anyway. Even so, my family invited over one thousand people for my ceremony. In the end, closer to fifteen hundred turned up.

Afghan weddings are also normally segregated, women and children on one side and men on the other. In a wedding hall, that usually means either a separate room for each gender or a large curtain dividing the room down the middle. Our solution was to have the wedding in two houses—one in my brother's house and one in his neighbour's. The men went to the neighbour's and the women to ours. The night before the wedding, we have a traditional henna ceremony in which the bride has her hands decorated with henna ink. For that we went to a beauty parlour. Normally, I loved a trip to a salon, but now it didn't cheer me up. Nothing about this wedding— the quality of the dresses or even my hairstyle—was my choice or how I would have wanted it to be. I'd done my best, but deep down it all felt so cheap and make-do.

The henna ceremony lasts most of the night. Usually it's done a few days before the actual wedding so the bride can rest before the big day, but we had no choice but to do it the night before. The whole night long a circle of women played the *daira,* a drum-type instrument, and sang songs. In the morning, I was exhausted. But in truth, even if the henna night had been a whole week earlier, I would not have slept the night before the wedding.

MY WEDDING was bittersweet. My mother was dead and my living sisters, who were still scattered across the country, couldn't come. My mother, who at my birth had wanted me to die, had then worked so hard for me to have a future. My mother, who had effectively picked out my husband for me on her deathbed, could not be there. Preparing for my ceremony without her there to hold my hand and whisper words of encouragement was as painful as walking on burning needles.

At 6 A.M., the hairdresser put the rollers in my hair. She tutted at me, telling me I looked terrible and needed more sleep. I nodded off in the chair. I slept there until about 10:30, and then she started to do my makeup. She was still tutting at the state of me. I looked in the mirror and realized that she was right, I did look awful, with red-rimmed eyes and a spotty face. By the time we entered the house, I was feeling really blue. The other big disappointment was that I had wanted to have the wedding secretly filmed with a video camera or a proper photographer. The Taliban had banned video but some of the video operators still worked anyway; they just charged triple to compensate for the risk. But my brother wouldn't allow it. Some of my brother's old friends were now working in low-level government jobs, and he was worried they would report us to the Taliban authorities. I have no souvenirs of my wedding, except for a few grainy snapshots friends managed to take with their personal cameras.

I didn't know many of the people at the wedding. The guests were my brother's friends and their wives or his work colleagues. I started to feel a bit angry, wondering if they had come just for the free food. It certainly didn't feel like they were there for me.

For the actual religious part of the marriage—conducted by a mullah—Hamid and I and our two witnesses were taken to a separate room. That was when I cried for the first, but not the last, time that day. And of course, all my makeup, the only thing making me look in any way attractive, started to run down my cheeks. I wiped my eyes then forgot myself as I inadvertently wiped mascara over my pretty pink dress. Fortunately, after the ceremony it was time to change into the white gown, and in its lacy sleeves and long veil I like to think I looked a little bit more beautiful.

Later in the evening, the tradition is that the elder of the family, either a father or brother, takes a cloth containing some sweets and fabric, and ties it to the bride's wrist. It is a symbol that the new bride is being sent to her husband's home. It's a very moving and personal scene. When Mirshakay took the braid and began tying it on my wrist, I started to cry. He started to cry too. We were hugging each other and both crying our eyes out. I think it was more than the moment that had got to us. We were crying because of all the people who weren't there: my mother, my brother Muqim, my father. We cried for all the family we had lost, as well as our status, our homes and our way of life. In those private few minutes, my brother and I hugged and cried in silence, both of us understanding the enormity of loss, the joy of moving forward and the pain of change. Eventually, he gathered himself and with a stern "Come now, Fawzia jan," he gently touched the tip of my nose, smiled and led me out of the room.

Dear Shuhra and Shaharzad,

Your father was the love of my life. He was more than enough for this "poor girl." In marrying him, I was a lucky girl indeed.

Marriage is an important rite in a woman's life, but I truly believe marriage should not prevent her from living her dreams. Rather, her dreams should become those of her husband, and her husband's dreams should become part of hers. This new couple should stand together and make the world theirs and theirs alone.

Sometimes, I long to see the day you will get married, but other times I don't want it to happen because I know that on that day you will stop being my little girls and become grown women. I don't want that to happen too fast.

But of course, I hope you will find love one day. Love is important. But not everyone thinks so. Many people believe duty, respect, religion and rules are more important than love.

But I do not think these things have to be separate. Love can exist alongside duty. Love thrives on duty. And on respect.

With love,
Your mother

THIRTEEN

An End before a Beginning

{ *1997* }

MY WEDDING DAY marked the next new chapter of my life—as a wife. But I had no inkling just what a short and tragic chapter it was destined to be.

My husband lived in 4th Makrorian, in a three-bedroom purpose-built apartment. It was simple, solid and functional. He had made a real effort (I suspect with the help of his sisters) to decorate our bedroom nicely, buying new pink curtains, a pink bedcover and even some pink silk flowers in a pink vase by the side of the bed. It was such a thoughtful gesture, but everything looked so very . . . pink. I had to stifle a giggle when I first saw it. By the time my wedding night arrived, I had been awake for twenty-four hours. Thankfully, my husband was also exhausted after such a long day and didn't make any sexual demands on me. We both fell fast asleep.

In the morning I awoke first, and for a second I panicked. My eyes opened, and I saw a pink curtain with hazy sunlight outside. I was in a strange bed with a man beside me. For a split second, I struggled to work out where I was, and then I remembered. I was married to Hamid, to the man sleeping next to me. He snored gently, and I smiled indulgently at him as I stroked his cheek. This was the first day of my new life.

Hamid's sister and her two children were also living with us. She had recently been widowed and had nowhere else to go. I was happy about this, thankful for the comforting presence of another woman about the place. She had been a teacher and was an intelligent, feisty woman. We got on famously. At last, I felt some contentment with my life. Hamid was the kind, warm man I always suspected he was. We basked and glowed in each other's company, laughing and making plans for our future. I hadn't felt a joy like that since the first day I started school at age seven. Life was finally going my way.

A week after our wedding, we had another ceremony called *takht-jami.* The bride and groom sit under decorations, flowers and ribbons, and visitors come and congratulate them and give them gifts. In childhood, my sisters and mother would regale me with stories of all the riches I would receive on my *takht-jami,* a new car perhaps, or a house in the mountains, or a whole ton of gold. But of course, life during the time of the Taliban was not so ostentatious. Friends and family came, bringing what they could. A tablecloth, some new dishes, fifty dollars.

We said goodbye to our last guests, and Hamid popped into his office for half an hour to check on things. His sister and I were about to make a cup of tea when there was a knock at the door. My sister-in-law went to open it, and there stood bearded men in black turbans. Mullah Omar, the Taliban leader, had heard Mirshakay was back in Kabul and had an arrest warrant for him. They had been searching for my brother for the past three days; he'd already gone into hiding. The family had not informed me of this because they wanted me to enjoy my honeymoon period.

Now here were the Taliban at my door. They barged into my newly married bliss like the battering rams of doom. Without asking, they walked into the living room where I was sitting under flower garlands in all my silly makeup and finery. As they looked at me, the colour drained from my face. I had had enough trouble in my life already to know that their arrival meant the end of this happy chapter. They barked at us to stay where we were and then went into my bedroom. They started tearing the bedsheets off the bed, where so recently Hamid and I had begun our married life together.

It was such an invasion of privacy and of decency and an affront to our culture. But these brutes didn't care about that. They started looking under the bed and pulling things out of cupboards. They said nothing, just turned the house upside down, tearing at the nice furniture with their dirty, unwashed hands.

Then they started yelling at me: "Where is Mirshakay?" "Where is the police general?" They waved an arrest warrant in my face. I felt sick to my stomach as I realized who they wanted. I told them calmly I had no idea. By now, they'd ripped apart my house so they knew I wasn't lying. Then my heart stopped again. Hamid! "Please don't come back from the office yet," I silently willed my husband. "Stay at work, don't come home yet. Please. Don't come home yet."

They left, and I listened with bated breath as they walked down the five flights of steps to the door of the main building. With each click-clack of their boots on the stair treads, I breathed a little easier— four floors to go, three floors, two. Then, on the first floor, I heard a door open. I gasped in horror. "No, please, please, don't let that be Hamid." He was seconds away from danger. He had come back to the house and bounded happily through the front door, carrying a gift of chocolates for me, and walked right into them. If he had only paused to buy some fruit, chat to a neighbour or even bend down to tie his shoelaces he might have missed them.

Angry at their failure to find my brother, they arrested Hamid. He had done nothing. He had committed no crime, but they took him. I ran down the stairs screaming. "We've been married only seven days, he knows nothing. This is my husband's house, we are newlyweds, we are innocent people, leave us alone," I begged them.

They simply asked me again, "Where is Mirshakay?" Then they handcuffed Hamid. He barely moved or spoke. He was in shock. The flowers he'd been holding for me dropped to the floor. A few neighbours had gathered to watch the scene. Nobody said anything. I grabbed my burka and followed my husband. Hamid knew me better than to tell me to stay at home and wait.

They put Hamid in a red Taliban pick up truck. They pushed me aside, laughing when I tried to get in after him. I flagged down a taxi. The driver wound down the window and said, "I am sorry, ma'am, I am sorry, sister, do you have a *muharram* with you?" I snapped at him. "What? Just let me in. I have to follow that car." He shook his head. "You need a *muharram* with you, sister. These stupid people, these men you want to follow, if they see you alone with me they will put both of us in prison." Then he drove away.

I followed the pickup with my eyes as it turned down the street and along the main road; then it took a left towards the new town. I was desperate not to lose sight of it. I hailed another taxi. This time, I spoke before the driver had a chance to. I begged for all I was worth. "Brother, dear brother, please, please help me. Please. They are taking my husband. I need to follow him. I'm alone. Can you please take me?"

He told me to get in. As we drove, he spoke hurriedly. "If they stop the car, say you are my sister, my name is . . . , I live in . . ." This kind man, this complete stranger, outlined to me all the key details of his life in case I, just a random passenger, should have to pretend he was my brother. It was so absurd. But the driver's actions were another reminder that whatever those in power threw at the ordinary men and women of my nation, Afghan values of decency and kindness prevailed.

They had taken Hamid to the intelligence agency office, a building in the centre of town close to the Ministry of the Interior. I don't know how much money I gave the driver, but I know it was quite a lot. I was just so grateful he was prepared to help a woman despite the risk to himself. I thought if I paid him well, he might just help another woman in the same circumstances.

I went to the gate, but they refused me entry. Now I took a massive risk. I lied to the Taliban at the gate. I told them that other Taliban had arrested me and ordered me to come into the building but that I couldn't go with the men in their vehicle. I said if they didn't let me in they'd be blamed. They let me in.

Once inside the main gate, I found the prison building. Hamid was standing there, surrounded by two Talibs. Hamid was barely reacting, I think from shock. One moment, he was dashing home with chocolates for his new wife, the next he had been arrested. I ran over and grabbed his hand. I looked directly at the Talibs through my burka and spoke: "Look, look at my hands. This is bridal henna. You are talking about Islam but you do not act as Muslims. We are just married. If you put him in prison, I will have no more *muharram*. How will I live? How will I survive? I have nobody to do shopping, to take care of me. I am just a young girl. I am helpless."

I was hoping that I could appeal to their sympathy and that they would let him go. But these were men who could remain unmoved by the pleas of a mere woman. They ignored me and walked Hamid to another gate with me following, still holding his hand and still pleading. When they opened the gate, my heart sank as I could see hundreds of prisoners inside. Some were handcuffed, some bound, others were standing, all crammed into a stinking central courtyard.

One of the Talibs took Hamid's hand, while I continued to hold the other. We had just started our new life, and now they were taking him away from me, tearing us apart. I was terrified that they would just execute him with no trial. They had arrested him without charge, so it was entirely possible. I was holding on tight and begging: "I'm coming too. How can I go alone? I am a woman, I cannot live alone outside. You are a Muslim, how can you do this?"

The Talib answered me in Pashto. He spoke crudely with the accent of an uneducated village man. "Shut up, woman, you talk too much." Then he pushed me hard, so hard that I fell over into a puddle of stinking water. I was still wearing my high heels and a fancy dress. Less than an hour ago we had been receiving guests. Hamid turned his head to try to help me up, but the Talib pushed him in the opposite direction, inside the gates. My last glimpse of my husband was as I struggled to stand up. The gates closed.

With Hamid behind the gates, my thoughts turned to my brother. It was him they had come to arrest. Was he safe? Where was he? I had no money left for another taxi, so I ran as fast as I could in heels across the city, back to my brother's house. His wife was there and she told me he was hiding in different relatives' houses. For the past three days, he had been changing places every night so as not to be discovered. Right now, she told me, he was in Karte Seh, an area west of Kabul that had been badly damaged during the civil war. I couldn't do anything for Hamid now, but I could still try to help my brother.

When I got there, I entered the house brusquely. I didn't stop to say *salaam* or greet the family. I just needed to see my brother with my own eyes. The couple who owned the house were both teachers. The husband was a professor in the economics faculty at Kabul University, and the wife one of the brave Afghan women who, under the ban on female teachers, took great personal risks secretly running a school from home. She and her husband had no children.

The room had no sofa, just lots of cushions lining the walls. My brother Mirshakay was lying on a mattress facing the wall. When he saw me, his face registered alarm. It was the first time he'd seen me since my wedding day, when he'd hugged me and wept as I went to my new life. Now we had entered chaos again.

Very quickly, I told him about Hamid's arrest and how they were searching for him now. It wasn't safe for him here; they would be searching all of our relatives' houses one after the other. It wasn't safe to take a taxi either. There were Taliban checkpoints everywhere, and if they stopped us they might have my brother's photo and recognize him. We started to walk. I was still in the blasted heels and my feet were killing me.

This was the first time I'd worn a burka to walk such a long distance. I was never very good at walking in them anyway, but when I was wearing heels and had such anxiety it was even worse. I stumbled over what felt like every stone and crack in the pavement.

We walked out of the city towards the outer suburbs. We didn't have anywhere to go as such, but we had limited choice in any case. Anywhere too public or central would have checkpoints; in the outer suburbs, there would be buildings we could hide behind, and not so many people. So we headed out. As we walked, we chatted. My brother asked me about Hamid and whether he had met my expectations as a husband. In some ways, I was happy to tell my brother that yes, indeed, Hamid had, and I had been right to marry him.

I told him how Hamid and I had discussed where we would live, whether we should leave Afghanistan. Hamid had suggested a new life in Pakistan, but I'd told him I couldn't leave while my brother was still in Kabul. Then we'd discussed moving back to Faizabad, the capital city of Badakhshan province and the place I had first gone to school. Badakhshan was not controlled by the Taliban. My sisters were there, as was Hamid's family, and we both missed the region. So that had been our plan. We would move back to the countryside, where I was to teach and Hamid could run his business.

Telling my brother these plans was more painful than the weeping blisters that now coated my heels. All those newlywed dreams and plans were now in ruins. After four hours of aimless walking, we hailed a taxi. I had remembered one of Hamid's relatives, a lady who lived alone with her son. I didn't know the exact address but knew it was 4th Makrorian, near where Hamid and I lived. On the way we passed a checkpoint. We sat inside the car terrified that they would wind the window down and see my brother, but we were lucky. They waved the car past without looking inside.

My brother had met this woman before; she was one of Hamid's relatives who had come to ask for my hand in marriage. He had not warmed to her. He said she wore too much makeup and her nails were too long. In Mirshakay's view, those were signs of a lazy woman. But now he had to throw himself upon her mercy. I asked around and was pointed to her apartment. I quickly explained the situation and asked if she could prepare a room for my brother for one night. She said yes, but she wasn't happy. She was understandably scared; if she was caught sheltering a man who was not a blood relative, she would be arrested and taken to the Vice and Virtue Department. I felt awful putting her in that position, but I had no choice.

I left my brother there and walked home. By the time I reached the house, my feet felt like they were on fire, sweat caked my eyes and ears and my hair was like a mattress of caked grease on my head. I threw the wretched burka up and off my head, ran into the bedroom and wailed with sorrow and frustration.

Dear Shuhra and Shaharzad,

Loss is one of the hardest things for any human being to bear.

But loss of those we love is a part of life and a part of growing, and no one can be protected from that. Perhaps you are reading this letter because I've died or been murdered and you've lost me. We know one day that will happen; we've discussed it, and I want you to be prepared for that inevitability.

Losing a home, as we did many times during the war, is also a horrible thing. Losing a home is hardest on children. It's something that has happened to millions of poor children in Afghanistan. Be aware of how lucky you are to have a house with a warm fire, a nice soft bed to sleep in, a lamp to read by and a table to do your schoolwork on. I know it doesn't sound like much, but not all children have this.

But perhaps the worst thing that can happen to any woman is to lose herself. To lose the sense of who and what she is or to lose sight of her dreams—these are some of the saddest losses a woman can experience. They are not inevitable but are forced on us by those who do not want us to dream or to succeed. I pray you will never lose your dreams.

With love,
Your mother

FOURTEEN

The Darkness Pervades

{1997}

I BARELY SLEPT that night. I was half mad with worry and fear, and my brain was racing, desperately trying to think of anyone who might be able to help me and to formulate a plan. As I stood in front of the mirror brushing my teeth in the morning, an idea came to me.

I remembered a friend who told me she had been teaching embroidery to the wife of a Taliban official. I threw on the burka and ran to her house. She listened, wide-eyed with shock and sympathy, as I recounted what had happened to Hamid. We didn't know if it would do any good, but she said she would take me to the official's house and make the necessary introductions.

We walked there together across the eerily quiet roads of this once-bustling city. A few cars and taxis spluttered noisily into life, the early morning sun dancing in the dust of empty street stalls and boarded-up shops. I saw a dejected-looking woman with hunched shoulders in a blue burka. For a second, I didn't recognize her. Then I realized I was looking at myself. I had caught my reflection in the grimy window of an empty photographic shop. The burka had stripped me of so much identity I didn't even know myself.

Startled by the strangeness of that sensation, I peered into the shop. It was long deserted. Faded photographs lined the walls, young men posing like Bollywood actors in front of backdrops of waterfalls, babies holding aloft balloons and smiling toothlessly at the parents who would have been standing just behind the camera trying to make them laugh, little girls in lacy dresses and ankle socks grinning shyly, brides in white veils standing proudly next to besuited husbands.

I stared at the images wondering what had happened to all those smiling faces. Who were they? Where were they now? By the time Taliban rule came to Afghanistan, almost a third of our original population of eighteen million was dead, killed in the fighting. Another third were refugees overseas. Only around six million of the previous population remained. Were all the faces I was staring at dead? And where was the studio owner? All photography was now banned by diktat of the Taliban. With his livelihood gone, he might have just closed the door and found another way to survive. Or he may have continued to work in secret, breaking Taliban law. He could be in prison right now. With Hamid. The thought of the unknown photography studio owner lying next to Hamid in a cell brought me back to reality. My friend touched my arm gently, and we walked on until we reached a gated apartment block. The Talib's house. A little boy was playing outside. The scent of boiled mutton wafted out the door.

The man was there with his wife, a pleasant woman with green eyes who seemed to share her husband's sympathies for our plight. They welcomed us into their home and gave us hot green tea. He was a youngish man, perhaps thirty. He said he wasn't sure if he could do anything but kindly promised to try to help. He would go and make inquiries as soon as the official offices opened that morning. I was frustrated, but not ungrateful. I was surprised a Talib, any Talib, could show humanity. This man was trying to help me, a stranger. He did not have to do so. He changed my opinion of many Taliban. I realized that just because he didn't share my ideals or my politics that didn't necessarily make him a terrible person.

Many Afghan men aligned with the Taliban because of a shared ethnicity and culture, a sense of shared geography or economic necessity. It was the same then as it is today. If the Taliban pay wages in a village where there are no jobs, what is a poor man to do? And many Afghan men, particularly in southern provinces like Kandahar or Helmand, agree with these more hard-line aspects of Islamic culture. This is the opposite of what I believe, of course, but I have always had a strong understanding of and respect for the many different views, ethnic groups, languages and cultures that make up Afghanistan. Not many people in the West know that over thirty languages are spoken across the country. For me, that diversity is our strength—at least during peaceful times. In wartime, those ethnic divisions are our greatest weakness and the main reason for so much senseless slaughter.

As we left the Talib's house, he kindly walked me and my friend to the gates of the apartment block—again making it clear that he wasn't sure he could do much. On the walk home, I began to prepare myself for the worst: news of Hamid's execution or a life sentence based on false charges. I didn't want to think about it, but I knew I had to be ready to face what was very likely to be bad news. I tried not to think of Hamid being dragged, hands tied, into the prison courtyard to be shot. Or lying in a filthy, freezing prison cell, emaciated and slowly going mad with hunger and cold. The thought of it was enough to drive me insane too.

I arrived home preoccupied with my tortured thoughts to see a familiar face emerge from the bathroom.

There Hamid stood. Water was still glistening on his hollow cheeks, droplets hanging off his beard.

I thought I was dreaming. Or that I'd lost my mind.

My husband was standing in the hallway smiling at me as if it was the most normal thing in the world. He moved towards me uttering my name, his weak legs faltering beneath him. I rushed to him, embracing him before he could fall. His usual male strength had been sapped by the violent abuse meted out by his jailers. The unexpected emotion of his sudden appearance was too much for us to bear and we both sobbed with relief. Hamid, my Hamid, my love, was home.

It had been just over twenty-four hours since his arrest, but without warning they had released him. I made him a breakfast of eggs and sweet tea, and he lay down to rest. I was exhausted from the roller coaster of emotion, but I had no time to rest myself. Now that Hamid was released they would surely renew their attempts to imprison my brother. We had to find another house for him to hide in. Fast.

I remembered a woman, a very tough character, who used to go to my English class. She lived nearby, only a few blocks away. She had a bad leg that made it very hard for her to walk, and since her husband died she had struggled to take care of her two daughters alone. They weren't a political family; they were just ordinary people trying to survive in the craziness that had become Kabul. No one would look for Mirshakay there. I knew their house would be a perfect place for him to lie low until we could work out a way to get him out of the country.

I put on my burka and ran to the woman's house. It was a very modest home, made all the more spartan by the shortages of the war. A few threadbare rugs lay on the living room floor. There were very few luxuries, and I guessed that others had long since been sold to buy rice, cooking oil and gas to fuel the stove. The woman limped around her living room, urging me to take a seat as she ordered her elder daughter to make tea for us. I explained that I wanted my brother to stay with her but that it might be dangerous for her if the Taliban caught him there. Her tone immediately became a little offended. She was not angry because I had come into her living room and made such an outrageous request but rather, in true Afghan style, because I thought such a request was even necessary. Of course he could stay—what a silly question!

I finished my tea and hurried off to collect Mirshakay. We gathered a few clothes and some extra food—I knew the lady would probably feign offence if I brought food, but she was already taking a great risk hiding my brother. An extra mouth to feed would stretch her meagre resources to the limit. We returned to the lady's house together. It was imperative that I go with my brother—not because he didn't know the way but because the surest way to arouse suspicion was for a strange man to enter the house alone. A man and a woman in a burka look like a social visit; a man by himself looks like a morality crime in progress and would surely set local tongues wagging, provoking a visit from the Taliban.

The woman and her family were very kind to Mirshakay, and I think he was able to relax a little. He stayed in that house for ten days. After that, we decided things had cooled down enough for him to move to my house. It was still too dangerous for him to move home with his family. As it was, the Taliban often harassed his wife, dropping by uninvited and unannounced, threatening her with quietly menacing voices: "Where is your husband? When did you last speak to him? Tell us." He was a hunted man, and they watched for him daily.

In the end, his wife became so scared she also moved into my house.

Hamid and I were still newlyweds—we should have been enjoying our new life together, but I was so busy running the house it was hard for us to snatch more than a few moments of quiet together. I suppose young wives all over the planet have romantic ideas of how those first few months of marriage will be, but for me, and I think for a lot of other women, the realities of adult life soon overtook the girlish notions of marital bliss. At first, I was quite resentful of the intrusion on what was supposed to be one of the happiest periods of my life, but such feelings were short-lived and my sense of duty soon took over. Also, this was my brother, whom I loved dearly. I remembered how kind he had been to me as a child, and how much of an influence he had had on my life. I felt guilty for having such selfish thoughts. Now it was my turn to take care of him and his family. I knew he would do the same for me, no matter what the risks or hardships.

Mirshakay was determined to flee Afghanistan. It was the only way to guarantee his safety, even though it meant a life of uncertainty as a refugee abroad. For the next three months, he didn't trim his beard but let it grow long, thick and dark. After a while, we barely recognized him. We prayed the Taliban wouldn't recognize him either.

The plan was to get a taxi to Torkham, the busiest town at the border with Pakistan. It is close to the famous Khyber Pass and lies on the edge of Pakistan's Federally Administered Tribal Areas, a region ruled by tribal elders and over which Islamabad has little control. The border between Afghanistan and Pakistan has never been formally recognized in Afghanistan. It's known as the Durand Line, and even today it is one of the greatest sources of tension between the Pakistani and Afghan governments. The Afghans refuse to recognize the line. The Americans and other NATO forces fighting the War on Terror claim that this loose border is home to thousands of al-Qaeda fighters. Pakistan denies this but does little to control fundamentalism in the area.

The local codes of honour are so strong that even when American bomber planes have pounded the area while ground troops look for bin Laden or his sympathizers, the villagers refuse to reveal their whereabouts. Bombs may rain down on their houses, but "honoured guests" will never be betrayed. I realize it is hard for people in the West to understand this. Going to the region is like stepping back five hundred years. Understand that and you begin to understand the area. Fail to understand it, as successive governments and foreign forces have, and you will always be defeated.

Unlike nowadays, in 1997, when we were planning my brother's escape, Afghans didn't need a visa to enter Pakistan across the main border crossing. My brother was hoping he could slip across the border unnoticed amid the noisy chaos of trucks, traders and travellers that continually flock through Torkham.

Mirshakay had arranged for a taxi to come to collect him early in the morning. I was rushing around helping get him ready to leave—organizing food for the journey, some *naan* and hard-boiled eggs to sustain him—while his wife packed his suitcase. There was a knock at the door, and before I had time to stop and think I opened it wide, expecting to see the driver. Two black turbans stood in the doorway—Taliban. They pushed their way into the apartment waving their guns. Everybody froze. There was no time to react, and nowhere to hide. We exchanged looks—this was it—we were caught.

The two men were openly triumphant as they grabbed my brother, forcing him to the floor. The larger of the pair—both looked like they were only in their twenties—jammed his knee hard into the small of my brother's back, making him yelp with pain. The other, in an act of barely concealed spite, grabbed Hamid by the neck and pushed his head towards the living room floor as though he were a rag doll. They laughed and jeered at my sister-in-law and me as they dragged and shoved our men into the hall and down to their pickup truck. As they went, my brother shouted at me not to follow them and to stay at home. Even in a moment as bleak and desperate as this, his male pride could not allow the disgrace of a woman coming to jail to try to get him out.

At the police station, my brother managed to persuade a guard to smuggle a note to the family. It contained instructions for us to contact an old colleague of my brother's who had held a senior position at the Ministry of Defence during the Communist years and was now working for the Taliban government. Under Communism, this man had been a general and now he was a senior Taliban military advisor. My brother hoped this man might be able to pull some strings to get both him and Hamid out. The note included an address for an apartment near the airport.

Once again, it was a brutal waiting game. For once, my strength left me and I lay on the bed for two days, paralyzed by frustration and fear. Hamid had been taken from me again. But this time, it was not only me he'd left behind. It was also our unborn child.

Three days earlier I had learned I was pregnant. Like many new mothers, I had my suspicions when I started being very ill and vomiting in the mornings. Hamid and I were delighted, of course. But the excitement we felt was tempered by the turmoil in our lives. There are perhaps few things as worrying as being a first-time mother in a time of war. In war, everyday survival is a battle in itself and only the strongest survive. Was it fair to bring a helpless infant into that kind of hell? Perhaps not.

But I also knew that life goes on despite the bullets and bombs. And in some ways, the desire to celebrate life and creation, however bad the circumstances, is an intrinsic part of the human spirit. Yes, I was scared but I also thought it would be wonderful to have something as precious and positive as a newborn child to focus on.

But despite my joy, it was clear from the outset that this was not going to be an easy pregnancy. Afghanistan has one of the highest maternal and infant mortality rates in the world. A lack of health resources and a cultural reluctance to openly talk about gynecological and pediatric care means that doctors can be hard to find, and the few who do exist can sometimes be badly trained. Families often resist seeking medical attention for a woman until there is absolutely no other choice and it's clear she will die without medical help—by which time it's often too late to save either the child or the mother. To be a doctor and work in these conditions takes great skill, patience and dedication. In earlier times, some of Afghanistan's best doctors were women. I'm sure women everywhere feel more comfortable being treated for intimate health issues by someone of their own gender. For a long time, I wanted to qualify as a doctor myself and join their ranks.

However, the Taliban had banned women from working, a decree that had completely depleted Afghanistan's medical staff. And then, in a further twist of insane cruelty, they banned male doctors from treating women. A male doctor was not even allowed to prescribe aspirin for a common cold to a woman. The result? Hundreds of women died unnecessarily under the Taliban—from flu, untreated bacterial infections, blood poisoning, fever, broken bones or pregnancy. They died simply because these brutal men who ran the country thought a woman's life as worthless as a fly's. These men, who claimed to be men of God, had no sense of sanctity for one of God's greatest creations: woman.

My morning sickness was really bad. And it wasn't just limited to the first few hours of the day. I can joke about it now, but trying not to vomit into the face covering of my burka was no laughing matter at the time. I hope no other young mother ever has to learn to pull up the hood of her garment, tilt her head forward and aim for the gap between her feet—all while fighting the natural urge to drop to her knees.

For three months, I vomited most of what I ate. It was a burden I could have done without—especially on the day I took my brother's letter and set off to find the house of his former colleague. My brother knew it was a long shot asking this man for help, but long shots were all we now had to cling to.

I was feeling very sorry for myself when I entered that house. But as my eyes adjusted to the gloom, I realized I still had an enormous amount to be thankful for. Most Afghans are desperately poor, but they are also immensely proud. They take pride in their homes, however simple they may be, and always offer food, tea and sweets to guests. Perhaps that is why I was so shocked by the terrible state of the living room. The floors were filthy and had clearly not been swept or washed in a long time. I wanted to take the carpets outside and give them a good dusting. The walls needed wiping, and I wanted to throw the windows wide open to let in some light and fresh air to clear the musty smell that filled the house.

The lady of the house greeted me. That was when I realized she was just a very simple woman who had never been taught any better. Even her manner of greeting a guest and the very way she carried herself were stilted and awkward. Looking around the room, I scanned a row of dirty faces of her children and other members of the extended family, each one grubbier than the next. That at least explained the smell.

I couldn't find anywhere clean to sit but squatted down in the least dirty spot. I felt desperately nauseous. I kept my burka on, even though I was indoors and prepared for a long wait. I was becoming familiar with dealing with the Taliban now. The first rule was patience. I was told the man would speak to me in twenty minutes, but I was prepared to wait all day if necessary. It seems strange in retrospect, but I was now far less worried about Hamid. The fact that he was in prison with my brother, not alone, was a big comfort. I knew they would both draw a lot of strength from each other, no matter what terrible things were being done to them.

I sat waiting, idly watching the woman clean the river of black and green snot oozing out of a boy's nose. We made small talk, but it was difficult. I found it hard to be civil sitting in a filthy room, in a filthy house, waiting for a filthy man who was now one of the key security advisors of my country's government. What sort of nation can you create when even your own home is filthy and the women and children who live there are trapped in ignorance? What hope was there for Afghanistan, I thought, while these uneducated people are in power? And then I shivered with horror. The realization had come to me. If this was the family living room of a senior Taliban advisor, what must Taliban prisons be like?

When the man finally appeared, he looked as rough and dishevelled as the rest of his family, not the man of power and authority I had expected. I explained how Hamid and my brother had come to be in jail. The man was not unpleasant and told me he remembered my brother well. He listened patiently and assured me that he would get them released. He asked me if I would wait while he made some phone calls in private, then excused himself. I made myself as comfortable as I could on the dirty floor and sat back to wait. The smell had gone now. My nose must have become accustomed to it.

When the man eventually returned, the news was not good. With a sigh he looked at his filthy hands and told me it would take time to get them out. He promised he would keep monitoring the situation and would contact me with any news. His tone had the half-baked sincerity of someone who felt reluctantly obliged to help but who would certainly not go to any great lengths to do so. This worried me. I walked home dejected. Hamid was still very weak. He'd only just begun to recover from his first incarceration. The air was getting cold and crisp now. We were well into autumn, and the winter snow was already settling in the mountains around the city. Soon Kabul itself would be covered with snow and temperatures would drop as low as minus fifteen degrees Celsius. I could imagine Hamid and my brother huddling together for warmth in the freezing prison courtyard, wearing only the clothes they were arrested in. No warm jackets, no thermal vests, no woolly socks. I bit my lip hard to stop the tears flowing as I thought of Hamid's toes freezing and turning blue. I didn't know how much more my husband's fragile body could take. His mind was a fortress of strength and intelligence and could sustain whatever tortures they threw at him. But everyone has a physical breaking point. In the freezing grip of the night breeze, when the air becomes so cold it hurts to catch your breath, I knew Hamid's breaking point was fast approaching.

Early the next morning, I was in my usual position—doubled over the toilet being violently ill. But today, my morning sickness seemed to have another cause. It had snowed in the night. As I dashed from my bed to the bathroom I glanced out a window to see the rooftops below covered in a fresh blanket of sparkling white. Had Hamid and my brother stood all night in the snow? Or were there two more dead bodies in the prison yard, fused together by the layer of ice that now covered them?

I dressed and hurried to the Talib's house, this time accompanied by Khadija, Hamid's sister. We went slipping and skidding along the icy streets that had turned to treacherous skating rinks. My burka provided an extra layer of warmth, but it also prevented me from making out the frozen contours of the road and limited my agility, so that each time my feet took off in a direction of their own choosing, I would throw one arm out in front of me to balance myself and break my fall, while the other went low around my waist to protect my unborn child in case I hit the ground.

Something had changed at the house when I arrived. The smell was still there, but I could see somebody had made an effort to sweep the floor, and the children's faces were smeared where a dirty cloth had been rubbed over them in an attempt at cleaning. The man was different too. He smiled widely at me, showing blackened teeth.

"I want you to teach my children English," he said. It was a request, not an order. But not a request I could refuse. "Of course," I answered. "Perhaps they could come to my house. There is room for them to play, and I can teach them better there."

Thankfully, this seemed to please him. I really didn't want to spend any longer in that home than was absolutely necessary. I needed to keep him happy, but part of me was also encouraged; if I could teach children such as these even a little of life beyond these grubby walls, then perhaps there was hope for my country after all. I had no idea what was happening in my life from one day to the next or whether I'd ever be able to make good my promise to teach them, but it made me see that children, all children, have value. With the correct help and learning, any child can grow up to change the fate of a nation.

I left the house feeling optimistic. The man had spoken little of my beloved prisoners, but the talk of English lessons and the changes I saw in the house were encouraging signs that he intended to help us.

Later that night, a fist banged on my apartment door. I cautiously inched it open. Hairy knuckles shoved it back hard into my forehead, and I reeled backwards. Two dark eyes beneath heavy brows and a black turban stared hard at me. But I felt no fear. In fact I barely noticed the Talib's face, because standing next to him were Hamid and Mirshakay. He shoved them both hard through the doorway, like a spoiled child who had been forced to share his toys. He muttered some impotent threats as I closed the door in his face and launched myself into Hamid's arms. My sister-in-law squealed her way across the living room and flung herself against her own husband. The former Communist general turned Talib had in fact been as good as his word.

We wasted no time. A taxi was arranged to pick us up the following morning. We had to get to Pakistan. The men were free, but it was not enough to rely on the whims or good graces of the Taliban. They could change their minds in a heartbeat and rearrest them. That was a risk we couldn't take.

The next morning, Hamid, I, my brother and his wife and their baby all squeezed into the waiting vehicle. Hamid sat on one side of the back seat, I was crushed next to him in my burka, my brother tucked in the middle, where we hoped no one would recognize him, and his wife next to the other window. A family friend sat in the front passenger seat—yet another retired general, an ethnic Pashtun who had kindly offered to help us. If we ran into problems, we hoped his stature as a general could help us. Failing that, his ethnicity would also lend weight both at the Taliban checkpoints and once we got closer to the border, as most of the Taliban were also Pashtun. For him to travel with us was an act of pure generosity. It still amazes me when I think of all the friends and neighbours over the years who risked themselves helping us. It's one of the reasons my door is never closed to those who need my help today. My Islamic faith teaches that each good turn done to us must be repaid by doing another good turn for someone else.

The taxi driver chatted nervously, trying to assure us his taxi was sturdy and reliable. I wasn't convinced, but Mirshakay had been insistent that we all go to Pakistan with him this time. And I agreed. After all the tensions of the previous weeks, I felt I needed to get out of the country, even if just for a week. It was also a good opportunity for Hamid to get some medical attention. This second spell in prison had left him even weaker. I could almost see his health deteriorating before my eyes. I was still suffering morning sickness, and for most of the journey I carried a bowl beneath my burka to vomit into. It was a terrible journey. We were squashed and uncomfortable, and all of us were on edge, expecting at any moment to be stopped and detained at a Taliban checkpoint. The general was unflappable, keeping up a steady banter with the gunmen each time we encountered them. Most of the Talibs relaxed when they heard their mother tongue being spoken in the familiar Pashtun accent. His natural authority demanded respect, and even the bravado of the young Talibs wilted in the glare of the general's old-soldier demeanour.

"You may pass, Uncle." My heart heaved a sigh of relief each time I heard those words, but when we crossed the border at Torkham my spirits soared. The car erupted into laughter as we entered Pakistan. You could feel the freedom. The fearful oppression of the Taliban had been lifted. And with it, a huge weight was taken from each of us.

By 4 o'clock that afternoon, we were in the southern Pakistani city of Peshawar. From there, we boarded an overnight bus to Lahore, the ancient city of kings. There, we went to my brother's house, where we were met with a warm welcome from his first wife and her parents, who were living there. That night, we ate *chappali kabab,* a wonderful local dish of ground beef mixed with pomegranates and red chili, washed down with Coca-Cola. It tasted as divine as any meal I had ever eaten, all the more so for being the first meal I had eaten in months that was not tainted by the poisonous coating of Taliban rule.

It was wonderful to be in Lahore. For the first time since our wedding, Hamid and I were able to go out and relax and enjoy ourselves as a perfectly normal young married couple. Lahore is a truly beautiful place of centuries-old tiled mosques and winding bazaars. Hamid and I walked around for hours sightseeing. We picnicked in a beautiful park reserved for women and families. He had fought to marry me for years, and since our wedding we had hardly had even a few seconds like this, just sitting and relaxing together, enjoying breathing the same air.

The city was so functional and clean after the turmoil of Kabul. Many of my city's great buildings had been destroyed in the civil war, and I marvelled at the historic architecture of Lahore. Between the sixteenth and eighteenth centuries, the city had been ruled by the Mughals, an Islamic Indian dynasty of emperors who controlled much of the Asian subcontinent. The Mughals were famous builders; the Taj Mahal, for example, was built by the Mughal emperor Shah Jahan. In Lahore, they created many of the city's most notable landmarks, including the spectacular Lahore Fort and the Shalimar Gardens, both of which are now UNESCO World Heritage Sites.

I was now three months pregnant and still not feeling very well. Hamid was also fragile from his two bouts of brutal treatment by the Taliban. For a few short days, however, we drew emotional and physical strength from the tranquility of Lahore. "Tranquil" is perhaps an odd word to use to describe a bustling Pakistani city of almost five million people, but that is how it felt after all we had been through.

After a week in Lahore, we got word that Afghan president Rabbani was in Peshawar. He had been deposed by the Taliban, but as far as we and the rest of the world were concerned he was still Afghanistan's legitimate leader. Rabbani's ambassador still represented Afghanistan in the United Nations General Assembly. Only Saudi Arabia and Pakistan had recognized the Taliban as the official government. My brother had once worked for Rabbani at the Interior Ministry and knew him well. He made contact with the president, and he and Hamid were invited to meet him. They readily went to pay their respects and to hear our president's plans for regaining control of our country.

Burhanuddin Rabbani, like my family, was from Badakhshan. He and my father had been friends and occasional rivals, and we respected him deeply. He had been a key voice against the rise of Communism in Afghanistan during the 1950s and '60s, and during the Soviet occupation he had organized military and political resistance from Pakistan.

When President Najibullah fell from power after the Communists lost power, Rabbani was selected to replace him. But the Mujahideen government of the time was very factional, and these divisions pitted Rabbani and Ahmad Shah Massoud's forces against those of Generals Dostum and Hekmatyar and launched the civil war.

There were a lot of people at Rabbani's compound, and both men returned from their meeting very excited. They were convinced Rabbani was the key to a stable Afghanistan—although with the Taliban firmly in control, it was hard for even Rabbani himself to envisage how that might happen. Their sense of optimism was infectious, and from the calm and safety of Lahore I found myself entertaining thoughts that perhaps all was not lost for Afghanistan.

We were all so excited by the prospect of Rabbani regaining his rightful role of president that Hamid and I decided, almost on the spot, that we should return to Kabul immediately. Apart from our newfound sense of optimism, Hamid's widowed sister was alone in Kabul with her children, and Hamid and I wanted to be there to support her. My brother decided it was too risky to return and that he would stay in Pakistan, switching between his houses in Peshawar and Lahore. Leaving my brother and his wives was awful because I had no idea when or if I might see them again. But I was a married woman now, and my rightful place was with my husband.

Winter was closing in, and the snow was getting heavier. As we retraced our steps back to Kabul, the landscape through the high mountains of the Khyber Pass had become white and crisp. Perhaps the jagged rocks were like the Taliban and the fresh snow was a new beginning for Afghanistan—covering their hard, unforgiving ways. I certainly hoped so.

Hamid and I crossed back into Afghanistan without incident and were soon back in our apartment in Kabul. A week away had refreshed me enough to give me a new sense of enjoyment at being in my homeland again. Even under Taliban rule, I never lost my patriotism. This was my Kabul and my Afghanistan.

It was the beginning of Ramadan, and like all observant Muslims we fasted between sunrise and sunset. We were up before dawn for *sahaar,* the substantial breakfast eaten while it was still dark to sustain us through the day's fasting until we were allowed to eat again after sunset. Typically, we would eat early and then go back to sleep for a while before morning prayers.

Hamid and I had just returned to bed when there was knocking at the door. Hamid went to answer; we thought it was a neighbour coming to ask a favour or something similar. I heard voices, then Hamid's footsteps on the floor as he came back to the bedroom. His face was ashen grey and he looked like he was going to be sick. He asked me for his coat. The Taliban were at our door. They had a car waiting for him outside. Hamid had no choice but to go with them. I wanted to rush to the door with him, to beg the Talibs to leave him alone, to leave us alone. We had come back to Kabul in the hope we might have an ordinary peaceful existence. And now here they were taking him away again.

Hamid was his usual dignified self. He gently ordered me to stay in the bedroom. I was dressed in my nightgown and not properly attired to be pleading with strange men, even on the doorstep of my own home at 5 o'clock in the morning. It wasn't clear what they wanted with Hamid. There were no charges. They just told him his presence was required and he was to go with them. I heard the door bang closed and lay back on the pillows sobbing, clutching my pregnant belly and once again wondering what would become of us.

I knew of a man from Badakhshan who now worked with the Taliban. I found his address in an old notebook. He had a job in Puli

Charkhi prison. Built in the 1970s, it was notorious for the brutal torture of inmates during the Soviet occupation. I didn't know where the Taliban had taken Hamid, but we were running out of people who might help us. You can really only ask someone to intervene once on your behalf—more and it becomes too dangerous for them—so it was impossible to go back to any of the people who had helped us previously.

I didn't know this man very well, but I hoped that the fact we were from the same region and that he knew who my father was might make him more sensitive to my pleas. The following day, I woke early and, donning my burka, I slipped into the cold morning air and went in search of him.

Puli Charkhi prison is about ten kilometres outside Kabul. I walked out of the suburbs as they faded away first into small villages, then into nothing but a few scattered mud houses and finally into dusty desert tracks. It is not a place a woman should be walking alone, especially not in those days. The tracks appear to lead nowhere—then suddenly the prison rises out of the earth. The guards' bayonets and the razor wire ringing the walls glinted in the sunlight. The rough, mud-plastered walls have a medieval feel with their imposing stone watchtowers. It is a terrifying place, known as the Alcatraz of Afghanistan because escape is impossible. I entered the guardhouse and explained my situation, asking for an audience with the man from Badakhshan. A guard went away to ask. He returned with a one-word answer: "No."

"What kind of Badakhshani are you?" was the message I sent back. Didn't he have any *gharor,* pride, that he would not even allow a wife to ask about her missing husband?

I hoped the accusation might sting the man into action. I was a newly married Muslim woman, and it is considered culturally inappropriate that I should be left alone without any support. The guards looked ashamed and promised to relay the message to their boss. But he still refused to see me. I could see why. I had chastised him in front of his men, and he probably felt humiliated. I was told to go home and come back a few days later.

I walked all the way home again on an empty, thirsty belly with a kicking baby, and with still no idea about where they had taken my husband.

I got home at lunchtime in a foul mood. One of Hamid's elderly relatives had recently died, and my sister-in-law and I were expected to attend the funeral to pay our condolences. I really didn't want to go, but family duty and honour dictated that I must. I don't remember much of the afternoon. My mind was overwhelmed with worry about Hamid. As I sat quietly on a carpet, lost in my own thoughts, an elderly man approached me. News of Hamid's arrest had spread quickly, even though it had been only a couple of days since his detention. The old man's dark eyes conveyed sympathy, and his long grey beard danced as he whispered to me that he had news of Hamid's whereabouts. According to one of his relatives— the old man didn't explain who, or how this person came to the information—my husband was being held by Intelligence Service Number 3. This was the most dangerous of all the intelligence wings. Their job was to root out dissenting political voices and make them go away. I was terrified for Hamid, but at least I knew now where he was.

Every day for a week, I went to the intelligence office and every day I was turned away by sneering guards. On the seventh day, I was allowed inside to see my husband. His naturally slim frame was gaunt and hunched. He had been repeatedly beaten and was in too much pain to stand up straight. His dark features were silhouetted against his unnaturally white skin, his eyes sunken and his cheek-bones protruding.

We sat at a rough wooden table and whispered to each other. I tried to hug him, but a Taliban prison is no place for affection, even between a husband and wife. He told me they had forced him to stand outside all night in the snow, while by day he endured endless interrogations and beatings. They asked him, "Why did you go and see Rabbani? What was the purpose of the meeting? What is your connection with Rabbani?"

President Rabbani was guarded by Pakistani security agents from the ISI, the Inter-Services Intelligence. It had long been suspected that many of the agents had sympathies with the Taliban, and here was proof. The Pakistani agents had clearly been feeding the Taliban the names of Rabbani's visitors, including Hamid, and presumably my brother as well.

As I was leaving the prison, a senior Talib came to me and asked, "How much is your husband's release worth? $2,500? $5,000?"

They obviously knew by now that Hamid was not political. They could beat him all day and all night and he wouldn't tell them anything. He couldn't because he didn't know anything. But his detention still created an opportunity for them to profit. I would have given them all I had but I didn't have any money. We weren't that rich, not cash rich anyway. And even if we could arrange financing from Pakistan via my brother, the Taliban had effectively ruined the banking system, so transferring money or borrowing large amounts of cash was now impossible. I just could not pay it. Something I will forever feel guilty about.

Hamid was now getting very sick from all the abuse he was suffering. He was half starved and frozen to death. A cold entered his lungs and became more and more serious. The lethal combination of his failing immunity, close proximity to many very sick prisoners and lack of a place to wash led to him contracting tuberculosis.

I prepared a letter pleading for his release and planned to give it to the executive board of the intelligence service. In it, I talked of Hamid's innocence and the fact that he now carried a communicable disease that threatened the health of the other prisoners. I delivered it myself to the office of a career bureaucrat. He wasn't a Talib but rather an ordinary, bespectacled man seemingly a little bemused and baffled by his latest masters. Given his age, I imagine he had served the Russians, the Mujahideen and now the Taliban. Different bosses for the different ages of Afghanistan.

He took the letter from me, and I burst out with the story of Hamid, his illness and our recent marriage. I wanted to gain his sympathy so that he might present the letter to the board with greater urgency. He peered through his glasses as I stood on the other side of the partition in my burka. Then he looked down at the letter and said, "Sister, who wrote this letter for you?"

"I did," I replied. "I am a medical student and just want to get my sick husband out of prison."

"Your husband is lucky," he said. "He has a wife who cares for him and is educated. But sister, what if they put me in prison? Who will take care of me? My wife is not educated; who would write the letters for me?"

He let out a long, dramatic sigh and put the letter underneath a pile of other letters, doubtless written by other desperate relatives. "Go now, sister, I cannot promise. But I will do my best to take your letters to the executive."

With tears stinging my eyes, I left his office. Hamid's life and liberty was just another letter underneath a hundred others. I knew it had little chance of being delivered by the bespectacled bureaucrat.

I walked home in the snow. As I climbed up the stairs to our apartment, I felt that my home without my husband was as empty as my stomach. As I entered the apartment, Hamid's sister Khadija ran to greet me, asking if I had any news about his release. I had no answer for her. I went straight to my bedroom and lay down trying to hold back the tears. I dozed off to sleep. Hours later, the sound of a mullah calling *iftar* (the evening meal that breaks the fast) woke me up. I lay back and listened: *Hai Alal falah, Hai Alal falah!*

Feeling hungry, I got up and went to the other room, expecting to see Khadija and her children about to eat. But she was feeling as low as me and she had also slept the day away. No one had prepared any food. I felt a pang of guilt. This was Hamid's home, and I was his wife. In his absence, it fell to me to keep the home running and look after his family. After all, it was the fault of my family that he was in prison at all. I went out to buy some rice and a little meat and came back to cook it. Khadija came into the kitchen fussing over me, telling me I was pregnant and should rest. She took the knife from my hand and took over the job of cutting the onions. We continued to cook together in companionable silence. It was a cold winter night in Kabul, snow was falling thickly and the city was silent with both fear and boredom.

I turned to Khadija with tears in my eyes. "I'm so sorry, jan [dear].

I feel all I have done is bring trouble to your family. I wish poor Hamid had never wanted to marry me. I have brought all this pain on him."

She put down the knife, wiped away an onion tear and took my hand. "Well, Fawzia, he is a strong man. And prison will only make his character stronger. You should not be sorry, you should be proud of him. He is a political prisoner, not a criminal."

This was the first time we had discussed the reasons why Hamid was in jail, and I was amazed she could be so calm and balanced about the situation. She had every right to be resentful of me and my family. Khadija has always been a woman I admire; she was strong, intelligent and reasonable. I was so touched by her tone, I couldn't reply because the tears choked my throat. I carried on stirring the rice pot and tried to convey my thanks with a silent look.

She hugged me and then ordered me into the dining room to find a date or a piece of fruit to break my fast with, telling me I needed to put my baby's health first.

I went and sat alone in the dining room, memories of my childhood starting to flicker across my mind. Long forgotten and half hidden until now, they came to the surface because of my melancholy mood. I recalled *iftar* at the *hooli* back in the days when my father was alive. A traditional napkin, like a large tablecloth but for the floor, would be laid out in the centre of the room.

Local village women made the napkin by hand with delicately woven threads. It had the most beautiful vibrant colours, stripes of red and orange created by natural dyes made from mountain plants and flowers. Mattresses and cushions would be placed around the edge of the napkin, and everyone would sit cross-legged on them to eat.

The napkin would be piled high with nutritious and delicious fast-breaking foods such as *bolani* (a tasty flatbread filled with vegetables), *manto* (parcels of steamed mincemeat with onions and yogurt) and *qabuli pilau* (rice mixed with raisins, lentils and carrots). My elder sisters would all rush to prepare the meal, usually finishing minutes before the fast ended and the hungry hordes of family members descended.

All the family would sit together, apart from my father who was either away or sitting with his guests: all the wives and their children, my half brothers and sisters. We would sit and eat, talk and laugh. I was only a very small girl then, but I used to love those moments. It was a time when everyone relaxed and shared stories of the day. My heart ached to think of those pre-war days when we were a whole family untouched by grief and loss. I missed my mother and my brothers and sisters so much. I yearned to be back there again, an innocent village child whose only preoccupation was stealing chocolates or dressing up in a pair of wooden shoes.

My thoughts were broken by Khadija entering the room with a plate of steaming *pilau*. I smiled gratefully at her. Her presence was a reminder that I wasn't alone: Hamid's family was also my family now. Khadija's children ran in to join us, and my heart gladdened as we all tucked in.

Every day, I tried to visit Hamid and on the few occasions I did get to see him he put on a very brave face and pretended he was being well treated. He didn't want me to worry. But I could see the uncontrollable trembling that had developed in his hands and the bruises on his increasingly thin face. I pretended to believe him and tried to be a dutiful wife, knowing that to confront him with the evidence of his abuse would only make life even harder for him to bear. I think that trying to hide his ordeal from his young pregnant wife helped give him the strength to endure it. So we spent those few precious moments together talking about ordinary events of family life, as if he had just come back from a business conference or the bazaar or some other mundane occasion that husbands and wives everywhere take for granted every day. It was easier to pretend that this was just our ordinary life—as if nothing was strange or scary or out of place. Some people will tell you denial is wrong—perhaps it is—but when you are being tossed in the stormy seas of helpless despair, denial can become the tiny raft to which you fervently cling. Sometimes denial is the only thing that keeps you afloat.

I decided to make another attempt to persuade the Badakhshani man who worked at Puli Charkhi jail to help us. After the long and tiring walk to get there, I was relieved when this time he invited me into his office. I told him how Hamid was innocent of any political crime, how he was being tortured and would soon die if he wasn't released. But again it was to no avail. He said there was nothing he could do for us. I started to cry. He let out a long sigh, then reluctantly promised me he would try to talk to the guard in charge of Hamid's section of the prison.

It was a Friday afternoon, a day I could usually gain access to meet Hamid. Khadija put on her blue shuttlecock burka and I the black Arab-style *niqab,* and we walked to the prison together.

As we waited at the gate, the guard went inside to call Hamid. As he did so, he left the door open and I was able to peek inside the main building. I watched as a second young guard, barely out of his teens, washed his hands and feet for the ablutions required before Islamic prayers. The first guard approached him and the man asked in Pashto, "*Sa khabara da?* What is up?"

The guard replied, "*Hamid khaza raghili da.* Hamid's wife is here."

The young man put down his water pot and started to walk towards us. I turned away so they didn't see I had been watching. Some other men walked past and I heard them speak in Urdu, the most widely spoken language in Pakistan. They weren't prisoners, and I can only assume they were Pakistani Taliban sympathizers working in our prisons. I took Khadija's hand, hoping the young man might have good news about Hamid's release. He walked straight up to us and asked, "*Hamid khaza chirta da?* Who is Hamid's wife?" I stepped forward, holding my *niqab* across my face with my left hand. "I am."

Without saying another word, the man bent down, picked up a stone from the ground and threw it at my head. I recoiled in shock. "You woman. You complain to your Badakhshanis about us? Who are you to do this? Go, get out of here, woman." For a few seconds I was too shocked to move. I started to speak, to try to explain that I had only been trying to free my innocent husband. The man picked up a second stone and threw it again. It just missed my head, and as it did so I moved my hand protectively, giving the man a glimpse of my painted fingernails.

He sneered and spat at the ground. "Look at your nails! You are a Muslim yet you have the fingers of a whore."

The blood rushed to my cheeks in anger. I wanted to tell him that he had no business judging or commenting on another man's wife. I was a Muslim woman unrelated to him, so he had no right to talk about me. He was the bad Muslim, not me.

Khadija could read my thoughts and stepped forward to stop me. The man grabbed another stone and threw it. "Get out of here, woman." Khadija grabbed me and we half ran, half walked back to the gate. Once at a safe distance, I turned and said to her loudly, so they could hear me, "These men are not Muslims; they are not even human beings." The man waved another stone at me menacingly and then turned to go back inside, cursing and swearing with words no decent Muslim I know would ever use.

Then, the awful reality of what had just happened hit me: I had been insulted and my attempts to speak to the Badakhshani in Puli Charkhi had backfired badly, which would now make things even worse for Hamid.

I started to shake and cry loudly under my *niqab*. Khadija also cried. Luckily we managed to find a taxi driver who was prepared to break the rule against driving female non-relatives. I don't think I trusted my legs to walk; I was shaking too much from a combination of anger, fear and pure humiliation. Once home, I threw myself on my bed and howled.

That evening, Khadija and I reached the awful decision that it was safer not to try to visit Hamid for a while. We feared it would only make things harder for him and lead to more beatings. The guards had decided his wife was an insolent whore for trying to protest his imprisonment and for wearing nail varnish. I was furious with the Badakhshani from Puli Charkhi. I suspected that not only had he chosen not to help us, but he had deliberately caused trouble for us. The fact was, I hadn't even complained to him of conditions. I had spoken only of Hamid's illness and his innocence.

That night, my last hopes for Hamid's release died.

FOR TWO weeks I didn't attempt to see him. I didn't want to be insulted or humiliated by those guards, and I feared that even if they did let me see him I'd break down and cry in front of him. The last thing he needed was to worry about my being upset. But by the following Friday, I could bear it no longer. I needed to see my husband. I also needed to ask him something important. As a married woman, I needed his permission to travel and I had decided that I wanted to go to my brother's in Pakistan to give birth. I couldn't bear the thought of delivering my first baby in Kabul, where the Taliban had banned all female doctors from working and male doctors from treating women.

Khadija insisted on coming with me for safety, and as we approached the prison gates I was a bag of nerves. I wasn't very optimistic that they would let me see him. I stayed a few paces back, while Khadija approached the guard and asked for Hamid. He disappeared, then came back accompanied by the same young guard who had thrown stones at me. I kept quiet, and so did Khadija, expecting a rock to come flying at my head at any moment. He looked straight at me and ordered, "Come close, woman."

Slowly I inched forward, promising myself that if he threw another stone at me, I would throw it right back at him.

"Show me your left hand," he ordered. I said nothing and I didn't show him my hand, instead hiding them both under my *niqab*. The man was coarse and rude and, in my eyes, totally unfamiliar with the Afghan custom of showing politeness and manners at all times.

He laughed as I hid my hands and said, "I am telling you. Don't put nail polish on your fingers anymore. If you do, you are not a Muslim."

I glared at him through the safety of my covered face. He dared to tell me I wasn't a Muslim, but then permitted himself to comment on the makeup worn by another man's wife! "Why do you wear it? Tell me," he ordered.

I replied as calmly as I could. "We have been married for only four months. It is customary and cultural for a new bride to wear makeup and nice clothes for the first year of marriage. Surely as an Afghan man you know this?"

He laughed a mocking and guttural laugh, showing a hint of his yellow teeth as he did so. "I see. So do you want me to release your husband?"

I didn't know what to say. I assumed he was just mocking me. I answered, "What is his crime? He has committed no crime."

The guard shrugged his shoulders and said, "Go, and come back with a male relative. Bring a man who is prepared to show me evidence of property. If the man will use his property as a guarantee that your husband will not attempt to leave Kabul, then I will release him."

I didn't say a word but turned and ran out the gate as fast as my legs could carry me. Khadija ran after me. We didn't know if he meant it, but we knew we had to try. We stood looking at each other, two women standing on the streets of a male-dominated world gone mad. We didn't know who we could ask or what to do next. My brothers had all left Kabul, and Hamid's family were mostly living in Badakhshan.

Then I remembered a cousin who owned a shop. We ran across the streets to get there. We reached it, both panting and out of breath, only to find it closed. In our excitement, we had forgotten it was Friday, the day of prayer and rest.

I didn't want to give the prison guard the chance of changing his mind and losing this possibility of releasing Hamid. We ran back to the prison. The guard was sitting on a chair enjoying the sunshine. I was pleased to see he looked relaxed.

I didn't want to go close to him in case I made him angry again. So Khadija went and explained the situation. He stood up, not saying a word to her, and went back inside the prison for what seemed like hours but was in reality only a few minutes. Then he reappeared with Hamid and another, even younger-looking guard. Then he spoke. "Hamid can go with you and this man will go too. If you can bring a letter back from a neighbour or friend, then I will release him."

He ordered a Taliban driver with a Hilux pickup truck to take us. We all got in. I dared not look at Hamid for fear of the guard, but I sneaked a sideways glance at him and saw he looked white as a sheet and on the verge of collapse.

The young Talib who was accompanying us told us he was from Wardak province. He seemed kind but very young, and I doubted he had any power or influence in the prison. I was terrified none of the neighbours would be able to help us and he'd drive Hamid straight back to prison. Dusk had fallen by the time we drove into Makrorian. Khadija recalled that one family among our neighbours owned their apartment; she didn't know them very well but we had no choice but to approach them for the guarantee. She went to talk to the man while Hamid and I and the young Talib went upstairs to wait in our apartment. It was emotional agony. Hamid was sitting in his own living room, but I couldn't even talk to him and at any second he might be taken back to prison.

I was still wearing my *niqab* but I noticed the young Talib was looking at my face, trying to read my eyes. I was scared and looked down. I think he saw how sad and scared I was. He was a native Pashto speaker but he spoke to me kindly in broken Dari, the language he knew Hamid and I spoke. "Don't worry, sister. I too am newly married, only twenty days. So I understand your pain. Even if you don't find a guarantee, I will leave Hamid here tonight and will come again tomorrow to get the letter."

He risked the wrath of his superiors by making that offer. It was another one of those surprising acts of random kindness when least expected. Hamid and I both thanked him.

We all sat and waited in silence for Khadija to return.

I heard male voices in the corridor of our apartment. I went out and saw half a dozen male neighbours. They smiled and said how happy they were that Hamid was being released. All of them told me not to worry; they would collectively offer Hamid his guarantee. I was so grateful to them that I could do nothing but cry. They went into the room and Hamid hugged them all. Two of the neighbours who owned property signed the letter of guarantee, which stated that Hamid, an engineer, would not leave Kabul and would attend appointments at the Interior Ministry whenever the Taliban required it. Failure to do so would result in the two men forfeiting their property. It was an awfully big risk for our neighbours to take, and once again I was amazed at the generosity some people show to others at such times of war and conflict.

I took a small lace handkerchief I had recently embroidered and gave it to the young Talib as a gift for his new bride. He thanked me sincerely. I wondered how this kind and sweet young man had come to join the Taliban's ranks. He was so unlike the rest.

It seemed like an age before the kindly neighbours left and I could finally be alone with my husband. He looked like a ghostly shadow of himself. Khadija and I tried to make him smile and told him jokes; he started to laugh and as he did so, his breath caught and he coughed. A terrifying, hacking cough that refused to stop. Khadija and I looked at each other, grim-faced. Hamid had TB. The cough was a sign of worse to come.

Dear Shuhra and Shaharzad,

There will be times in your life when all hope and strength leave you. Times when you just want to give up and turn your face away from the world. But, my darling daughters, giving up is not something our family does.

When your father was arrested in those early days of our marriage, I wanted to give up. Perhaps if I had not been pregnant and feeling Shaharzad kicking in my belly, I might have done so. But knowing I was about to give a new life meant I had to fight even harder for the life I had. I also remembered my mother, your grandmother. Imagine if she had given up after my father died. Imagine if she had taken the easy route and married a man who didn't want us and placed us in an orphanage or neglected us. She never would have done this because giving up was something that woman did not know how to do.

Imagine also if your grandfather had given up when the central government had told him it was not possible to build the Atanga Pass. Think of how many lives would have been lost on the mountains. By refusing to give up the project, he saved countless lives over the years.

Thank God I have both of their blood in me. Because of them, giving up is not something I can do either.

And you, my dear daughters, come from that same blood too. If there comes a day in your life when the fear takes hold of you and squeezes the fight out of you, then I want you to remember these words. Giving up is not what we do. We fight. We live. We survive.

With love,
Your mother

FIFTEEN

Back to My Roots

{ *1998* }

DURING HIS WEEKS of incarceration, Hamid had been beaten sense-less, manacled and left outside for days in the wind, rain and snow as punishment. He had contracted a fatal disease. And for what? Nothing. He was guilty of nothing and they had charged him with nothing. Sadly, Hamid's story is not an unusual one for the Taliban era. Many other innocent men and women found themselves in Taliban prisons and suffered similar fates.

The year was 1998. It was the beginning of spring, and the heavy snows of winter were thawing fast as each day got progressively warmer. It was a welcome relief to feel the sun again. It was good for Hamid too. He was still very sick and coughed constantly.

By now, I was almost seven months pregnant and my baby was very active, kicking and wriggling inside me. I was having trouble getting a good night's sleep with my unborn child testing her grow-ing strength and Hamid exploding into coughing fits at regular intervals throughout the night.

He was too ill to work, and the medication the doctor had pre-scribed didn't seem to be making much difference to his condition. Despite the sun's increasingly warm rays, Kabul felt very oppressive.

Taliban rule in the capital was absolute. We lived in constant fear that they would show up at our front door and drag Hamid back to prison. It was not a question of if they would do so but when.

But his time in prison had taken such a toll on Hamid's health that a fourth detention would most certainly constitute a death sentence. We knew we had to flee Taliban control, and Pakistan wasn't really an option. Hamid had become a target for the Taliban after Pakistani spies reported his visit to President Rabbani's compound, and we feared he would be followed if we went back there.

Despite having promised the Taliban we would stay in Kabul, we decided to escape to Badakhshan. Our kindly neighbours who had signed Hamid's guarantee told us they supported our decision and we should flee while we still could.

Ahmad Shah Massoud and President Rabbani's forces were still holding out against the Taliban in this northern provincial stronghold. Even the mighty Soviet war machine had been unable to defeat the Mujahideen in Badakhshan, so we felt hopeful that we would find genuine refuge from the Taliban there. Our journey was to be fraught with danger, however.

Hamid was prescribed six months' worth of medication from his doctor and we set off. It was a difficult journey under any circumstances, across rough tracks and winding mountain passes, without taking into account the risk from the Taliban. Hamid's poor health and my pregnancy made us even more vulnerable. It was a measure of our desperation to get away from Kabul that we even considered travelling at this time. The city that had once been my safe haven now felt like a prison overrun by sadistic guards.

I packed a few belongings for the journey—mostly wedding gifts and things that reminded me of my family. I wanted to hide the few precious photographs I had of my mother and my murdered brother Muqim beneath clothing in the bottom of a suitcase, away from prying Taliban eyes. But I knew that if the Taliban found the photos they would be destroyed, and I dared not take the risk.

My sister-in-law Khadija was determined to stay with her children in Kabul. I argued and pleaded with her, but she could not be budged. I think she felt she owed it to her dead husband, Hamid's brother, to stay in Kabul and raise her children. She had become such a close friend that it was hard for me to leave her there alone in the house, but I respected her decision to stay.

Had I felt there was even a chance the Taliban would leave us alone, I might have stayed too. But Hamid and I were living on borrowed time. Sooner or later, some Taliban administrator would review the list of all the people they had detained and released and decide to send more fanatical young men to rearrest Hamid out of mere suspicion. Their attitude seemed to be "He's bound to be doing something wrong. Let's arrest him and torture him and then he will tell us." Of course, if you torture people for long enough they will tell you anything. And if they don't, then by Taliban logic they die guarding some terrible secret.

Ordinary people were being imprisoned for the most trivial of so-called offences. When Hamid was in jail, he spoke to taxi drivers who had been arrested for taking unaccompanied female passengers. Ironically, although the driver would be thrown in jail, the woman in question often got far worse for having "tempted" the driver. Taliban rules and their enforcement were often as arbitrary as the man holding the gun. This created an environment of paranoia in which it was safer to stay home than to leave and risk breaking some new law.

The situation was both terrifying and infuriating—these men thought they were ruling my country, but they were ruining it. And all their actions were cloaked in the name of Islam, which they used as a political catch-all to silence their critics. You don't like the way we treat women? You're un-Islamic. You want to listen to music? You're un-Islamic. You disagree with our justice system? You're un-Islamic. You say we are misinterpreting the Koran for our own ends? You're un-Islamic. These uneducated men had a two-dimensional view of the world that seemed firmly anchored in the Dark Ages, and that's exactly where they were determined to take my country. So as much as it pained us, we felt we had no choice but to leave Kabul.

We left the city early one morning, creeping through the city streets as dawn broke over the mountains, the springs in the taxi creaking over every bump in the road. Our plan was to drive east, following the path of the Kabul River until we reached Surobi. Taliban influence extended only a few hundred kilometres to the north of Kabul; beyond that, Ahmad Shah Massoud's forces had so far managed to keep them at bay. But to get to them, we had to find a way through the battle lines, one that wouldn't get us killed or draw too much attention from the Taliban, who suspected people going north of being spies.

Surobi is a small town in a lush valley surrounded by lakes, which have provided much of the capital's erratic supply of electricity from as far back as the 1950s. It's a relatively short drive of only seventy kilometres, but because the valley had seen some of the heaviest fighting during the civil war the road was (even by the standards of hardy Afghan travellers) in an appalling state, full of potholes and craters. This meant we had to drive at walking speed most of the way, nose to tail with all the other traffic. On either side of the gravel road, the earth was embroidered with a deadly lattice-work of landmines. During the past twenty years, over ten million landmines have been littered across Afghanistan. These evil weapons maim and kill our population to this day, the majority of their victims being children.

Frustrated or fatigued drivers would occasionally stray from the safe middle road, sometimes without consequence. Other times, their vehicles would erupt in a geyser of smoke and flaming metal. The largest landmines are designed to destroy sixty-ton armoured battle tanks, so driving a rusting nine-hundred-kilogram sedan over one is like holding a dandelion in front of a screaming jet engine. The most terrible scenes occurred when gung-ho bus drivers would try a shortcut. Sadly, drivers were the first to die in these blasts, which would usually rip the wheels and the entire front of the vehicle off. The terrified and shaken survivors faced an awful choice as the flames from the explosion grew in intensity: either perish in the blazing wreck of the bus or leap out of a broken window and take your chances in the minefield. There was really only one option, but it was a life-and-death gamble that not all of them won.

The road to Surobi passes over arid dusty plains outside the capital and passes Bagram Airbase. Today, Bagram is the main U.S. military base in Afghanistan but even then it was a huge installation, having served as the Soviets' centre of air force operations.

The expanse of valley soon gave way to steep and rocky mountains, and the road cut its way through the narrow gorge. Once we got to Surobi, our car turned north towards Tagab. The road from Surobi to Tagab was even worse. This area is not more than 150 kilometres northeast of Kabul and saw some of the heaviest fighting during the Soviet era. The road had been heavily bombed, parts of it blown up by the Mujahideen to prevent the Red Army advance. When we got to Tagab, I was shocked to see how many of the simple mud houses were in ruins. Many of the people there were living among the rubble, sheltering in whatever part of their house still stood.

Hamid and I were very anxious. So far, we had managed to get through the Taliban checkpoints without any problems. The next leg of our journey would be more difficult. Tagab marked the end of the Taliban front line in this part of the mountains. There was a lot of military equipment and large depots that appeared to be full of fuel for the tanks and trucks, and ammunition for rifles, artillery, mortars and rockets. Tired-faced, bearded young men stood on guard, and the traffic backed up as we neared the main checkpoint. Hamid and I stiffened. This would be where our escape succeeded or failed. We were worried that Hamid's name might be on a Taliban watch list and that his presence here might be enough to cause the Taliban to arrest him again.

As the line of cars and trucks crept forward, I could see nervous men and their wives in burkas being ordered out of their vehicles and made to present their luggage for inspection. Fervent young men with black turbans rifled through open bags and suitcases, tossing neatly packed clothing and treasured personal possessions on the ground. One stood up suddenly with a whoop of excitement, holding a videotape aloft like a trophy. This was contraband. A woman lurched at the cassette as the Talib dangled it out of her reach. She was wearing a burka, but I could tell she was young. I imagined she too was a new bride, torn between her anger and frustration at the injustice being dished out by her tormentor and the fear she felt knowing that by protesting she risked provoking more serious consequences. Her husband stayed a few paces behind, murmuring to his wife to stop. He would not let himself restrain his bride, knowing her actions were just, but neither could he challenge the Talib and be seen to condone her dissent.

The gunman pushed the woman hard in the chest, his hand lingering on the outline of her bust, which showed vaguely beneath her burka. She recoiled in shock for a moment before rushing back towards the Talib, fuelled by anger at the sexual assault. He just laughed and groped her once more before ramming his shoulder under her chin and knocking her to the ground. For a moment, she lay there stunned, and as she got onto her hands and knees the young Talib dropped the black plastic videocassette onto the ground in front of her and brought his heel heavily down upon it, smashing the brittle case. The woman didn't utter a word, but she lifted her head so she could better see the cruelty etched on the man's face. He bowed, then grinned at her theatrically and scooped up the spilled entrails of tape. He let the coils of plastic drip between his fingers as he walked backwards, watching her for any reaction. Turning to face a tree, he hurled the tangled remains high into the branches, where the ribbon tumbled through the leaves. Her head fell forward, and she sobbed as her husband stooped to help her up. The Talib's dark eyes blazed triumphantly; he was clearly pleased by another apparent moral victory. The branches of the tree glistened in the midday light, filled with the innards of dozens of similar tapes. This was clearly a game that was played out on a regular basis.

My decision to leave the photos of my family at home had hurt at the time, but now I was thankful that I hadn't taken them. I hurriedly began unloading our luggage from the car, while Hamid quietly asked some other men where we could hire a horse and a guide. Our plan was to go through the narrow mountain passes and strike out northwest to Jabul Saraj, which was not under control of the Taliban. We aimed to loop west through the mountains and around the front lines of the fighting rather than go directly north, which was the most direct but also most dangerous route.

I was worried the Taliban would take our passports and tear them up, but when it was our turn to face the checkpoint, the armed men didn't actually pay us much attention. Their friend's game with the newlyweds had put them in a good mood, and after a cursory search of our luggage, they let us pass. A woman a little farther back in the queue was not so lucky. It was obvious she was from a northern province because she was wearing the white burka that is traditional in that part of the country. The Taliban turned on her for daring to wear such a garment, beating her with sticks and lengths of wire cable.

I wasn't looking forward to the horse ride, but after what we had witnessed I couldn't wait to get away from these terrible, inhuman men into the comparative safety of the hills beyond. At more than seven months pregnant, I struggled to mount the horse that Hamid had managed to hire. But with his help and my desire to escape, I managed to get on. Hamid walked beside the animal, and I felt very odd as we left the Taliban behind. It was as if my life had been diverted to some strange parallel universe. As a couple, Hamid and I were the image of what I felt the future Afghanistan should be: an educated, ambitious young woman, with her equally educated, urbane, intellectual and loving husband. Yet here I was dressed in a burka riding on horseback as my long-haired, bearded husband walked beside me through the mountains. This Taliban ideology threatened to shackle my country to the Dark Ages.

But beneath this fear, I also had a powerful sense of optimism. The Taliban didn't represent the true spirit of the Afghan people I knew and loved so well. They were an aberration, a disease that had taken hold after so many years' sickness brought about by war and suffering. As we climbed through the mountains, fording streams and negotiating narrow paths, I felt the weight of oppression begin to lift. With each cautious step, I seemed to get lighter, until finally, after several hours of hard trekking, we made it to Northern Alliance lines.

Not that there was any great fanfare when we got there. We simply arrived at a small town, where people were going about their business in a very ordinary way, at which point our guide turned to us as if to say, "Here we are."

We arranged another car, which would take us to Jabul Saraj. It was just a few hours' drive, but it really was like entering another world. The markets were thriving and full of shoppers. Women were walking and talking to men without the strict supervision demanded by the Taliban, and the restaurants were busy with diners. Hamid and I checked into a hotel, something that would have been impossible in Kabul but that felt incredibly normal here.

As I stood in the foyer of the little hotel, I felt overwhelmed by the events of the past year. Life under the Taliban had changed me in ways I hadn't really understood until now. I wasn't the same person I had been; my confidence had evaporated and the daily fear had exhausted my reserves of strength. I stood there quietly, like a good Taliban wife, whereas once I would have been organizing our check-in, inspecting the room and making sure the porter brought in our bags. Now I was passive, just waiting for my husband to make all the arrangements. It saddened me to realize how much I had changed. Even as a little girl I was a great organizer, something my mother always commented on when telling stories of my childhood. The Taliban had taken that confident girl and determined teenager and turned her into a diminutive, cold, scared and exhausted woman living beneath the cloak of invisibility that was her burka.

I couldn't bring myself to talk to the hotel manager or the owner, who was cheerily waving his hands about in greeting. My attitude towards men had changed. They were cruel and not to be trusted, merely waiting to exploit women at the first opportunity that presented itself. And this terrible shift in my attitude had occurred in the name of Islam—though it was not an Islam I recognized. This division between the sexes was born of fear and suspicion, not respect as I had been raised to believe.

My mother came from a much more conservative generation, yet even she enjoyed the kind of liberation and empowerment that was being denied to me and hundreds of thousands of other women under the Taliban. She was allowed to visit her family when she wished and was given the responsibility of managing my father's businesses in his absence, of supervising his cattle herds on their annual journey to the higher pasture. Yes, my father beat my mother, which, as wrong as it seems now, was normal for village culture at that time; but for all that, I know he truly respected her. The Taliban were as violent towards women and more, but had none of the respect.

There was a huge silence inside me. Until now, I hadn't even noticed it. Little by little, it had grown with each prison visit, each woman I saw getting beaten on the streets and each public execution of a young woman who was just like me.

We went up to our room, which was typical of Afghan guest houses: small, with a mattress on the floor. I was in a weird mood; the emotion of being free of the Taliban churned up feelings I had buried deep for a long time. Hamid was in good spirits and almost danced around our little room with a boyishness I thought had been crushed out of him by those frozen nights in the prison yard. His enthusiasm was infectious, and I finally allowed myself to relax. Taking off my burka, I threw it in the corner of the room, casting some of my cares aside with it. Looking at the crumpled, dirty burka lying there in a heap, I wanted to jump on it and grind it into the floor.

"Put your scarf on, my darling wife," Hamid said. "We're going out."

The words seemed so foreign that for a moment I felt like he had just dared me to do something very naughty, as though we were mischievous children plotting something forbidden.

That's when the wave of euphoria washed over me. I could. We could. Go out in the street, like a normal couple. And I needed to cover only my hair, not my face. My pregnant belly was very large, but to this day it seems to me that my feet did not touch the stairs as we scampered outside like a pair of giggling teenagers.

The wind on my face was like the kiss of freedom. My scarf covered all my hair and my clothes were modest, in accordance with the teachings of Islam, yet without my burka I felt strangely naked.

I began to think about how much the Taliban had damaged Islam. These were men who acted in the name of Allah, but they didn't respect the God they claimed to represent. Instead of following the Koran, they placed themselves above the teachings of the holy word, believing they, not God, had the right to become the moral arbiters, who decided what was righteous and what was forbidden. They had hijacked and corrupted Islam, turning it into a tool to achieve their own selfish ends.

The following morning, we took a small bus to Puli Khumri, the capital of Baghlan province. Afghan buses can be very chaotic. Hamid and I climbed aboard and sat waiting for the other passengers to finish saying goodbye to friends and relatives, or argue with the driver, or try to stack an extra piece of luggage onto the already overflowing roof. Nearby, a street hawker was selling *Ashawa panir*—a type of cheese that is a regional specialty and a favourite dish at many Afghan picnics. Like most pregnant women, I had a very good appetite and I asked Hamid to go and buy me some. As a kind husband should, he dutifully indulged my request. The bus was nearly ready to depart when he climbed back on board, out of breath but clutching a small piece of the white cheese, which is mild and chewy and not unlike mozzarella. However, in his chivalrous dashing out to buy the mother of his unborn child some cheese, he hadn't remembered to get raisins—the traditional accompaniment to the cheese that helps bring out its flavour. I didn't want to seem ungrateful, but I was a little disappointed. The bus was beginning to move and there was no time to go back and get some. I was just resolving to enjoy the cheese despite the absence of raisins when a sharp knock at the window startled me. I spun around, expecting to see the black menace of a Taliban turban. Instead, I was greeted by the kind eyes of the elderly cheese merchant.

"Here, sister," he said, passing a small plastic bag to me. "The man forgot to get raisins."

Under the Taliban, we would have been considered criminals. Yet here we were treated with courtesy, good manners and respect. It was a simple act of human kindness, nothing more, nothing less, but it was so unexpectedly touching that my eyes pricked with tears.

The incident put me in a much better mood, and I enjoyed the spring landscape. The mountain peaks were beginning to cast off their wintry jackets of snow, while the new growth of grass and flowers farther down the slopes sprouted towards the sun's rays. It gave me a sense of hope for my country. No matter how cold and cruel the Taliban might be, I felt that they too might, one day, melt away like the snow.

At Puli Khumri, we stayed at the home of one of Hamid's aunts and her husband. This couple had once come to my brother's home to negotiate Hamid's marriage proposal, and I liked them very much. But I was mindful that I had a lot to live up to. Their neighbours all knew that our marriage had cost Hamid's family twenty thousand dollars, an enormous amount of money. They would all be curious to see and assess me. And that brought with it a huge sense of expectation that, after months of stress and days of travel and only weeks from childbirth, I couldn't help but feel I was struggling to live up to.

Hamid's aunt was kind. She knew exactly how I felt and had already begun to make preparations for a bath. By that, I mean a bucket of water heated over the cooking fire. But when you are exhausted and caked in dust and sweat, pouring enamel jugs over your head from a bucket filled with what had hours earlier been pure mountain snow is an experience as indulgent as the most luxurious five-star-hotel spa visit imaginable.

With each splash, I scrubbed away the stress, the strain and the filth of my life under the Taliban. Days before, I had left Kabul, accorded no more value than a dog. With each soaking, I regained a little more humanity and a little more self-worth. All I had to deal with now was the scrutiny of the neighbours, and as self-conscious as I might have felt, the terrible rule of the Taliban had also given me an inner strength that I was only just beginning to realize. The fact is I wasn't the young and naive bride I had been not so long ago. Now, I was a wife who had negotiated with fundamentalist tyrants, an expectant mother who had climbed mountains and an idealistic and hopeful woman who was finally beginning to find the firm ground of maturity beneath her feet.

However, when I emerged, the neighbours made it clear from their faces that they didn't think Hamid had got much value for his twenty thousand dollars. They barely bothered to conceal the raised eyebrows and pursed lips. I can only imagine what they said about me once they were home.

When we were alone, Hamid laughed about it. He kissed my forehead gently and told me not to care what people said or thought. We had each other and that was all that mattered.

After a night's rest, we continued our journey north. When we got to the town of Talakan, we had to hire a Jeep because floods from the winter snow melt had washed out parts of the road to Kisham, the next part of our journey. From there, we had to go by truck to Faizabad, the capital of Badakhshan. This wasn't the news I wanted to hear. Travelling atop a truck is the most basic form of transportation in Afghanistan, and usually the preserve of the Kuchis, Afghanistan's small nomadic gypsy population. I asked Hamid to see if he could find us a car, but despite his best efforts there were no small vehicles going to Faizabad. The spring thaw had caused havoc with the roads here too.

I was horrified when I saw the truck. I was an educated city woman of high breeding, and this was a lorry normally used for transporting goats. Today, it was piled high with sacks of rice. If I had been offered this vehicle to escape Kabul I would have gladly climbed aboard, but now I was safe and as I began to regain my confidence my pride was getting the better of me. Hamid gave me an ultimatum: this was the last truck going to Faizabad and if I didn't get on it, we would be stuck here in Kisham. I had no choice but to swallow my pride and get aboard. I had put my burka back on, for warmth and to protect me from the dust as much as for any other reason, but even with the anonymity it afforded I spent the next four hours with my head tucked into my knees, in case we should pass somebody I knew and they recognized me. Occasionally, I would look up to enjoy the view, but the shame of being seen swaying on top of that goat truck always got the better of me and I quickly buried my head again.

The road was incredibly steep and rough. As we crawled our way up Qaraqmar, the most notoriously dangerous part of the road, the driver lost traction and came to a halt. But when he stepped on the brakes, he discovered they didn't work. They had become over-heated on the downhill sections, and the truck started rolling back-wards towards the river. That gave me cause to look up: we were gathering speed towards the icy clutches of the fast-flowing flood waters. Hamid, the other passengers and I perched on the rice sacks and braced ourselves for the expected explosion into the river. An image of the freezing water clawing at my sodden burka, dragging me under and smashing me against the rocks, filled my head.

I closed my eyes in sheer panic, fingers digging into the rice sack as if it might offer some protection. The tires of the truck skidded backwards, fighting to gain a hold on the slippery gravel as we bounced and lurched amid shouts and screams of passengers and driver alike. Suddenly we stopped, just metres from the water's edge. I turned to Hamid, whose hand was being crushed in my adrenaline-fuelled grip. We turned to each other and laughed a relieved, nervous laugh. The driver tooted the horn in feeble celebration as cries of "*Alhamdulellah,* praise be to Allah" rang out. My knees felt weak as we climbed down from the truck. I was glad to be back on my own two feet, any thoughts of social embarrassment purged from my mind by the near-death experience.

The truck wasn't going anywhere. The brakes were cooked and it was beginning to get late. Besides, as close as I was to Faizabad, the last thing I wanted to do was get back on top of the truck. Instead, I walked around the rocks on the river bank, drinking in the land-scape. I was free of the Taliban, free of the threats of beatings, free of their persecution of Hamid, free of the burka if I chose. That night, we slept on top of the truck. I didn't care anymore if anyone saw me. Tomorrow I would be in Faizabad, sleeping underneath the moun-tain skies of my home province.

Dear Shuhra and Shaharzad,

When I was a young village girl and desperate to go to school, I felt dirty and rough. I had so few clothes and always wore my wellingtons and a big red scarf that I trailed in the mud. I normally had a disgustingly runny nose.

Today, it makes me smile when I look at you two dressed in your fashionable clothes and worrying about your hairstyles. You have grown up in Kabul, our capital city, and are properly sophisticated city girls. If you saw how I looked at your age, you'd probably recoil in horror.

I know when I take you home to Badakhshan these days, you sometimes find it hard to fit in because the village children look so different to you.

But girls, the one thing I do not ever want you to be is a snob, or someone who looks down on others. We came from a poor village and we are no better than these children in their rags. Negative circumstances may take either one of you back there to live in poverty one day.

And remember this. This place you come from will always welcome you back if you need it to.

With love,
Your mother

SIXTEEN

A Daughter for a Daughter

{ 1998–2001 }

HAMID AND I settled into Faizabad life quickly. I was delighted to see all my relatives again. All my full sisters, my mother's other daughters, had married local men and remained in our province. Many of my half brothers and sisters had also stayed behind there when war broke out. I hadn't seen any of them in years and was delighted to be reunited with them. My sisters hadn't even known I had got married or was pregnant.

Faizabad itself became a haven for me, just as it had been in my early childhood, when we had fled there from the Mujahideen. I had forgotten what a beautiful city it is, with a highly elevated position and fresh air, an ancient bazaar of mud-plastered shops selling anything and everything and a clear turquoise river running right through the centre of the city.

We rented a small three-bedroom house from where Hamid was able to run his finance business. He also started teaching at the university. I was able to relax and prepare to give birth. I was as nervous as any first-time mother and had no idea what to expect from labour, except that it was likely to hurt. The hospital in Faizabad wasn't hygienic, and I knew I'd rather give birth at home than on a wire-framed bed with a paper-thin mattress in the dirty public ward.

My first-born daughter made her entry into the world on July 8, 1998. I'd been invited to lunch at one of Hamid's relatives, but when I got there I felt so sick I could barely touch my food. At 3 o'clock, I went home, and by 10 that evening my little angel was born.

The labour was relatively short but it was tough. I had a female doctor friend with me but no pain relief. In our culture, it is hoped and almost expected that a woman will give birth to a son first. But I didn't care what sex my baby was, as long as it was healthy. After my baby was delivered, it was taken from me to be washed and dressed in swaddling clothes. No one had yet told me its sex.

Then Hamid was allowed to enter the room. In most Islamic societies, it is not normal for men to be present during the birth. He came over to the bed and stroked my hair, smoothing the perspiration from my forehead. He spoke softly: "A daughter, we have ourselves a daughter." He genuinely wasn't bothered that he didn't have a son. Our baby was a perfectly formed 4.5 kilos of delight, and we were both overjoyed. She looked like Hamid with thick black hair.

In the days after her birth, when like all new mothers I struggled to learn how to breastfeed and deal with sleepless nights and exhaustion, I became very reflective. As I stared at her tiny sleeping form, I prayed so hard for a better world for her, a better Afghanistan. I didn't want her to know any of the discrimination and hate that women suffer in our country. As I held her to my breast, I had the sense that she was my world now. Nothing mattered but her. My clothes, my appearance, my own petty and selfish desires all just melted away.

I had to argue with my family to be allowed to breastfeed immediately. In Badakhshani tradition, breastfeeding does not begin until three days after the birth. People believe that something bad is in the milk in those first few days. Because I had studied medicine at university, I knew that of course the opposite is true. In those first few hours, breast milk contains colostrum, which is essential for a child's immune system.

Without food in those first few hours, the baby gets weak and cold. And if a woman doesn't start to express her milk straight away, she's at greater risk of infections like mastitis or of not being able to express milk when the time comes. This faulty perception about immediate breastfeeding is yet another reason why maternal and child mortality is so high in my province.

I had to argue with my sisters to stop them from preventing me from feeding her. They tried so hard to stop me, shouting that I was hurting my baby by feeding her so soon. I tried to explain to them that it was good for her, but they just looked at me accusingly, as if I was being a bad mother. In their eyes, years of tradition and being told the same thing far outweighed whatever their sister may have learned at university.

But my sisters were kind to me in other ways, forcing me to stay warm and wrapped up in blankets (even though it was July and baking hot), cooking me my favourite foods to keep my strength up and forbidding me to do housework. But the joy of the baby was tempered by the acute agony of missing my mother. I wished so much she had lived to see her granddaughter. She'd have known that another one of us had been born, that another woman of strength and determination had entered the world.

Six days after her birth, Hamid and I threw a big party to celebrate. We invited half the town and we had music and a video camera—everything we had not been allowed at our wedding. In some ways, that party became the wedding day we'd never had. It was a genuine celebration of our love and of our new little family.

I decided to teach again. I advertised myself as an English teacher and rented a house near the centre of town as my school. Within a month, I had three hundred female students, ranging from young girls to doctors, university students and teachers. I didn't have a lot of teacher training, so I ordered audio and visual material from overseas. Such things had never been used in Faizabad before, and my school earned a reputation as a modern, professional place of learning. I couldn't believe my luck. I was earning a good income of around six hundred dollars a month running my own business doing something I loved. I brought my baby into the classes with me and the students loved her; some of them became my close friends. For the first time in my life, I was experiencing real independence.

I still wore my burka every day and strangely it no longer bothered me. There was no Taliban rule in Badakhshan and no law forcing me to wear it. But nonetheless, most women here seemed to wear them and all my students did. It was important for me to be respected for the sake of my school, so I decided to wear it too. I think I did not mind wearing it precisely because it was my choice to do so rather than it being imposed on me.

The only blot on this happy landscape was my husband's health. He enjoyed his teaching job at the university, but the chalk dust from the blackboards got into his lungs and made his coughing worse.

When Shaharzad was just six months old, life took another unwanted twist. I got that familiar nauseous feeling again. I was pregnant. I was devastated. I didn't want another child so soon. My school was running successfully; I had my friends and my life. I didn't want a baby.

Hamid gave me permission to have an abortion. Abortion was not legal (and is still illegal in Afghanistan today), but back then there were doctors at the hospital willing to carry out the procedure. I went to see them and was shown all sorts of suction machines that they used to carry it out. I was afraid of what the machines might do to my insides. So the doctor suggested giving me an injection to induce miscarriage. I don't know what it contained but I allowed them to inject the needle into my arm. No sooner had they done so than I panicked. I had changed my mind. I jumped up shouting, "No, no, I can't do this. I want my baby."

I was terrified it was too late and that the injection would work. I clutched my stomach and talked to the tiny embryo inside me, willing it to live, telling it I was sorry. Just like my mother before me I had wanted a child to die, only to realize later that I would do anything to keep it alive.

Hamid stayed at home, battling the issue out with my sisters. They had been truly horrified by my desire to abort a child. They screamed at us, telling us we were breaking God's code, that it was against Islam. And they were right to say that. When I look back now, I admit I cannot defend my initial decision to do it, other than to say that I really didn't think I could cope with another baby at that time. Hamid understood this, and that was why he had supported me.

I came back from the hospital still pregnant. My eldest sister was still there with Hamid. She was overjoyed I hadn't aborted the child but was so disgusted I'd even considered it she could barely look at me. Hamid just held me in his arms and whispered that it was going to be okay. I wasn't sure he was right. But I also knew now that it was not my unborn child's fault that we were where we were. My duty was to her as a mother.

My daughter Shuhra knows the whole story. My sister told her about it all when she was about six. Sometimes she uses it to tease me. If I'm telling her off or asking her to tidy her room, she places her hands on her hips and looks at me squarely with a mischievous glint in her eye. "Mother, you wanted to kill me, remember?" Of course, she knows full well that saying that will leave me racked with guilt and she'll get away with not cleaning her room.

The pregnancy continued, but it was hard. I was breastfeeding Shaharzad, which tired me, as did standing in the classroom from 8 A.M. until 5 P.M. Also, the Taliban were encroaching. They took control of Kisham, the border town of Badakhshan. We were terrified they would get as far as Faizabad. If they did so, Hamid and I decided we would try to flee to the mountains and make our way back to my father's village in Koof district.

At one point, Taliban fighters were only twenty-five kilometres away. I stood outside my school listening to the familiar sound of heavy artillery and watching as the men of the city boarded trucks, volunteering to go fight the Taliban alongside the Mujahideen army, which was loyal to the Rabbani government. Part of me wanted Hamid to join them, but I told him not to go. He was a teacher, not a soldier—he didn't even know how to fire a gun. Besides, he was too weak to fight anyone. Many of the young men who got onto trucks and went into battle that day never came back. But they were successful in keeping the Taliban out of Faizabad and managed to push them back.

In the middle of all this, Shuhra decided to make her entrance. I had a terrible labour that lasted for three days. My sister and a female doctor friend were with me. Hamid stood waiting outside. This time, he wanted a boy. I had already given him a girl, so now I really was supposed to produce a boy. His family, my family, our neighbours, our entire culture of boys before girls expected it thus.

But I failed to deliver them the son they wanted. Instead, my second daughter, Shuhra, came kicking and screaming into the world. She was tiny and red faced, just 2.5 kilos, a dangerously low weight. When I saw her, I was reminded of how I might have looked when I was born. I was the baby that was described as ugly as a mouse. The same description could be applied to Shuhra. She was wrinkled and bald and red and screaming non-stop. But as I looked at her, my heart filled with so much love that I thought it might burst into hundreds of pieces. Here she was. This little girl who was almost not born, whom I had shamefully almost killed, here she was alive and screaming and looking just like I had.

I was overjoyed, but Hamid was not. This is Afghanistan, and sadly even the most liberal, modern-thinking man cannot be untouched by hundreds of years of culture. And that culture dictated that I had failed in my biggest duty as a wife by not giving him a son. This time, the cruel gossip and innuendo got to him. I think somebody made a joke to him about the twenty-thousand–dollar girl being bad value for money. Perhaps he had heard these jokes at his expense so many times over the years that something just snapped inside him.

He didn't come into my room to see me for almost nine hours. I lay back on the pillows with Shuhra in my arms, waiting for him, unable to understand where he was. She was so tiny she almost disappeared into her swaddling clothes, and I could hardly hold onto her.

When he finally came in, Shuhra was asleep in a crib next to me. He refused to look at me. When Shaharzad was born, he had burst into the room excitedly, stroking my hair and cheek as he gazed in wonderment at his child; this time he offered his wife no tender touch or reassuring words. His angry face said it all. He looked into the crib and at least managed a wan smile at his sleeping baby daughter, another of Afghanistan's "poor girls."

In the weeks that followed, I found it difficult to forgive Hamid for how he had treated me the day she was born. I knew he was only behaving like countless other Afghan men, but I had not expected it from him. He had always been so supportive, taking pride in his ability to fly in the face of the gossips and the patriarchy. Perhaps I had expected too much from him. But I felt disappointed and badly let down. His coughing kept me and the baby awake at night, so he moved into a separate room. That marked the end of our physical relationship.

But despite being upset with him over this, I was aware of how lucky I was that he was such a wonderful, tender father to his girls. He loved both of them openly and deeply, and if he was still angry at not having a son he never once let that show to his daughters. For that, at least, I was truly grateful.

By now, he was barely strong enough to teach, cutting down his days at the university to just two a week. The rest of the time he stayed at home and looked after Shaharzad. She has wonderful memories of a father who sang, played games and dress-up, even allowing her to make him up as a bride and put ribbons in his hair.

Hamid was everything to me and he was an extraordinary Afghan man. In many ways, he was very ahead of his time. We were in love when we married, deeply in love. But I suppose the years together, the trials and tribulations of his imprisonment and his illness meant that over time we just grew apart. The casual intimacy, the laughter, the joy of being in the same room and sharing secret glances had gone. I think it's probably a sad truth that over time that happens to couples all over the world, wherever and whoever they are. We forget to take a moment to listen to what our partner is trying to say to us, we jump too easily to harsh words and impatience and we fail to make the special little efforts that we used to. Then, one day, we wake up and our intimacy and love is gone.

Up until she was about six months old, I was desperately worried that Shuhra would not survive. She was so tiny and frail that I was scared that even washing her might give her a fever. I was also terrified and tormented with guilt that the injection I had taken to try to abort her had somehow affected her development. If she had died, I don't think I would have ever forgiven myself. As my mother had experienced before me, my initial rejection of my child gave me an even greater debt of duty to her now.

Gradually, she grew stronger and put on weight, growing ever funnier and more clever as she did so. Today, she is the brightest, cheekiest and sometimes naughtiest little girl that ever lived. I see much of myself and both of my parents in her. She has my father's wisdom and my mother's wit and strength. She is also immersed in politics and says she would like to be president of Afghanistan when she grows up. Thankfully, she is far removed from the image of a "poor girl."

A couple of weeks after she was born, I received a part-time job offer to manage a small orphanage. I didn't want to return to work so quickly, but with Hamid sick we needed the money. I left Shaharzad with her father and wrapped baby Shuhra in a big scarf I tied around me. She would lie quietly against my breast, hidden under the burka. I would attend meetings with my baby hidden this way, and people wouldn't even realize she was there. She didn't complain and rarely even made a noise. I think she was just happy to be alive and to be snuggled so close to her mother. I carried her at work like this until she was five months old and she became too heavy. I think it's one of the reasons she's so secure and confident as a child today.

As Shuhra and Shaharzad blossomed and grew, Hamid was dying before my eyes. He was losing weight almost daily. The skin on his once-handsome face had turned dark, as though coated with a translucent layer of black. His eyes were bloodshot and he coughed almost constantly; by now he was beginning to cough up little drops of blood.

When Shuhra was three months old, I was asked to take part in a provincial medical survey for an aid agency. This meant joining a team of sixty nurses, doctors and support staff to travel across twelve remote districts assessing the medical and nutritional needs of the people. It was an incredible offer and the type of community outreach work I had dreamed of doing when I had wanted to be a doctor. Despite the bad timing of a new baby and a terminally ill husband, I couldn't turn it down. Hamid understood this and gave me his blessing to go.

I almost didn't, though. It was a gruelling trip for anyone, let alone a mother with a tiny baby. It would be hard to find clean water or proper washing facilities, and we would be travelling across remote and barely accessible mountain tracks. The journey was to take in many of the country's Ismaili communities—devotees of Shia, Islam's second-largest sect. In Afghanistan, they predominantly live near the Tajikistan border. Our trip would also take us to the wild and rarely visited Wakhan Corridor, a finger of land that connects Afghanistan with China. It was created during the so-called Great Game—the period in the nineteenth century when the Russian and British Empires were wrestling for control of central Asia—when it had served as a buffer between the military ambitions of the British Lion and the Russian Bear.

Despite my reservations, I knew I'd regret it if I didn't go. Good opportunities rarely present themselves at the perfect moment; that's just a fact of life. And I felt I could play a real part in the success of the survey.

As we set off in a convoy, I was reminded of the trips my mother used to make each year, driving my father's cattle herd out to graze the spring pasture. She would sit proudly on her horse, still wearing her burka, and go off on her annual adventures complete with a caravan of donkeys, horses and servants. I remember sitting on the horse in front of her, feeling so small against the huge mountains but so important in our mission. As we set off across rugged tracks on our survey I felt similar emotion, only this time it was me with the baby on my lap. The trip was to change my life. We visited some of the most remote places in the region—places I have never been able to visit again. The levels of extreme poverty we found crystallized once and for all my political awakening. I knew my calling was to help.

We began the survey in January. It was so cold that people were actually using fresh animal dung to keep their babies warm while they slept. Their biggest fear was that their children would freeze to death; they had no idea that the dung could cause disease or infection. Hygiene was non-existent, with children going barefoot in the snow, most of them malnourished.

By night, we would eat and take shelter in the religious leader's home. Usually the largest house in the village, it would typically have running water and a drop toilet, literally a large, deep hole in the ground. This was similar to the house I had grown up in, and although the western doctors on our survey team found it hard I found it reassuringly familiar. But, community leaders aside, the villagers lived in a level of poverty I had never seen before, not even as a child. Often we would find a one-room house with an entire family living inside, the animals in one corner and a toilet in the other. And when I say toilet, I don't mean even a bucket, just a corner of the room with feces piled high and babies crawling around all over the room. It was shocking. I tried to explain to the patriarchs of these families the dangers such poor hygiene posed, but digging a latrine—even one that might save children's lives—a safe distance from the house is sadly often more than these uneducated village men can bear, and they will not lower themselves by doing it.

I tried a different approach: "Doesn't your good Muslim wife deserve to have her dignity preserved when she performs her bodily functions?" But sadly, the indignity suffered by a woman defecating in the corner of the living room, or outside in full view of her neighbours, is outweighed by the male indignity of providing a facility that would give her some privacy. Seeing such things helped me understand why Badakhshan province has the world's highest infant and maternal mortality rate.

In Darwaz, one of the poorest districts, the women told me they had to go out at 4 o'clock in the morning in the snow to feed the animals. Sometimes, the snow can be as high as a metre. No one helps them, and when they get back in they have to cook the bread on an open fire and prepare food for the whole family. It is more than a life of domestic drudgery. It is a life of hard labour. The men too work hard, going out into the fields at 6 A.M., not returning until after dark, trying to grow enough crops in summer to last the family and the animals through the winter. It was a forceful reminder to me of how poor and marginalized people can be. Seeing their suffering triggered something of an epiphany about who I was, where I had come from and what my calling in life was to be.

We were in an area called Kala Panja, one of the Ismaili communities. We had been invited to have dinner and stay the night at the house of the local leader. I had never met him, but he greeted me like an old friend. I was rather embarrassed, and my colleagues were beginning to laugh at me when he revealed the reason for his effusiveness. He had known my father. As we sat, he told tales that depicted my father as a hard-working, dedicated man who did all he could to bring changes to the poor. He smiled at me and said, "Now, Miss Koofi, I see you sitting here and I see you are the same as your father."

It was the first time that anyone had likened me to my father, and I flushed with pride. As I sat in the room surrounded by elders, doctors, villagers, all people coming together to try to make a difference, I was transported back in time—to a time when my mother ruled her kitchen, and servants and brothers stood in a line to hand out piping-hot pots of rice to that mysterious room where my father met with his guests. As a child, I had yearned to enter this mysterious secret room, to see what happened there and to hear its discussions.

I smiled to myself as I realized the mystery had lifted now. Those meetings my father had were actually just like the one I was in now. They were simply dinners with delegations of aid workers, doctors, engineers and local elders. How many nights had he sat and dined and discussed plans and projects and ways to bring development to his people? How many meals had my mother cooked for visitors like this? I sat there barely engaging in the conversation, lost in my thoughts and feeling secretly thrilled to be here, finally understanding such a critical part of my father's life.

When we left in the morning, the man made me a gift of a sheep for baby Shuhra. Wakhan sheep are short and fat and famous for their tender meat. The other Afghans on the trip were jealous and teased him: "Where is our sheep? Why did you give it to Miss Koofi?"

But the man just smiled and said, "It's a gift for Miss Koofi's father. I am honoured to have welcomed his daughter and his grand-daughter into my home. And to see how his daughter has grown to work for good, just like him." The words made me very proud.

As we travelled the districts, I met more people who had known my father and gained a deeper understanding of the political role my family had held. I had been hired only as a translator on the medical survey, which was not a senior role. But people heard my name and thought I was somehow here representing my father, that the Koofi family was back in Badakhshan mobilizing communities.

Villagers started to come and seek me out personally, presenting problems to me. I tried to explain that I hadn't organized the survey but was just a low-level helper. But they kept coming, with issues unrelated to the survey such as salary problems or land disputes. I found it a little unnerving and overwhelming. But it also gave me a growing sense of purpose and determination. And of belonging. It was here, with my father's political legacy and my mother's personal values, my baby at my breast, that I realized I wanted to be a politi-cian. I don't even know if "want" is the right word. It was what I *had* to be. It was the role I was born for.

The survey took six weeks. Shaharzad was only eighteen months old, and I missed her terribly while I was away. Hamid was more than happy to take care of her because I think he knew in his heart that his days were limited; those few weeks of bonding alone with his beloved elder daughter were precious to him.

After the survey ended, I went back to my job at the orphan-age. This further mobilized me. There were 120 students—sixty boys and sixty girls. Each child had a different story. They were ter-rible stories. Some had lost both parents, but not all were orphans. Some had a living mother who had remarried and a stepfather who refused to allow them in the house; others had been placed in the orphanage by parents too poor to feed them. It was heartbreaking, and I wished I could have taken every one of them home with me. I spent the first three months of the job interviewing children about their backgrounds and organizing their individual histories into a database.

Despite the sadness of the children's stories, the orphanage was a happy place. I was able to take both my daughters to work with me. Baby Shuhra stayed quiet, hidden under her scarf, and Shaharzad played with the children. I still occasionally see some of those same children. Several of them are at university now, and I still try to help them as much as I can. When some of them came to Kabul to study, I rented a house for them. In the absence of parents, they had no one else to help them. I don't have much money and it is a financial struggle for me to do these things, but I do them willingly and from a desire to help.

But things really changed for me when a few months later the United Nations opened a UNICEF office. I applied for and got a job as a children's protection officer. It was a small office, and I was effectively the second in charge. Working for the UN was a big step up for me. And the job was tough. It involved working with children and internally displaced people who had lost their homes during the fighting.

Part of my job was to network with youth and civil society organizations. One of them was called the Badakhshan Volunteer Women's Association. I worked for them voluntarily in my spare time, fundraising and organizing things like micro-credit loans for women wanting to set up small businesses. I was also involved in a team planning International Women's Day celebrations every March 8. International Women's Day is not celebrated everywhere and certainly not all over Afghanistan, but in Badakhshan we recognized it as an important commemoration. We travelled the villages giving gifts and organizing a Mother of the Year contest. It was a way of giving the village women a sense of pride in themselves.

We organized a big day of events in Faizabad, and it was there in 1999 that I made my first-ever public speech. I talked about how women were treated and how the civilians were treated in Kabul during the civil war. I spoke freely, angrily, about the strength and power of Afghan women, how during all the atrocities of the civil war, when they had seen husbands and sons murdered and suffered rape and torture themselves, they didn't lose their strength or their pride. I called them the "unstoppable Afghan women."

Although the Taliban controlled the rest of the country, they still didn't control Badakhshan. Rabbani's government was very much in control in the region and because Rabbani was once with the Mujahideen, many people thought my speech went too far in blaming the Mujahideen for torture. In those days, people didn't want to criticize the Mujahideen—in fact, that's true even today. These were the men who had saved us from the Russians, so criticizing them is seen as unpatriotic, almost treasonous. I admire what the Mujahideen did in defeating the Russian invaders, but there is no denying that in the civil war years that followed they were responsible for many barbaric acts committed against innocent civilians, including my own family.

There were a few angry faces and shocked silences among disapproving government officials when I spoke of this. But afterwards, many ordinary people, including teachers, doctors and community volunteers, came up to me and told me what a good speech it was. I was finding my voice. And I was finding my rightful place.

Hamid was getting weaker and weaker, and in a desperate attempt to stave off the inevitable I spent most of my wages trying to source new medical treatments to help him. My sisters were harsh with me and told me not to bother wasting my money and to face the fact that he was dying. But this was the man I loved. Just as I could not sit back and wait when he was in prison, I could not now sit back and calmly wait for him to die. He was so supportive of me at that time, so happy to see his wife succeeding, that I felt I owed it to him to keep him alive. After Shuhra's birth, our physical relationship died, but in some ways our love came back. I think he felt guilty about the way he had treated me for giving him a second daughter and worked even harder to prove to me he was completely behind my work. When I came home in the evenings, he always made a point of asking me about my day, persuading me to share my problems and work worries with him. He was in so much emotional pain. After years of having waited for me, when he finally persuaded my brothers and married me the result was a slow descent into death. With sorrow in his eyes, he once held my hand and told me I was like having a dish that you'd wanted to taste for so many years, a dish you dreamed of eating every day and that you could taste and smell in your imagination. When this dish was finally served to you, you found you had nothing to eat it with, no spoon or fork, and all you could do was look at it.

Part of my job involved travelling to Islamabad in Pakistan for conferences. I would fly to the city of Jalalabad in the south of Afghanistan and then across the Torkham border pass, the same drive Hamid and I had taken with my brother in that brief, happy week we had spent in Lahore before he was arrested for the third and final time. I loved the trips to Pakistan, and they enabled me to buy Hamid more medicine. But arriving in Jalalabad, which was under Taliban control, was horrible. I hated seeing the Taliban when I got off the plane and hated the way they snarled at me when I showed my United Nations identification. I felt their stares as I walked past them to the waiting UN vehicle; they scared me, even though I was under UN protection and they couldn't do anything to me. I used to repeat a little mantra to myself to calm down: "You're UN now. You can work. You can deliver. They can't stop you."

One day, I was about to board the plane to Jalalabad when I was stopped by Afghan security officials. They told me that Rabbani government officials had informed them that my husband was a suspected member of the Taliban and that I was a security threat. I was incredulous with rage. I said, "Thank you so much. My husband was in prison for three months just because he met Rabbani in Pakistan and now you are telling me he's a traitor?" I later discovered that someone, I don't know who, had deliberately given the intelligence services false information about us. It was a reminder that enemies can be hidden anywhere and that gossip in a country like Afghanistan can be deadly.

Badakhshan was the only place in Afghanistan where women could work, and I was the only Afghan woman in the whole country working for the UN. It was high profile, and of course that involved certain dangers. Pretty much all of Faizabad now knew who I was and what I did. Many people were pleased for me and liked having the UN presence. To others, I was a constant source of scandal and gossip. Even my direct boss couldn't get his head around having a female deputy and used to tell me to close the door so I couldn't be seen if he had male visitors to the office.

There was a mosque close to our house, and one Friday afternoon the mullah started preaching about women working for international organizations. He declared that it was *haram*, forbidden, and that no husband should allow his wife to do it. His view was that women should not work alongside non-believers and that any salary that resulted from such work was also *haram*.

Poor Hamid was sitting in the yard playing with Shaharzad as he heard this. He told me he managed to laugh before going inside so that he wouldn't have to listen anymore. His wife was the only woman in the entire province working for an international organization, so it had to be me the mullah was referring to. There he was looking after his daughter while I worked, listening to us both being denounced. Of course, such reversal of roles is much more common today. Not only in the West but also in Afghanistan, many younger men of the modern generation share child-care duties, and in many households both husbands and wives work out of economic necessity. Back then, though, we were almost unique. I was desperately upset by what the mullah had said. Perhaps it was easier for him to try to turn an entire community against one family than to speak to my husband man to man about what he perceived as his wife's errant behaviour.

Ironically, when I became an MP a few years later, this very same mullah, who was also a teacher of religion, came to ask for my help. He had been kicked out of his job and wanted me to intervene with the Ministry of Education. When he had preached against me, he would never have come to me for help but years later even a man like that could accept that women now played a role in government and society. I did help him, and in 2010 when I stood for election again he helped campaign for me. It is so important to have women in public and governmental roles because this is what allows people's views to slowly change.

The UN was a wonderful organization to work for and was very helpful to me at that difficult time. Sometimes I was able to take the kids and Hamid with me to Pakistan. One time, I took him to the Shifa hospital, one of the most famous hospitals in Islamabad, where he received a new type of medicine. It was very expensive, however: five hundred dollars a month. I managed it for six months, but after that my salary just couldn't cover the expense.

I suppose I was still in denial that he was dying. He was so young. It was early 2001, and he was only thirty-five years old.

By now, the fighting between the Northern Alliance and the Taliban had almost stopped, and there were rumours that the UN Security Council was about to recognize the Taliban as the legitimate government of Afghanistan. That was a prospect that many Afghans found terrible. It seemed the world couldn't see what we saw, nor could it see the danger the Taliban presented. In the spring of 2001, Ahmad Shah Massoud went on a political trip to Europe on behalf of the Rabbani government. He had been invited to address the European Parliament in Strasbourg (a place I would visit in later years) by the European president, Nicole Fontaine.

He used his speech to warn of the emerging threat of the Taliban and the imminent risk of a large-scale al-Qaeda strike on western targets. During his brief visit to Europe, he also travelled to Paris and Brussels, where he held talks with European Union security chief Javier Solana and Belgian foreign minister Louis Michel. He carried with him the hopes of many Afghans, and we were pleased to hear via BBC radio that he was well received. His message was simple and clear: the Taliban, and the al-Qaeda fighters they were sheltering, were a growing threat not only to Afghanistan but to the world. In a personalized message to American president George W. Bush, Massoud warned, "If you don't help us, these terrorists will damage the U.S. and Europe very soon." But, alas, the West's political leaders did not heed his warnings in time.

There was very much an air of sad resignation among my friends at that time. It really seemed like the Taliban were here to stay. For fourteen years, we fought the Soviets and now we had to fight this new and strange form of Islam. And if the United Nations did recognize them as the government, that meant the Rabbani government that ruled in Badakhshan would become the illegal government. Which, on a personal level, meant I would almost certainly lose my job.

At the same time as General Massoud was in Europe, a lot of foreign delegations came to Badakhshan to meet Rabbani, who had returned from Pakistan and was now based in Faizabad. It was clear that the UN was actively trying to broker peace and some kind of agreement between the Taliban and the government.

It was September 9, 2001, a sunny autumn day. I had just gotten into the UN car and was on my way to an internally displaced persons' (IDP) camp where I was supposed to be monitoring the children's play activities. The lives of these IDPs were truly awful; they were living in tents with no sanitation, but they never lost their spirit and would always smile and joke. But when I arrived, they were all in floods of tears. A young man told me why. Ahmad Shah Massoud had reportedly been killed. My head spun and my knees buckled underneath me. It was just like the sensation I had had when my mother died and I had felt like the stars were falling from the sky. The hero of our nation could not be dead. It wasn't possible.

Later that night, we got more details of the story on the BBC. The situation was still very confused, and it was not clear whether he was dead or just badly injured. On the ground, there was wild rumour. But over the course of the coming weeks and months, the picture became clearer. Two Arab extremists posing as television journalists had detonated a bomb that was hidden inside their camera as they interviewed the famously cautious Massoud. One died in the explosion and the other was gunned down by Massoud's men as he tried to escape. Massoud was badly injured in the blast and died while being flown by helicopter to the hospital. Police in France and Belgium later made a string of arrests and convicted a number of al-Qaeda-linked North African men for having provided the killers with forged documents and cover stories. It seems Osama bin Laden had correctly judged that in the wake of his network's infamous terrorist attacks on the United States two days later, Washington would naturally turn to Massoud to ask for assistance in capturing or killing bin Laden. If anyone could have caught bin Laden, it was Massoud. In the end, the Northern Alliance did go into battle to help the fight against al-Qaeda. But it did so without its great commander.

I can liken the day Massoud died only to the day when President Kennedy died. Americans of that generation always say they remember exactly where they were when they heard the news. It was the same for us Afghans. Even Shaharzad, who was just a tiny girl of three, remembers the day Massoud died.

For many, Massoud was the hero of the Mujahideen, the man who had led the battle against the Soviets. He was a skilful tactician and a brutally efficient soldier. His victories earned him the title of the "lion of the Panjshir." But for many of the younger generation who had been damaged by that war, including me, he began being a hero when he started to fight against the Taliban. He was so often the lone voice speaking out and warning against the extremism they carried with them. He warned the world about the terrorists and he paid for that with his life.

To this day, I struggle to understand how the West ignored his message that Islamic terrorism was a threat to the world. He told world leaders that if terrorism was not stopped right here in Afghanistan, tomorrow it would come to their borders. He tried to explain that he was a devout Muslim, but that the Islam the Taliban propagated was not one he agreed with nor one that represented the culture or history of the Afghan nation. He had five children, four daughters and a son. All his daughters were educated, and he often spoke about that. He tried to educate people that Islamic values do not prevent a woman from being educated or from working. He knew the Taliban were creating a negative image of Islam around the world, and he tried to counter that.

He was such an inspiration to me. He taught me that freedom is not a gift from God. It is something men must earn.

When he died, I felt Afghanistan had lost all hope.

Just forty-eight hours later, Massoud's warnings about Islamic terrorism came horrifically true. The Twin Towers of the World Trade Center in New York and the Pentagon in Virginia had been hit by three planes, each taken over by five hijackers, while a fourth airliner crashed into a field in Pennsylvania, killing forty passengers and crew along with the four hijackers on board, bringing the total number of al-Qaeda victims that day to nearly three thousand.

Two thousand nine hundred seventy-seven innocent people.

The world had heeded the warnings too late to save these poor people.

And many more innocent lives, mostly in Afghanistan and Iraq, would be lost in the so-called War on Terror that followed.

Dear Shuhra and Shaharzad,

It saddens me so much that many people in the world have a negative view of our country and our culture. Many people in the world believe all Afghan people are terrorists or fundamentalists.

They think this because our country has so often been at the heart of the world's strategic battles—wars over energy control, the Cold War, the War on Terror.

But beneath this is a country of great history, of enlightenment, of culture. This is a land where our own warriors built great minarets and monuments. It was even a land where travellers and those of other faiths were made welcome, some even building their own monuments, such as the Buddhas of Bamiyan.

It is a land of giant mountains and skies that never end, of emerald forests and azure lakes. It is a place where the people show hospitality and warmth like no other. It is also a nation where honour, faith, tradition and duty know no bounds. This, my dear girls, is a land to be proud of.

Never deny your heritage. And never apologize for it. You are from Afghanistan. Take pride in this. And make it your duty to restore our true Afghan pride to the world.

This is a big duty I ask of you. But it is one your grandchildren will thank you for.

With love,
Your mother

SEVENTEEN

The Darkness Lifts

{ *2001* }

ON SEPTEMBER 11, 2001, I was sitting at my desk when a colleague ran in clutching a radio. We listened in shock to the news that the Twin Towers had been attacked.

I had tears running down my face as I thought about all those people trapped inside. We had no skyscrapers in Afghanistan and I had never seen a building so high it touched the sky, so I could only imagine the terror of being unable to get out of the burning building.

For the first time, I felt a strong connection between what was happening in Afghanistan and what was happening on the other side of the world. For me, the whole story was like one big jigsaw puzzle. A puzzle that had been coming together for years. Now, someone somewhere had placed the final piece on the board. And the world was shaking with shock.

Bitterly I thought that at least world leaders would now finally know Ahmad Shah Massoud's warnings had been justified when he said terrorism would come to their lands.

What I didn't expect was such a quick response from the world. Perhaps some Afghans disagree with me on this, but I personally believe very strongly that the United States was right to send troops into Afghanistan to topple the Taliban.

At work, emails started to flood in, warning international UN staff to leave Afghanistan and all local staff to stay in their main offices and not travel within the country. My boss was from another province and went to be with his family, so I was left to manage the office alone.

It was a very difficult time because we were in the midst of a large province-wide immunization campaign. We were also supposed to be distributing books for the forthcoming school year. For two months, our office managed, alone, to implement the immunization campaign for children and to keep the schools open. I was still the only Afghan female UNICEF staff member inside Afghanistan.

In America, the investigation into who carried out the attacks on September 11, 2001, quickly identified the hijackers and then traced their activities back to al-Qaeda sources. Washington demanded that the Taliban government hand over Osama bin Laden. They refused.

On October 7, 2001, less than a month after the attack on the World Trade Center, the United States launched Operation Enduring Freedom. American and British warplanes and cruise missiles struck Taliban and al-Qaeda targets across Afghanistan. At the same time, Massoud's Northern Alliance soldiers began to push south towards Kabul with the aid of their newfound air superiority, but sadly without their key general.

The West was hoping for a quick, clean removal of the Taliban and the death or capture of Osama bin Laden and his deputy Ayman al-Zawahiri.

It was a simple plan: U.S. and British air power would devastate Taliban forces, while new types of bombs would blow apart whole mountainsides to kill al-Qaeda fighters in the caves where they hid. On the ground, the Northern Alliance and other key forces, again predominantly from the north, would mop up what the bombs had missed.

Some of these men took to their task with a chilling enthusiasm. We occasionally heard news of atrocities against Taliban forces, such as prisoners being burned alive. In some of the villages that had been oppressed by the Taliban, people grew brave and began pelting them with stones and telling them to leave.

I knew that not all the Taliban had been bad. Some of the low-ranking officers were just people trying to survive. And hadn't I even been helped by some of them? For example, there was the Talib neighbour who didn't even know me but had helped me to get Hamid out of prison or the young, newly married Talib from Wardak who had been prepared to disobey his superiors in order to let Hamid stay at home. I was sad that individuals like these were getting killed, but I was thrilled the Taliban's theocratic regime was being destroyed and this dark period of Afghan history was coming to an end.

I didn't mind that the United States and a host of other foreign nations were leading the fighting. Many Afghans dislike the help of non-Muslims because they consider them infidels. But I didn't see it that way. I had never really considered the Taliban true Afghans. They were always controlled and led by other nations. I remember when I lived in Kabul seeing the entire neighbourhood of Wazir Akbar Khan taken over by the Taliban's "guests," the Arabs, the Chechens and the Pakistanis. Hearing their accents and seeing their wives dressed in black *niqabs,* I'd had the sensation that Kabul was no longer under Afghan control but that it had become an Arab city by proxy, like Riyadh in Saudi Arabia or Doha in Qatar.

And some of the Taliban's worst atrocities had foreign connections. When the Taliban attacked the Shomali Plain, an area north of Kabul, they did so with such ferocity that the land is still known as the "burning plains." During one battle, they killed thousands of men, then deliberately burned all the trees and crops, before bulldozing the remains into the ground. This totally annihilated the population's chances of future survival. Destroying crops and other scorched-earth tactics are things I associate more with Arab countries than with Afghanistan. And it is most definitely not something the Taliban would have been clever enough to have thought of themselves. After they had burned everything, they went from house to house forcing all the young girls and women outside. The last time people saw these women they were being herded into trucks and cars. The local suspicion was that they were taken to countries like

Pakistan, Saudi Arabia and Qatar and forced to work in brothels. Some of the Arab fighters also took these women as forced wives. No one can prove these local suspicions are true, but I have seen too many things like this happen to not believe they could be true.

So when non-Afghan forces were involved in the Taliban's defeat, I was grateful for their help and just so very pleased the Taliban were no longer going to be running my beloved country. One by one, the provinces of Afghanistan fell from Taliban control. In Tora Bora, which had been believed to be bin Laden's hideout, the fighting raged for weeks. Then suddenly, it was over. The Taliban were gone.

The men who had tortured my husband and destroyed my chance for a happy marriage were losing their power, just as Hamid was losing his final battle for his health.

Being the only UN female staff member in the country made me the subject of much curiosity. Journalists constantly visited my office wanting my advice on stories they could write—something that was hard to find time for, given that I was running the office alone. We were setting up a back-to-school campaign in which thousands of boys and girls who were past school age but who had missed an education because of the war or the Taliban were invited back to finish their studies.

UNICEF, in co-operation with other organizations, provided the children with temporary school tents, stationery and books. It was exhausting but hugely rewarding to know that I was helping to ensure these young people an education.

In addition to that campaign, I had to mobilize workers for a mass polio immunization drive all over the province. The work-load meant that I was out until late most evenings, and this made for problems at home. Hamid was sick and he needed me. I wanted to be with him, but I also wanted to be doing this essential work for my country. Usually, Hamid was supportive and didn't mind when I worked long hours, but by now he knew he didn't have long left and he resented the time I gave to my job over him. I was completely torn emotionally, which only added to the stress.

Some days I was literally running from one meeting to the next, with no time to eat. I was still wearing my burka, even during the meetings with foreign officials and aid workers. Then one day, the provincial governor suggested I take it off. He said it was okay. These people needed to see my face to communicate with me. After that, I stopped wearing it at work.

It was a hard time, but I learned so much, not least about my own ability to lead and to implement. As I gained the trust of both local people and my international colleagues, more trust and responsibility came my way. I knew I really had found my calling.

In the weeks and months that followed the fall of the Taliban, Afghanistan was a country transformed. The air of optimism in Kabul was so potent you could almost taste it. Overnight, hundreds of refugees started returning home. Those who had fled Afghanistan at various points during the last several years—the Soviet era, the brutal, bloody civil war or the harshness of Taliban rule—felt safe enough to return. Afghan investors who had made money overseas came home and started planning new businesses, hotels, banks, even golf courses and ski resorts.

The country was still on its knees economically, of course, and most people were living in truly abject poverty. In all the major cities, basic power supplies like electricity had been destroyed and few people had access to clean water or sanitation. Many of those returning found their homes had been destroyed or taken over by other people. Unemployment was rife and food shortages massive as the country struggled to return to a semblance of normality. It was chaos, but for the first time in a long time the chaos had an air of optimism.

The UN office expanded massively. Funds were coming in thick and fast from all over the world, and the race was on to distribute them where they were needed most.

I needed to spend time with Hamid, so I took a month's leave and went to Kabul. I tried to re-enrol at Kabul University so I could continue the medical studies I had been forced to abandon when the Taliban banned women from higher education. I was told too much time had passed for me to pick up where I had left off. But in reality, I think I was denied the chance because I made the mistake of taking Shuhra with me to the interview. The admissions officer made it clear to me he did not approve of mothers going out to work. I was upset they wouldn't admit me, but I had bigger concerns. Hamid was coughing up blood almost hourly.

I took him to Pakistan again, to the same doctor who had prescribed the five-hundred-dollar-per-month medicine. The doctor gave us the devastating news that because Hamid hadn't been taking the medication continuously, his tuberculosis had become too advanced for the medication to be effective. The condition was now so serious that the doctor said he could do nothing. He advised that we try a hospital in Iran that was experimenting with a new technique. I gave Hamid the money, and he went alone while I returned to Faizabad and my job. Hamid stayed in the Iranian hospital for four months. Our contact was limited to a few phone calls, but when we spoke he sounded upbeat and said he was feeling better.

Back in Faizabad, things were changing at the government level. For women, the future was looking brighter than it had been in years. Hamid Karzai had been declared interim president until formal elections could be held. Human rights activists who had been persecuted under the Taliban were now working openly to create a better society. But of course Badakhshan was no longer the seat of government, and the central power base had moved back to Kabul. Suddenly, I felt isolated and provincial. I wanted to be part of the action. So I applied for and got a job as a UNICEF women and child protection officer based in the capital city. Fortunately, UNICEF provided a daycare, so I was able to take the girls with me.

Normally, a man would take responsibility for arranging a family move to a new city. By now Hamid had come home, but he was too sick to go outside. Somehow, I had to find the time to move to Kabul with a sick husband and two little children. One of my brother Jamalshah's two wives and her children were also going to come and live with me. I took the afternoon off work and went to the bazaar to try to arrange a truck to drive all our possessions and furniture to Kabul. The drivers looked at me strangely. "Sister, where is your husband?" they asked. "Why don't you have a man to do this for you?" I snapped at them angrily, "Brothers, do you think a woman can't do the simple task of renting a car? Why do you always think women are useless?"

Once in Kabul, we settled back in Hamid's old apartment in Makrorian. It was now 2003. My job was busy, and I thrived on it. I became the representative for gender issues in the UN staff association and was expected to travel the country overseeing gender-related projects. I recall one trip to Kandahar, a city that had been the spiritual heartland of the Taliban. When I arrived, the community leaders I was working with barely spoke to me. These were deeply conservative men who had been Taliban supporters. In a few short months, they'd gone from Taliban rule to what they now saw as the indignity of a woman turning up to tell them what to do. Gradually, I won them over and after a few days we were all co-operating as if we'd always worked together. Even today, I stay in touch with some of them, and they visit me when they come to Kabul. I truly believe that people change their opinions only from first-hand experience. Opinions on gender can and do change, even among the most conservative of men.

When Hamid came back from Iran, initially I was thrilled by how much he seemed to have improved. But within a few weeks, he was back to square one, unable to walk more than a few metres without coughing up thick globules of blood. It was heartbreaking to see. The disease is transmissible, and Hamid was terrified for our daughters; whenever he started to cough, he would put his handkerchief over his mouth and order the girls to leave the room. Our apartment was on the fifth floor, which meant that he was housebound because walking up and down the stairs was too difficult for him. We had long since ceased being able to have any physical intimacy, but he was still a good husband as far as his health allowed. The illness had not destroyed his mind, and he had great problem-solving capacities. Whenever I had a bad day at work or couldn't figure out how we were going to implement a new project, he would always be on hand with advice or a sympathetic ear. Even then he was my rock.

After a few weeks, he needed a checkup so we flew to the Aga Khan University Hospital in Karachi, one of the region's most modern hospitals. He was too weak to walk, and I had to push him through the ward in a wheelchair. He was so thin and grey-haired by now that one of the nurses assumed he was my father. We stayed overnight in the hospital. I slept by his side just as I had done with my mother in the days before she died. The following morning, the doctor gave us the news. It was too late. His lungs were now more like leathery shoe soles than essential organs. His medicine was so strong that the side effects made his whole body sick and he felt very nauseous. He said he wanted to stop taking it.

It was summer, and the sun seemed to perk him up. Now that the medicine wasn't destroying his appetite by making him vomit, his hunger returned. He started to eat proper meals again, and the colour returned to his cheeks. I had a week's leave from UNICEF and wanted to spend every moment of it with him. It was Wednesday, and I had decided to prepare a chicken broth for him. He hadn't slept well the night before and was tired. I was trying to get him to eat the soup, but he barely had strength to lift the spoon. That evening both my sister and his sister came to visit.

He was chatting with them, and as I watched I noticed how very handsome and fresh-faced he looked. It was as if the illness had lifted from his face, and suddenly he was the old Hamid again. "Hamid, my love," I joked, "you are kidding me, aren't you? I think you're teasing me—you aren't sick. How can you look this good?" He laughed, but as he did so his breath caught and he started gasping for air.

We carried him to his room, and I had to turn my head away so he wouldn't see me cry. It was late, and I lay down in the other room with the women for a while, but I couldn't settle. I went into Hamid's room and lay down next to him. I took his hand and we both started to cry. I was thinking back to the first week of our marriage when we were so happy, when we were planning our future together. We hadn't asked for much, yet all we had been given was sadness and sickness.

The girls came into the room. They'd dressed up like little Kuchi girls and started to sing a song for their father. It was their childish attempt to cheer us all up. It was beautiful and it was heartbreaking.

They twirled and spun veils over their heads singing, "I'm a little Kuchi girl, look at me dance." After the song, they asked Hamid to kiss them but he refused because he was scared of the risk of transmission. He wanted so much to kiss his little girls goodbye but he couldn't.

I was still trying to force food down him, begging him, "Please have this mulberry, please just try a little more soup. Just swallow one spoonful." After this vain attempt, I started to nod off. I was exhausted. My sister came into the room and told me to go and rest. I didn't want to leave Hamid, but he insisted. He was still joking with me. "Fawzia, your other supervisor will look after me. She will make sure I keep eating my food and my fruit and keep breathing. Go rest for a little while, please."

I went and lay down with the girls on their bed, holding them tight, wondering how these little creatures would live without the love of their father. About an hour later, I heard a scream. I will never forget it. It was my sister screaming Hamid's name. I ran into the room just in time to see him take his last breaths.

I shouted in terror, "Hamid, no. Please don't go yet." When he heard me, he opened his eyes to look at me. Just for a second our eyes met, mine full of fear, his calm and resigned. Then he closed them again. He was gone.

Dear Shuhra and Shaharzad,

When your father died, Shuhra was exactly the age that I was when I lost my father. A bitter irony that I wish fate had not repeated across the generations.

In the first days after your father died, I blamed myself. From a fatherless mother came fatherless daughters.

I had tasted the bitterness of not having a father. I knew how difficult it would be for you in our society. I knew that you would suffer not only by not having a father but also by not having a brother.

But just as my mother helped me find strength and encouraged me with enough passion for two parents, so I have had to do the same for you.

You have only me. But know that I love you with the might of a hundred parents.

And know your father would be so proud of you today if he could see you growing up into the beautiful young women you are.

When I listen to you talk about your futures, my heart bursts with pride. Shaharzad wants to be a rocket scientist and Shuhra wants to be president of Afghanistan. That's this week, anyway. Next week you will probably change your minds again. But I know that what will never change is how high you are both aiming. And you are right to aim high, my darlings. Aim for the stars. That way, if you fall, you land on the tops of the trees. If you don't aim high then all you see is the bottom of the branches.

I can't give you your father back. But I can give you ambition, decent values and confidence. And these are the most precious gifts from a mother to a daughter.

With love,
Your mother

EIGHTEEN

A New Purpose

{ *2003* }

HAMID DIED IN 2003 in July, the same month we had married.

My life now felt empty, bereft, all love and laughter stolen from it. For the next two years, I worked like an automaton in my UN role, but mentally I was lost. Aside from looking after my daughters, I felt purposeless. I didn't socialize. Weddings, parties, picnics: none of the things I used to love interested me anymore. My days followed the same routine of waking up, going to work, taking the girls home for dinner, playing with them, bathing them, putting them to bed and then getting back onto the computer and working until midnight.

I lived for my daughters, but as much as I loved them I needed more from life. I needed a sense of being. Remarrying was out of the question. Despite my family gently suggesting it to me, I had no desire for it. Hamid was, and remains to this day, the only man I have ever wanted to marry. To remarry would be to betray his memory. I still feel this as strongly now as I felt it in the weeks after he died.

But politics became a husband of a different kind. Politics was in my blood, and I believe it was my destiny. God wanted me to live for a purpose, and what greater purpose can there be but to improve the lot of the poor and bring pride to a nation torn apart by war?

In 2004, Afghanistan held its first-ever democratic elections. Back in the 1970s, when my father was an MP, Zahir Shah had promised to bring more democracy, and there had been similar elections for local MPs, but that process was derailed by the Russian invasion and then the war. Now, thirty years later, it was in motion again, and the country was elated.

Hamid Karzai had been interim president since the fall of the Taliban in 2001. He was still a popular figure and was elected in a landslide victory. There had been fears that this election day would be marred by violence, but it passed relatively peacefully.

It was a chilly autumn day with a thick grey fog swirling in the streets. Hundreds of thousands of people came out to vote. In some polling stations, a sea of women in blue burkas queued to vote from 4 o'clock in the morning. It was an extraordinary moment for Afghanistan, and despite my grief the significance of it was not lost on me. I think that was the first day since Hamid's death that I had allowed myself to feel emotion.

Back then, President Karzai had promised women's rights, civil society, all the things I believed in. Since his initial victory, his attitude has changed and he has become much more focused on appeasing the hard-liners, but in those days he was like a breath of fresh air. Sadly, the resounding victory he secured in 2005 was not repeated in 2009. He won that election too but amid allegations of widespread fraud. It was another reminder that in my country everything can change for the worse, in just four short years.

In 2005, it was announced that parliamentary elections would be held to select the members of parliament who would represent the various districts and provinces of Afghanistan. My family decided the Koofis should reaffirm their political history and be part of this new generation. One of us had to stand for election. There was much negotiation within the family as to who should run. My brother Nadir Shah, the son of Dawlat bibi, one of the two wives my father had divorced, wanted to stand. Nadir had been a respected Mujahideen commander. Later, he had become the first of us children to enter the family business of politics and held an important political post at the local level. He had the position of district manager in Koof district in Badakhshan. So understandably he believed he was the person best placed to represent the family.

But I disagreed. I thought I was the best and most experienced person for the job. Although I didn't yet have the local political experience Nadir had, my years with the UN had taught me much. I had contacts, both nationally and internationally, and experience in organizing and mobilizing volunteers as well as providing local services and running projects. I knew I would make a good MP. But I didn't know if any of my brothers would even consider allowing it.

First, I called my brother Mirshakay. As a child, Mirshakay had been one of my father's favourite sons. He had been made an *arbab* (community leader) at a young age. My father used to lift him up on his horse and allow him to sit at the front of the saddle. Mirshakay would look down at me from the horse with a snooty, proud expression. I hated him then and I was torn up with jealousy. I so wanted to be allowed to ride my father's horse too, but a daughter would never have been given that treat. But as we grew older, Mirshakay became one of my biggest supporters. We had shared our life together during Taliban rule, constantly moving. And it was he who had finally allowed me to marry Hamid and who was there on my wedding day at the emotional moment I left the family home for my husband's home.

After leaving Afghanistan for Pakistan, he had eventually gone to Europe, settling in Denmark with one of his wives. But he and I remained close, and to this day we still speak at least once a week on the phone. He listened quietly as I made my case and told him why I was the best Koofi to be an MP. He hung up the phone promising me he would talk to the others.

The family was split, and the debate raged for a few weeks; it was almost like an internal election within the family. But to my surprise, by the end of it most relatives supported me and Nadir was persuaded not to stand. The family decision was that only one person could stand for election, because to have two siblings stand against each other would have created too much disharmony among us all.

I wished my mother had been there to see it. I suspect she wouldn't have believed it was happening. In my childhood, my father didn't even speak directly to his daughters, and no one bothered to celebrate the girls' birthdays; that's how far down the scale we girls were. But here we were, only a generation later, electing a woman as the political leader of the clan.

I don't think my family is alone in accepting rapid change like this. Many Afghan families have gone through similar processes as more and more women have had to go out to work simply due to economics. The same thing has happened in many other countries. Once women become an economic force, they become emancipated. I believe that change in gender attitudes cannot be forced on a country from the outside, however well-meaning such forces may be. Where outsiders have tried to force change on people it usually only makes them dig in their heels deeper. Change can come only from within a country and it begins with individual families. I am living proof of this.

Several of my brothers and half brothers didn't believe I stood a chance of winning. My father had married all but one of his wives for their political usefulness. In doing so, he had created a local empire of allies, networks and connections. But my brothers thought these old networks had been too badly dismembered during the war and Taliban years, and that no one would remember the Koofis anymore. I had travelled to the villages in my work with the UN and knew that wasn't true. Many people I had met remembered my father, and the respect for our family was most definitely still there.

Furthermore, I was confident about my own networks. In the four years I had spent living in Faizabad with Hamid, I had volunteered for women's groups, taught over four hundred students English, visited internally displaced people camps and set up sanitation and school projects. People knew me there. My friends were civil society leaders, teachers, doctors and human rights activists. This was the new Afghanistan that I was part of and felt I could represent. I was still only twenty-nine, but I had also lived through Soviet occupation, civil war and the Taliban.

And my concerns went much wider than just gender and women's issues. Men suffer just as much as women from poverty and illiteracy. I wanted to promote social justice for all and education for all, tackle poverty and its root causes, and in doing so move Afghanistan out of the Dark Ages and into its rightful role in the world. It didn't matter if those prepared to join me in that struggle were male or female. I am the child of my mother, who was the epitome of the suffering and endurance of so many Afghan women. But I am also the child of my father, who was the very model of a committed and dedicated politician. Both of my parents have been equally major influences on my life. And both of them have led me to this great calling.

I went to Badakhshan to start campaigning. Within a couple of days, the news had spread that I was to run. I set up an office in the centre of Faizabad and I was thrilled when I began receiving phone calls from hundreds of young people, both male and female, volunteering to campaign for me. The youth wanted change and they saw me as the candidate to bring change. My office was buzzing with vitality and optimism.

The campaign was gruelling. We didn't have much time; we had very limited funds and a massive geographical area to cover. My days began at 5 A.M., more often than not to face a five- or six-hour journey across dirt roads to reach a remote village or town before nightfall. Then back again to Faizabad the following day and a different town the day after.

I was exhausted but determined. And I was elated at the reception I received. In one village, women came out to greet me, singing and playing a *daira*, an instrument similar to a tambourine and made of goatskin. They sang and clapped and threw flowers and sweets at me. I already knew for sure I would win the women's vote because I spoke a lot about the issues that mattered to them: maternal mortality, lack of access to education, child health. In some areas of Badakhshan, women work just as hard as men and are out in the fields from dawn to dusk. Yet they still don't have the right to own property. If their husband dies, then the house is often passed to another male relative instead of to the wife. To me, that's wrong.

I understood these women and admired them. My life now was radically different from theirs. I dressed in the latest fashions and used a computer, while they came to greet me with filthy hands and had never read a book. But I had grown up with their way of life. My mother's life had been just like theirs. I understood their daily struggles and respected them without patronizing them. I know many people in the West will consider these women to be the nameless, faceless victims of our country, but I don't see it like that. They are proud, strong, intelligent and resourceful females.

Convincing male voters, especially the older ones, was harder. In another village, I was supposed to give a speech in a mosque, the largest building in the place and the only venue able to hold a large number of people. But the speech almost didn't happen because some of the elders didn't want me to go inside the mosque. I had to sit in the car while the local men and male members of my campaign team debated it. When they finally agreed I could go inside, I was so nervous I forgot to say "In the name of Allah" when I started my speech, a very silly mistake on my part. I expected a hostile response after that. But as I talked, I saw some of the old men at the back were crying. They were wrinkled, grey-haired men in turbans and traditional long striped coats who had tears streaming down their cheeks. After I had finished, they told me that they had known my father and that hearing me speak had been a reminder of the passion and sincerity he also used to put in his speeches. Hearing them say that made me cry too.

I didn't wear the burka when I was out campaigning because I needed to look people in the eye and communicate with them. But I did make sure I wore respectful and extremely modest local clothes, a long baggy dress over loose trousers—the same type of dress that had once been used to hide my six-year-old brother from would-be assassins.

As the campaign rolled on, so did my levels of support. In one extremely remote district called Jurm, I was thrilled to arrive and find a convoy of over seventy cars waiting for us while elders and young men sat waving Afghan flags and my campaign posters. This wasn't an area I knew particularly well or one that my father had represented. But they supported me because they really cared about the elections. They were interested in the democratic process and wanted to make their voices heard by selecting their own local leader.

Critics of the United States often say that America has forced democracy on an unwilling Afghanistan and that it is pointless to have democratic processes in such a seemingly underdeveloped country. I strongly disagree. America has supported democracy in Afghanistan but has in no way forced it upon us. Afghanistan has had democratic traditions for centuries, whether in selecting *arbabs* (community leaders) or in the tradition of elders voting on local issues at *loya jirgas* (community councils). Voting for national government is only one step further on from that. And I had no doubt that the people I met, even the illiterate and poor, wanted this chance to vote for change. Who in the world would not want to vote for their own leader if it was safe to do so and they were given the opportunity?

As I drove around the province, it felt strange to see my poster and picture staring down at me. My face on the poster adorned cars, shop windows and houses. I began to feel a sense of rising panic. What if I let these people down? What if I couldn't justify their belief in me? What if I couldn't deliver the services they badly needed?

At night, I would be racked with self-doubt. I was afraid that I would win this time but then lose all trust by the next set of elections. I could not bear the thought of losing the trust of these kindly old men with their honest faces or the women who grabbed me with their callused hands and told me my struggle was their struggle.

People liked me, but only because they needed someone to help them. However, realistic delivery is one thing. Convincing people I wasn't able to make them rich or wave a magic wand was another. One woman asked me if I could make sure she was given a free house in Kabul. She really believed I could do that for her. I had to explain that that is not an MP's job, at least not an MP who doesn't believe in corruption.

As the campaign wore on, I got more and more excited. Dawn broke at 4 A.M., and with it my day began. Most days I didn't get to bed until after midnight. I got as many as two hundred calls a day from people wanting to ask me questions or offering to volunteer. The whole thing took on a momentum of its own.

I remember one man who rang me and told me none of the women in his family, his wife or his mother, had voting cards because he had not given them permission to vote. But these women had all been urging him to use his own vote to vote for me. He had no idea who I was or what I represented so he called me up to ask. He was so traditional; a man who would not let his wife vote but who respected her view enough to bother to find out about the candidate she liked. He reminded me a little of my father. At the end of the conversation, he promised me his vote. I hope in later years he let his wife vote too.

Some of the calls were hostile. I had several men, complete strangers, call me and tell me I was a whore because I was standing for election. Some simply screamed over the phone at me, telling me to go back home and leave politics to the men. Others told me I was a bad Muslim and should be punished. I tried not to let such calls upset me, but of course they always did.

In one town, we visited the house of some of my mother's sisters. As a child, I used to love visiting these relatives because I remembered the woman as highly glamorous, particularly one aunt who always wore makeup. Their house then had been noisy and warm, and I remember being smothered in hugs and kisses and the scent of perfume. Now the house was silent. Only two old ladies had survived and living with them were several children, assorted relatives who had been orphaned. It was so heart-rending: a house of widows and sad-eyed children.

One boy, Najibullah, about nine years old, stood out to me. He had lovely, deep brown eyes that resembled those of my brother Muqim, the brother who was murdered. I asked who he was and learned he was the grandson of my mother's favourite brother—the brother who had once galloped his horse back to our house after learning of my father's beatings and offered to take my mother away if she wanted to leave. He and his family had all been killed during the war, leaving only this little boy named Najibullah. I couldn't leave him there in that house of sadness, so I offered to take him home with me. Today, he's a lively teenager and he lives with Shaharzad, Shuhra and me in our house in Kabul. He goes to school and is excelling at his studies. He's wonderful with the girls and is a great help to me in the house.

Thirty-six hours before the election, I still had two districts to visit, both of them five-hour drives away in opposite directions. The rules dictated that all campaigning must cease twenty-four hours before voting began. I don't know how we managed it, but we made it to both districts. In one of them, I was touched to find that my local campaign had been led by Uncle Riza, the father of Shahnaz, my father's seventh and last wife, my half brother Ennayat's mother. All these years later, and here he was supporting and helping me. The poor man had lost most of his children, including Shahnaz, in the war. By now he was a very old man but he was still sprightly and fit, and he insisted on walking everywhere with us. We ate dinner and spent the night at his house. It was another reminder to me of how powerful the tendrils of the extended family system can be.

But the district I had been both dreading and longing to visit was my ancestral home of Koof. I hadn't been there since I was four years old. The last time was the day my mother had grabbed me and my siblings and we had run for our lives along the river bank while being chased by gunmen. Going back had dredged up all those old feelings of fear and loss. As our car bumped along the precipitous tracks and over the high plateau where my father had been murdered by the Mujahideen, I felt an ocean of pain wash over me. This was where my family had begun and where it had been destroyed.

I could barely breathe by the time we reached the village. As we drove along the main track that wove its way through the houses, the same track my father had ridden down in procession each time he took a new wife, the reality of the damage wrought by the war was all too devastatingly clear. The spring where we had played as children was now almost dry. The once fresh, clear water that had gushed and gurgled was now just a trickle of brown. My mother's gardens and orchards, which had been her pride and joy, were dust. In her day, the gardens had shone with seasonal colour: greens in the spring, pink berries and blossoms in summer, fat red and orange pumpkins and peppers in the autumn and brown nuts and purple vegetables in the winter. Now there was nothing, just the branches of a few dead trees poking into the sky like twisted skeletons.

The *hooli*—our house—was still standing, but only just. The whole west wing, including the guest house, had been destroyed. The huge pear tree that had stood in the centre of the yard was just a stump. It had taken a direct hit from a rocket during the war. This tree had witnessed so much. It was where I hid from my mother when I'd been naughty, where my father had hidden his weapons and where my sister and sister-in-law had been whipped with rifle butts by Mujahideen trying to steal my father's guns.

My father's suite of rooms, the Paris suite, was still there. The gaily painted murals on the wall were still visible. This was the room where my mother and father lay together as man and wife, where I had been conceived, where my mother had washed my father's dead body with half its skull missing in order to prepare him for his funeral. I touched the cold plastered walls with my hands, tracing what I could of the patterns. Those murals had been my father's pride and joy. In his eyes, they were like the ones from the French royal palace at Versailles—only in his view, his were better.

Finally, I plucked up the courage to go into the kitchen. This was the room where my mother had reigned supreme. The room where we slept on mattresses we rolled out nightly, where she told me and the other children stories of faraway lands and kings and queens, where banquets and feasts were prepared. In here, we had watched the rain and snow fall and the sun rise and set from the high window set into the wall. Once upon a time, I thought the whole world was in that view from the window.

I took a deep breath and walked in. My knees nearly gave way underneath me. It was almost as if I could see my mother bent over a pan of rice with a ladle in her hand, could smell the meat cooking and feel the warmth of the open fire coming from the *tanur* (bread oven) in the centre of the room. For a moment, I was four again and there she was. I felt her. Then she was gone and I was left alone. Just me, the adult Fawzia, standing in a room that no longer seemed to contain all the world. Now I realized how tiny it was, just a mud room with a tiny window looking out onto a single range of mountains. Not the whole world at all.

I sat in the kitchen for a long time, watching through the window as the day turned to dusk and a half crescent moon surrounded by twinkling stars became visible. No one disturbed me. They knew I needed that personal communion with my mother.

Next, I needed to feel my father. I left the *hooli* by the back entrance and climbed the hill where he had been buried. His grave had the best view of the mountains, a 360-degree outlook onto his own paradise. I knelt down beside it and prayed. Then I sat and spoke to the grave. I asked my father for guidance and wisdom to help me on this path of politics. I told him I knew he'd be shocked that it was one of his daughters and not a son who had chosen to continue the family business, but I promised him I wouldn't let him or his memory down.

By now, it was getting cold and dark and one of my mother's friends, a lady who had been one of our servants, came to call me down. She cried and shook her head sadly at my father's grave and told me not a day went by without her remembering my parents. She said my mother had been a woman full of kindness, who saw no difference between rich and poor, and that my father had often been a fearsome man but one determined to improve the lot of his friends and neighbours, whatever the personal sacrifice for himself.

She stroked my cheek and looked me straight in the eye: "Fawzia jan, you will win this election and take your seat in the parliament. You will win it for them. You will."

It was not a statement of confidence in my abilities. It was more an order. The Koofi political dynasty was to rise once again.

Dear Shuhra and Shaharzad,

Politics has always been at the core of our family. Over the generations, it has shaped and defined our lives, sometimes even dictating who we married.

I have always shared the family love of politics, but I never thought it would be the career I chose. I wanted to be a doctor and to heal people.

I saw how politics killed my father. And for this reason, most of all, I never wanted a life in politics.

But it seems I had little choice. It was always going to be my destiny. And in some ways, your father's arrest was the start of my own individual politicization. When he was arrested, I could not and would not sit at home and wait, doing nothing. I had to gather resources, find allies, try to see the bigger picture and work with it.

I was tired of being told to stay quietly in the background and not dishonour the men. Where was that getting us? Nowhere.

I had an education and I had a voice and I was determined to use it to help Hamid.

That same voice and my desire to save those in trouble still guide me through my political life today.

Perhaps the ways in which I failed your father are an even greater motivation. For every injustice I can help solve in my job as an MP, *perhaps it makes up a little for what I could not ultimately do: save his life.*

With love,
Your mother

NINETEEN

A Movement for Change

{ *2005* }

ON ELECTION DAY, the mood was jubilant. My sisters had been mobilizing female voters, arranging free transport to take them to and from the polling stations. We did that not simply because we wanted them to vote for me; we wanted to ensure that the women with valid voting cards actually got a chance to use them, no matter what candidate they voted for. My sisters were dressed in their burkas so women voters on the buses didn't know who they were. That allowed them to take a rough poll of how the women intended to vote. After the buses had been dropped off at the polling stations, my sisters ran into my office excitedly and told me virtually all of the women on the transport had said they were voting for me.

I knew I was going to win by then, but I was still tense. This is Afghanistan and anything can happen. I was also worried I might be assassinated at any moment. There had already been several threats and incidents such as bombs under my car. But in some ways, I was more worried about what would happen after I won and about how I would cope with the expectations and the pressure.

The polling stations opened at 6 A.M. One of my sisters had hired a car and driver and intended to visit as many polling stations as possible to check there was no cheating or fraud, a problem that blights almost every Afghan election. She rang me from the first polling station. She was shouting, actually screaming, "Fawzia, something is wrong here. The election staff are supporting a candidate—they are not neutral. They are telling people who they should vote for!"

I called some of my contacts in the electoral commission and asked them to send monitors. A western member of staff went to check the situation and called me back to say everything was fine. But of course no one would commit fraud openly in front of a foreigner.

Then I got a call from another district to say the same thing was happening there. One of the candidates was the brother of a local police commander, and all the policemen in that area had been ordered to go and vote for him. My campaign office kicked into action. They started to call all the journalists we knew—the BBC, the local Afghan radio stations, anyone we could think of. We had to get the message out that we knew they were cheating because that was the only way to stop it.

My half brother Nadir had wanted to stand for election himself and had been very opposed to my candidacy, more because he didn't think it was a job for a woman than because he was angry at not having won the family selection. If another brother had decided to stand, Nadir would have been happier about it. Earlier in the campaign, he had allegedly been furious every time he saw my face on posters, even ripping some down. But on this day, his family loyalty took precedence over his resentment. He spent the day driving to some of the most remote polling stations to monitor them. When the roads were too bad to drive, he got out and trekked the mountains on foot. He had not wanted me to stand, but now that I was running he most certainly was not going to allow his little sister to lose because of fraud. I was very grateful to him for that.

At the end of the day, all the ballot boxes were collected and brought to Faizabad. They were locked overnight, and counting started the following day. My volunteer campaign team was so scared that election staff might tamper with the boxes that two of them decided to spend the night outside the election offices. They had no blankets but stayed there in the cold the whole night. I was so touched by the dedication these young volunteers were showing me; I knew they were really doing it to help their country and the democratic process. When youth do that, it is extremely moving to see.

The counting process took two very long weeks in total, but all early indications were that I would win the seat despite the fraud.

I felt the tension lift and was finally able to get some rest. That evening, I was enjoying a dinner with friends when my brother Mirshakay rang me from Denmark. He was crying and sobbing hysterically. His eldest son, Najib, had drowned that afternoon.

My brother had two wives. His second wife was with him in Denmark, but his first wife had opted to stay in Afghanistan. Najib was the son of the first wife and the only child she and my brother had together. He was a lovely, kind young man and been part of my campaign team. The morning after the election, he had gone with friends on a picnic and decided to swim. The current had taken him by surprise and swept him away. I struggled to believe what I was hearing. Why did every happy event in my family have to end with a tragedy or a death?

Towards the middle of the first week of the counting, we became aware that some of the election commission staff were cheating. They had been seen removing ballot papers with my name on them and not counting them. One of my supporters actually saw it happen with his own eyes. He was furious and began shouting, "Look, she is a woman and she is risking her life to stand. Why don't you count her vote? We are the young generation and we want her to lead us." The argument escalated so violently that the police were called. Fortunately, the police chief took the allegations seriously and ordered a recount of several boxes while they watched. On the recount, I received three hundred extra votes just from a few boxes. They most certainly had been cheating.

At the end of the count I had won eight thousand votes. The candidate who came next won seven thousand. As a female candidate, I was part of a quota system designed to ensure at least two women from each province entered parliament on reserved seats. I had needed only eighteen hundred votes to fulfill the quota but I was pleased the results proved I would have won anyway, quota or no quota.

I have mixed feelings about these quota systems. I can see why quotas are important in male-dominated countries like Afghanistan where women do need extra support to enter politics. But I also feel uneasy about them because I worry they can prevent people from taking women seriously. I want to win people's votes on merit and on an equal playing field.

By the time confirmation came that I had won, I was aware that politics had changed my life utterly. Privacy was a thing of my past. There was now a constant stream of visitors at my door, asking for my help on everything from employment issues to illness. It was overwhelming.

And without a husband, it was even harder. Most male MPs have a partner to help them manage daily life and deal with guests. Most female MPs are either unmarried or widowed like me; sadly, that is no coincidence—few Afghan men would allow or support their wives to take such a high-profile political role.

I had been lucky to have such a rare and supportive husband and I know Hamid would have done anything and everything he could to help me manage this new role. But with him gone, I had to cope with everything all alone. The girls were upset because I wasn't able to put them to bed every night like I had done before. I felt guilty and torn and wondered if I had made the right decision. Like working women all over the world, I wondered if I had selfishly put my own ambitions ahead of my children. But then I thought back to my father. Had it been so different for him? Didn't he also feel guilt at leaving his wives and brood of children for weeks on end because of his job? It was the price we had to pay in order to serve our people, and I was consoled when I reminded myself that part of the reason I wanted to work for change was so that my daughters would have a better country to grow up in.

But then the smears and rumours started against me. And I realized just how hard it is to be a woman in a man's world. My opponents, angry over my victory, started a stream of viciously untrue slander against me, ranging from the suggestion I had a rich businessman boyfriend in Dubai who had funded my campaign to the accusation that I had lied about my achievements on my CV. But the most hurtful of all was that I had divorced Hamid in order to stand for election and had lied about his death. According to this particularly nasty rumour, Hamid was alive and well and living in a mountain village.

I was still grieving so deeply for my husband that this false allegation made me shake with rage. How dare these people propagate such hurtful filth? It was nothing short of disgusting. Unfortunately, I was not alone. Most of the female politicians I know have suffered similarly vicious false rumours. And such rumours are more than just hurtful; they are downright dangerous. In Afghanistan, a woman's reputation and honour can mean her life. And my opponents knew that very well. They did not care if their lies would lead to my death—and that is something I struggle to understand. How can the gossips fail to see the consequences of their actions? I believe that to spread casual gossip or lies about another person without any factual basis is both un-Islamic and a sin. And those who do so will be judged for it.

The weeks after the election were a crazy period of adjustment. On some days, I had five hundred people come to see me. At times, people had to sit in corridors because there was no room. They all wanted to know what my policies were and what I was going to do for them. I had to sit and talk to everyone individually, explaining the same thing over and over again. It was clear I couldn't go on like this, so after a few weeks I managed to get a little more organized and hired staff to manage an appointments system.

In October 2005, the new democratic parliament opened after thirty-three years of conflict. On the day of the opening ceremony, I was beside myself with joy. The streets were closed to traffic because of the risk of suicide bombers trying to disrupt proceedings. But people still came out onto the streets to wave flags and dance the *attan*, the national dance.

A bus came to take all the female MPs together to the parliament, and as we drove past the dancing citizens I felt such joy in my heart. We passed a big poster of President Karzai and Ahmad Shah

Massoud, and I started to cry. I really felt that I was part of a new Afghanistan, a country that was finally leaving violence behind and embracing peace. Whatever personal sacrifices I was making now, it would be worth it to achieve this.

For the first time in my life, I had a sense of pride and maturity and a feeling that I could change things. I had both the power and a voice to make a difference. I was so very happy, but I still couldn't stop crying. Since Hamid died, I rarely cry. I've been through so much in my life: my father assassinated, my brother murdered, my mother dying, my husband dying, our house being looted. I've cried so many tears over the years that these days I have no tears left. But on that momentous occasion, I think I cried the whole day long. Only this time, they were tears of happiness.

I had never been inside the parliament building until that day and I was almost overcome with excitement at the thought that this was my new place of work and my office. Under the new post-war system of governance that had been decided for Afghanistan, the National Assembly was created as the national legislature. It is a bicameral body, composed of the lower house called the Wolesi Jirga (House of the People) and the upper house known as the Meshrano Jirga (House of the Elders). I was one of sixty-eight women in the lower house and twenty-three women in the upper house. The lower house is made up of 250 members elected to five-year terms directly by the people, in proportion to the population of each province; a quota requirement of two women from each province was instituted to ensure women got elected. In the upper house, one-third of the members are elected by provincial councils for four years, one-third are elected by district councils of each province for three years and one-third are appointed by the president. Again, there is a quota to ensure female representation. Finally, there is the Stera Mahkama, the Supreme Court, which constitutes Afghanistan's highest chamber in the judicial system. The Stera Mahkama is made up of nine judges appointed by the president to a ten-year term, with the approval of the parliament. Judges must be at least forty years of age, have a degree in law or Islamic jurisprudence and be free of any affiliation to a political party.

As I looked around the room, I realized some of my fellow MPs were former presidents, ministers, governors and powerful Mujahideen commanders—all now sitting in the same room as women like me. Zahir Shah, the former monarch who had promised to bring democracy so many years ago and the man whom my father had served, was also there. He was a very old man now and was living in exile in Europe, but for this historic day he made one last trip home.

The national anthem was played and we all stood up. As I looked around at my fellow newly elected MPs, I felt I could see all of Afghanistan in their faces. There were men in big turbans and long coats, intellectuals in smart suits and ties, young people, old people, women, and people from every different ethnic group. This is what democracy means to me: people with different views, cultural beliefs and experiences coming together under one roof to work alongside one another for a common aim. After so much bloodshed and tears, it was a beautiful thing to see and even more beautiful to be part of it.

More national songs were played, including one called "Daz Ma Zeba Watan" (which can be roughly translated as "This Land Was My Ancestors'"). It's one of my favourite songs and sums up how I feel about my country. The lyrics go like this:

> This is our beautiful land
> This is our beloved land
> This land is our life
> This Afghanistan.
>
> This country is our life
> This country is our faith
> Our children say this when they are crawling
> This is the land of our grandfather
> This is the land of our grandmother.
>
> It is very dear to us
> This Afghanistan.

I sacrifice myself to its rivers
I sacrifice myself to its deserts
I sacrifice myself to its streams.

This is the land that we know
My heart is made bright by it
This Afghanistan
Our heart is made bright by it
This Afghanistan.

This is our beautiful land
This is our beloved land
This land is our life.
This Afghanistan.

After the music and pomp of the opening ceremony was over, it was time to settle down to business. I was determined not to be dismissed as "just a woman," so from day one I spoke up about issues and quickly gained a reputation for being both outspoken and capable. I also made it clear that I would work professionally and cooperate with everyone. Many men in the parliament were opposed to the women MPs and did their best to intimidate us. When we spoke, they would try to shout us down or, on some occasions, even walk out. They also tried to belittle any male MPs who showed us support. One male MP was shouted down in a debate on education after he backed the view of a woman. Other male MPs started to heckle him and derided him as a "feminist"—a huge insult for a man in Afghanistan.

I've gotten used to those things now. The atmosphere in the Afghan parliament is loud and often verging on violent. A tug of the beard is an ancient way of telling someone they have offended you. Some days, an awful lot of beard tugging goes on. I have decided that showing hostility or shouting back in these situations achieves nothing. Instead, I have tried to create an atmosphere of mutual respect. I have listened politely to opposing views and tried to find common ground wherever I could. Democracy is about fighting for your beliefs, but it is also about learning to accept that sometimes you just have to agree to disagree.

At the same time, I made a vow to myself never to lose sight of my principles and values. If you always go along with the popular flow, then you are lost and lose sight of what you believe in. My core values of promoting human rights and gender equality, alleviating poverty and creating greater access to education will never change. Sadly, some of the female MPs found the process too much. To this day, I still haven't heard some of them utter a single word in the parliament. That makes me very sad.

Other female MPs, however, became too outspoken. A young female MP called Malalai Joya was suspended from parliament in 2007. MPs voted that she had broken the parliamentary rules by insulting fellow MPs when she gave an interview on national TV likening some members of parliament to inhabitants of a zoo or a stable. I had admired Malalai's ambition and passion and was genuinely sorry for her when she was voted out. I think most female MPs were. But her mistake was perhaps that she was too passionate. Serious legislative gains cannot be achieved by simply shouting loudly. Politics is a long-term game. And a clever politician needs to work within that framework. Co-operating, conceding occasionally and always striving to find common ground are sometimes the only ways to push forward legislative change.

The day parliament opened, all the new MPs had to put our hands on the Holy Koran and swear allegiance to the country. We promised to be honest to Afghanistan and to its people. When I put my hand on the Koran to swear, I felt engulfed by the enormity of the responsibility.

It pains me to say it, but given the rampant corruption that exists in my country today it seems not all of my colleagues took their vow of honesty seriously that day.

The next day, the debate began for the election of leadership positions, such as speaker, deputy speakers and secretaries, which are highly important senior political positions in the house. I had already made some good friends among other MPs, such as Sabrina Saqib, who had the proud honour of being the youngest member of parliament. I told her I wanted to run for the position of deputy speaker. My feeling was that I risked nothing by doing so and that even if I lost, the very act of running would ensure that the new female voices were being heard at the most senior level in the legislature. Sabrina was supportive and agreed that it would be good for all the women if I stood, but she also warned me that I was unlikely to win and would face a great deal of opposition from some of the men. She also feared I wasn't well known enough yet and did not have other big-name MPs supporting me.

Next, I talked to my family, who also urged caution. Nadir, the brother who held the local political role of district manager in Badakhshan's Koof district and had also wanted to stand for national election, was totally against it. He said to me: "Fawzia jan, it was more than enough for a woman to become an MP. You should not be more ambitious. If you stand for speaker, you will lose. That would not look good for the political reputation of our family. Politics is not just about you, Fawzia, it is about the political dynasty of our whole family."

Those words stung, but I understood what he was trying to say. Traditionally politics in Afghanistan is seen as just winning a battle or gaining power, not as a genuine means by which ordinary people can use their voice to demonstrate their will. In the past, if a member of one of Afghanistan's political families lost in an election, it damaged the reputation of the whole family. But that was a risk I was prepared to take. This was a much bigger battle for me. It was a battle to serve the people of my country.

Finally, I talked to Shuhra and Shaharzad. Here, I got the best reaction of all. Shuhra was only six years old and Shaharzad seven. Shuhra, in an early sign of her genuine political leanings, had a great campaign idea. She said, "I will gather one hundred children from my school and give them flags, then we will come to the parliament to ask the MPs to vote for you." I gave her a big kiss of thanks. I was surprised how sophisticated her idea was for a child of six and extremely proud that she was already learning to think big.

Shaharzad is a gentle and thoughtful child who reminds me so much of her father. She took my hand and gave me a long, earnest look as she said, "Mother, one of the women should have a senior position in this parliament. And it is better it is you who has it, because I know you are the best. I know it means you will be away from us even more and working very hard, but that's okay with us." I almost cried. It is exactly what Hamid would have said.

I decided to run.

The corridors in the parliament building resonated with talk of only one thing. Who was going to run for the positions? My candidacy seemed like a big joke to many MPs, especially the ones who had made plenty of money through war profiteering and involvement in criminal activities. This only strengthened my resolve to win the post of deputy speaker. The wealthier MPs started to court favour by throwing lavish evening parties at their homes and in some of Kabul's smartest restaurants and hotels, inviting those who might vote for them. I didn't have any spare cash for that kind of thing, and it had been noted that I was the only candidate who hadn't organized an event. The night before the voting, my sister helped organize a small dinner party for me at a very inexpensive, low-key restaurant. It was by no means a smart place, but it was all I could afford. Around twenty MPs turned up. The night of the dinner was freezing, and the restaurant was so cold inside that you could see your breath when you exhaled. I asked the restaurant manager to try to sort out some heating. He brought out a very cheap, old oil heater called a *bukhari,* which leaked noxious fumes. The food was awful, cold and congealed. After a while, guests could barely even see each other because the *bukhari* was giving off so much smoke. I was extremely tense, but I tried my best to cover it up and be a good hostess.

But when we got home, I shook my head and sighed, telling my sister that I'd blown it. After such a disastrous social function, no one was going to vote for me. Being able to entertain people and be a gracious host is an important part of our culture, and if you fail at it people judge you harshly.

The children were already asleep. I climbed into bed next to them, but I couldn't sleep. The voting was the next day, and all the candidates were supposed to give a short speech before it began. In the middle of the night, I got up to write mine. I sat there until the early hours staring at a blank piece of paper, not knowing where to start or what to say. Usually I love writing speeches and it comes straight from my heart, but not this one. I started to write, promising this and that, only to tear it up because it just didn't sound right.

All the candidates had been told to prepare only very short speeches. But I wanted to write something that defined me and my values, and it was almost impossible to express that in just a few sentences. Dawn started to creep across the clouds and into my bedroom. By now, I was on my third or fourth attempt; I looked at it again. It still didn't work. I tore up the piece of paper and resolved to just ad lib. I was sure that once I was standing there in front of my fellow MPs, I'd know what I needed to say.

The next morning, all the candidates and their supporters were running along the corridors of parliament making last-ditch attempts to win supporters. There were ten other candidates for the position of deputy speaker. All of them were well known except for me. Some of them were powerful people. Around 10 A.M., I had a visit from a staff member of one of my opponents, asking me to withdraw my candidacy and offering to pay me a substantial amount of money if I did so. I was horrified but sadly not shocked. How could these people try to win such an important vote by paying to win? And how dare they think I would be bribed?

The plenary voting session started. I sat quietly in a corner just gathering my thoughts and watching the situation unfold. If nothing else, it was certainly an exciting scene to witness and be part of. Then, I was called to give my introductory speech. I walked up to the podium, aware of some male MPs watching me with either mocking or angry eyes. Out of the corner of my eye, I saw my good friend Sabrina give me a supportive smile, which helped control my nerves.

This was the first time I had given any kind of speech in front of the other MPs, and I struggled to keep my body from shaking. Then suddenly I remembered that I had won over eight thousand votes. I had every right to be there.

As I looked around, my sense of confidence and self-esteem grew. I took a deep breath and started by introducing myself. Then I told them that I wanted to run for this position to demonstrate that women in Afghanistan are able to do big things and hold senior posts; that my mission would be to put my country's interests before my personal interests; that I saw an Afghanistan that had been severely damaged in every way and needed new voices and new energy to rebuild it. I told them that although I was only thirty, I was not a novice and already had a huge amount of professional experience.

I went on to say how much I loved Afghanistan and our culture, and how my entire commitment was to change this country for the better. I was talking quickly as I usually do when talking from the heart and I was so focused that I almost didn't hear the clapping at first. Then it became louder. By the time I finished, several MPs— men, women, traditionalists, the powerful—were clapping loudly. Many MPs came up to me, congratulating me on the sincerity of the speech. An old friend of my father's, a Pashtun man from Kunduz province, came and kissed me gently on the forehead and whispered that I had done my father justice. The reaction was so positive that for the first time I started to think I might actually win. I could barely breathe when the counting started.

I won with a large majority. It was the first time in Afghan history that a woman, a "poor girl," had been elected to such a senior political position.

I couldn't take it in. My face was as radiant as a blooming flower and for a moment I thought I was flying through the air. Suddenly, I was surrounded by journalists firing questions at me. What were my priorities on women? How would I bring change? How would a woman cope with the scrutiny of such a senior parliamentary position? This was my first real experience of a press conference and it was fairly intimidating, but I tried to answer honestly and clearly. I am not an MP who dislikes journalists. I think in our country many journalists do a fantastic job of sharing information with the public and challenging those in power, so I have always tried to treat the media with the respect it deserves.

Over the next few days, I was almost besieged by media attention. No one had expected a women to achieve what I had, and I became a national novelty. But I was determined make each interview show that I was more than just a point of curiosity; I was a serious politician who was more than capable of doing the job I held.

Next, Karzai announced his cabinet of ministers. The only female minister was Masooda Jalal, a former medical doctor. She had been the only woman to run against Hamid Karzai in the presidential race. She had lost, gaining only a small number of votes, but Karzai appointed her minister of women's affairs. To this day, a woman hasn't held any other mainstream ministerial post, something I find very disappointing. If a woman can be women's minister, why can't she be the minister for business? Or communications? Or indeed any of the other senior posts, provided she has the relevant experience, of course. Karzai did make one other high-profile appointment. A much-respected lady by the name of Habiba Sorabi had been given the post of governor of central Bamiyan province on March 23, 2005. She has since become a very well-known and popular figure in Afghan politics.

With all the roles in place, the parliament opened for business. That was another truly historic event, and it was broadcast on live TV both in Afghanistan and around the world. As the speaker was not present, I had to chair the first plenary session. I looked around and once again realized that here I was chairing a parliament in which former presidents, ministers and Mujahideen leaders were all sitting. But I wasn't nervous. Debating is one of the things I enjoy most in life, so to have the chance of chairing such an important debate was wonderful. I simply loved it.

That day went very well, and afterwards a number of male MPs commented on how surprised they had been that a woman had managed the task of keeping order so well. They too now recognized what an important symbol this was for Afghan women and for the nation.

But very soon the jealousy started. Some of the old MPs, the corrupt ones, are losing power and public support day by day. And they know it. These old-style politicians who use guns and intimidation as their means of communication could not stomach the fact that a young woman like me was growing in political popularity and influence. As I walked past them in the corridors or stepped down from the podium, I would hear them muttering, "What? A woman is chairing our parliament and we must just sit here and watch? She cannot be allowed to continue."

I tried to ignore them and started focusing on providing the services that voters had wanted when they elected me. The Kabul-Faizabad road, for example, was still a dirt track with no asphalt. I started to lobby for funds to build a proper highway that would for the first time link Badakhshan with the capital city. On a political visit to the U.S., I met President George W. Bush and his wife, Laura. I found Laura to be a very pleasant, warm woman and I liked her immensely. She seemed genuinely committed to civil issues—children's rights, education for women, school-building projects, human rights. I got a sense that as a mother herself she understood the plight of women and children in developing countries. She asked me many intelligent questions about the situation in my country and listened carefully as I outlined what I thought she and the U.S. could do to help. I felt encouraged by her support.

I also used my time in the U.S. to try to gain wider support for construction of this road. The U.S. ambassador told me he couldn't make me any promises, but that my request had been noted. Four months later, I learned that the U.S. Agency for International Development had approved the budget for the road. I was thrilled.

The road is now completed and it has improved the lot of Badakhshanis immeasurably. What was once a three-day journey to Kabul now takes less than a day. The road takes in some wonderful scenery, and I think it's the most beautiful in all Afghanistan. Some Badakhshanis have nicknamed it "Fawzia's road." The road on the other side of the Atanga Pass is still not completed, despite my best efforts. I will not rest until this road is built too. I feel I owe it to my father to complete the dream that he so bravely started.

In recent years, I have met several other famous international politicians, including Tony Blair, Gordon Brown and David Cameron, the previous and current prime ministers of the U.K. I have also met Hillary Clinton twice. I find her an incredibly inspiring woman who has a definite grace and power about her. I also met Stephen Harper, the Canadian prime minister, and Peter MacKay, the Canadian defence minister.

I have yet to meet President Obama, but I hope I shall. Afghans followed his campaign and subsequent election very closely, and he became a very popular figure here. There was something very inspiring to us about his journey to become the first black president of the United States. Many Afghans also regarded him as someone who would favour negotiation over war and who had a very strong understanding of foreign policy and global issues.

As the years have passed, I have made some very good friends and allies at the international level, among the fraternity of diplomats, aid workers and journalists. I believe we all have something to learn from each other and that co-operation between nations is essential. For too long, Afghanistan has allowed itself to be a pawn that is moved and shifted by the hands of more powerful players. I believe that Afghanistan can and will one day take its rightful role as a power player within the Asian region. As a nation, we need to learn to work more strategically with our allies and stand up to our enemies.

We don't have to be a nation that the world either fears as terrorists or pities as victims. We are a great people and we can be a great nation. Achieving this for my country is my life's ambition. I'm not certain what God's purpose is for me, only that he has one. It may be that he has chosen me to lead my country out of the abyss of corruption and poverty or simply that he wants me to be a hard-working MP and a good mother who will raise two shining stars as daughters. Whatever the future holds for me and my nation, I know that God alone wills it.

Dear Father,

I was almost four years old when you were martyred. In that short time, you addressed me directly only once, and that was to tell me to go away.

I do not know how you would react to seeing me in the position I am in today. But I like to think that you'd be proud of what the youngest child of your favourite wife has achieved.

I barely knew you, my father, but I know I have inherited many of your qualities. When I hear people tell stories about you, I am always proud of your honesty, frankness and hard work. Even now, so many years after your death, you are still widely remembered for these qualities. That is an inspiration to me.

I think that if a person is not honest to himself or herself, he or she cannot be honest to others. I know your openness and truthfulness made you different from the other members of parliament. I know you always believed in what you did and would stand by your values and the decisions you took on behalf of your people. These characteristics made you a great man.

In my job as an MP, the very same job that you held before me, I often think of you and wonder how you would react to a difficult situation.

Remembering you gives me the courage to remain fearless and determined. Over thirty years after your death, you still lead me and your family by example.

I inherited more than your values, Father. I inherited your political legacy. It is a legacy I will never betray. Even if I know that one day, just like you, I will probably be killed because of this work.

But I don't want that to happen, Father. And maybe, God willing, it won't. If I stay alive then perhaps one day I might even get to be president. What do you think of that, Father? I hope the idea of that makes you smile in heaven.

With love,
Your daughter,
Fawzia

A Dream for a
War-Torn Nation

{ *2010* }

LET ME SHARE a memory with you.

Two years ago, I went to a village in Badakhshan to hear the problems of the people and to find out what I could do to help them. The roads were difficult, and as dusk fell we got stuck in a village. We had no choice but to spend the night there. The family we stayed with was one of the richest families in what was an extremely poor village. The house owner led us to his home, and on the way we were greeted by the young people of the village, who had lined up on both sides of the road to welcome us. After talking with them a while, we went on towards our host's house.

A beautiful young woman, aged about thirty, wearing ragged clothes and a deep red *hijab*, came out of the house to welcome us. I greeted the woman, and she bent to kiss my hands. I was embarrassed. I hadn't done anything for this beautiful young woman or her village, so she had no reason to do it. I felt uncomfortable and didn't allow her to kiss my hands. The woman, who seemed unhappy and worried, invited us into the living room. The room was small and dark. It took a while for my eyes to adjust to the gloom.

When they did, I noticed she was heavily pregnant.

The woman brought us green tea, dried mulberries and walnuts. I asked her how many children she had. She replied that she had five children, all under the age of seven, and was now seven months pregnant again. I was worried about her: she did not look quite right to me. She left the room again and came back with a big plate of sweet Afghan rice pudding that she had made for us. She spread out a cloth and then put the big wooden bowl of rice on it.

Dinner was a good opportunity for me to try to engage her in conversation to get more information about her life. I started by talking about the weather.

I said, "It's summer, but your village is so high up in the mountains it still feels cold. In winter it must be very cold here."

The shy woman replied, "Yes, in winter we have a lot of snow. We can't even get out of the house, it snows so heavily."

I asked her, "How do you manage then? Is someone helping you with the housework?"

She replied, "No one helps me. I wake up at four in the morning, I clear the snow 'til the stable doors are clear, then I feed the cows and other animals. After that I prepare dough and bake *naan* in the oven. Then I clean the house."

"But you are heavily pregnant," I said. "Do you still do all this on your own?"

"Yes," she replied. She seemed surprised by my surprise at her answer.

I told her I didn't think she looked well and that I was worried about her.

She told me she felt very ill. "I work all day and at night I cannot move because I am in so much pain."

I asked her why she didn't see a doctor. She told me that it wasn't possible because the hospital was far away. I told her I would talk to her husband on her behalf and tell him he must take her.

She replied, "If my husband takes me to the hospital, then we would have to sell a goat or a sheep in order to pay for my treatment. He would never agree to that. On top of that, how would we get there? The hospital is three days walking and we don't have a donkey or horse."

I told her that her life should be more important than that of a goat or a sheep. If she was healthy, she could take care of the whole family but if she was sick then she couldn't look after anyone.

She shook her head and slowly gave a sad, wistful smile. "If I die," she said, "then my husband will marry somebody else, but the whole family is fed by the milk of the goats and the meat from the sheep. If we lose a goat or sheep, then who will feed this family? From where will this family get food?"

I have never forgotten this poor woman. And I doubt she is still alive. Multiple pregnancies, poor diet, exhaustion and lack of access to a doctor—any one of these things could have killed her. And there are hundreds of thousands of women like her across Afghanistan. The typical Afghan woman does not fear death and wants to keep her family happy and satisfied at any cost. Brave and kind, she is ready to sacrifice herself for the sake of others, but what does she get in return? Normally very little. And often, a husband who puts the cost of a goat or a sheep above his wife's life. When I remember this woman, tears come to my eyes and I feel more compelled than ever to help all those others like her.

I have a dream that one day all human beings in Afghanistan will have equal rights. Afghan girls have capacity, talent and skill. They should be given every opportunity to be educated and literate and to participate fully in the political and social future of the country.

I also dream that the culture of ethnic divisions that has so marred our nation will one day disappear. I hope too that the Islamic values that have shaped our history and our culture are kept safe from false and wrong interpretations. The Afghan people are the main victims of terrorism worldwide, yet Afghanistan is known to the world as the main producer of terrorists. I hope that with active diplomacy and good representation, we will be able to change this perception. Afghanistan is traditionally a poor country, but we have great resources. We have copper, gold, emeralds and oil. I hope our untapped mineral wealth can be used to combat poverty in Afghanistan and to give our country greater importance.

Afghanistan as a nation has witnessed great struggles. We have never accepted invasion nor have we ever been colonized or conquered. On the night in the nineteenth century when the British retreated from Afghanistan, in what is known as the First Afghan War, local tribesmen sang a song of victory. One of its lines went like this: "If you don't know our zeal, then you will know it when you come to the battlefield." This is an accurate statement. We are proud and fierce warriors by nature. We will always defend ourselves when required. But it should also be understood that we do not search for war.

The doors of globalization and global opportunities, open to so many other countries in the world, should no longer be closed for Afghanistan. I dream that one day, Afghanistan will be a nation free from the shackles of poverty. I dream it will no longer be labelled the most dangerous place in the world for a woman or a child to be born. Around a third of Afghan children die before their fifth birthday. Our future generations are lost to us through poverty, disease and war. I dream this will end. Since 2001 and the fall of the Taliban, billions of dollars of aid money has been spent in Afghanistan. I am grateful for every penny of it, but unfortunately much of it has been wasted, misdirected or diverted into the wrong hands, such as those of corrupt local politicians or profiteering contracting companies who take great profits but build poor-quality roads or new hospitals without proper plumbing.

Despite their good intentions, some of the decisions made by the United Nations and the international community have had mixed results. At a meeting in Geneva in 2002, it was decided the United States would train the newly formed Afghan national army, while Germany would be responsible for the police, Italy the justice system, Britain counter-narcotics and Japan disarming illegal groups. This so-called five-pillar approach had at its heart the issue of security, yet almost ten years after Operation Enduring Freedom began, Afghanistan is still far from stable.

A large part of the problem is that for far too long now, Afghanistan's leaders have acted as if the country is theirs to do with as they please. They forget that there is a whole nation of people living here—real people, good people with families and businesses and children and dreams for their future. Instead, Afghanistan has been run like the personal fiefdom of a few powerful men. The leaders' agenda has generally been entirely selfish. In the case of the Soviets, Afghanistan was used as a stepping stone in their ambitions for empire, as they jealously eyed Pakistan's warm-water ports. Afghanistan lay in the way, and as such was largely an inconvenience to be subjugated in the name of a political objective.

Then the Mujahideen cloaked themselves in nationalism. They were the liberating heroes of our nation, and while all Afghans are proud of their long and tenacious victory over the Soviets, their desire for personal power led to civil war and nearly destroyed my country. It was their infighting and the ensuing chaos that opened the door for the Taliban to take control. The Taliban strove for a kind of great leap backwards, propelling Afghanistan into a medieval era of Islamic conservatism and hyperbole rarely seen in the history of the world or indeed in Islam itself.

Little if any thought was given to the ambitions, hopes and welfare of ordinary Afghans. Ironically, it was perhaps the Soviets who got closest to doing so, building hospitals and learning institutions to improve people's lives. But it was done as a means of achieving a larger strategic goal, not for the greater good of the diverse peoples who call Afghanistan home.

Ordinary Afghans, be they Pashtun, Tajik, Hazara, Uzbek, Aimak, Turkmen or Baluch, have their own hopes for this country. Unfortunately, for far too long they have had leaders who are interested only in serving themselves, and in many ways that is still true to this day. The average Afghan politician has the attitude that once he comes to power, his office and authority becomes a personal plaything, to be used for giving influential jobs to friends and relatives completely unqualified for the positions or enriching themselves through bribe taking and outright theft. The last thing on their minds is the welfare and happiness of the people they are supposed to represent.

Nepotism is rampant in Afghanistan's political system. Family and friends are incredibly important in my country, just like anywhere else. However, our politicians have yet to realize that public office is about public service, not giving your nearest and dearest key positions in the administration—even when it arises out of a well-intentioned "I need someone I can trust; who better than my cousin/nephew/old family friend?" This is wrong. It is not the way to run an effective government and is a catalyst for greater corruption. The person appointed is not motivated by a desire to serve their nation; instead, his loyalty lies with the person who hired him. Decisions are made on the basis of what's best for them, not what's best for the people. Accountability and transparency breaks down, and the fundamentals of good government are cast aside.

Sadly, while most Afghans dislike the way our government runs, many are accepting of it. Expectations of political leaders are low, and all too often dissenting voices can be bought off with a job, a contract or even just cash. And if they can't be bought off? Well, sadly, my country is a dangerous place. People who speak out die here all the time, and very few of the murders are ever solved. Much is written in the world media about the kidnapping of foreign aid workers, a rare but very unfortunate occurrence. These people have come only to help us, and my heart weeps every time one of them lays down their life for a country that isn't even theirs. But what the media do not report is how commonly Afghans are kidnapped. Every rich businessman in our country knows someone who has been kidnapped for ransom. Even small children are not safe from the kidnap gangs who want their parents' money. For those reasons, most of the Afghan business people who came back here after the Taliban fell have left again—those holding dual passports went to Europe or America—creating a massive brain and skill drain.

And that won't change until the people whose job it is to run the country, in a parliamentary system, start to do things for the right reason. That reason is very clear in my mind. A person should be involved in public service only if he or she truly wants to serve the public. If all our politicians and government officials started to think like that, then there's no limit to what could be achieved. The billions of dollars of aid and development money that has been poured into Afghanistan would go to where it is actually needed. The contract to do the work would be performed by the contractor best able to perform the service, not the one who pays the biggest bribe. The police and army would be loyal solely to their uniform and to the nation it represents, not to a corrupt boss. Local governors would diligently and honestly collect taxes and duties and deliver them to the central treasury. The central government in turn would see that the money gets spent wisely and efficiently on the ministries and projects the politicians have designated. And politicians would be bound to listen to, and act upon, the wishes of their constituents.

I don't wish to sound politically naive. All governments have their problems. But the best governments have mechanisms for improvement. That requires parliamentary inquiries in which members are free and willing to investigate and present their findings in an honest and frank way. It requires a judiciary that can act independently of influence and has the teeth to fight off any corrupting influence. It requires a police force disciplined and proud enough to turn its back on petty larceny and bold enough to investigate any level of criminal activity, no matter who is implicated or how powerful he might be. The international media recently reported that Afghanistan had been ranked in the top three of Transparency International's world corruption index. That is a shocking statistic.

So where does one start? I believe a sound government has to begin with a proper parliamentary opposition. Only when there is the political will to listen to the people and act on their behalf with honesty and integrity can things begin to improve in Afghanistan. This is my personal opinion, but it is one formed by talking to thousands of ordinary people. Many Afghans have given up hope and have resigned themselves to ever having an honest government. But they deserve so much more.

Afghans have been fed a diet of rubbish politics for thirty years, and so it is no wonder the political health of this nation has suffered. As a country, we are politically malnourished and our national growth has been stunted as a consequence. This is beginning to change, though. I have several political colleagues who are genuinely listening to the electorate and acting with honesty and integrity. And in doing so, they are winning the respect and trust of the people.

Much of Afghanistan's success as a democracy hinges on two factors. The first is education. All children, both boys and girls, must receive a decent, affordable education. They need it for their personal future, but they also need it to make informed decisions about the future of their country. The second is security. There needs to be law and order so that ordinary Afghan families can build their lives in safety and peace. And when the time comes to elect a government, they need to feel safe during the act of voting and safe in the knowledge that their vote actually counts. Afghans generally want the opportunity to elect their leaders. They don't, however, yet know what it means to have free and fair elections.

If a genuinely democratic government can be established, then I hope that with time all aspects of government, including the security forces, will form the backbone of a stable, free and just society. This involves something of a chicken and egg argument. Does security produce better government? Or does good governance produce security? The answer is probably both.

And what about the Taliban, who stand for both and neither at the same time? As I write this book, the world's powers are talking about withdrawal from Afghanistan. In my view, they are planning to withdraw before the job is finished and while war and conflict still blight our land. This conflict could at any point explode on an international scale. The warning that the great Ahmad Shah Massoud gave the West that terrorism would come to its shores is more relevant than ever. Unless our international friends start to work on a wider regional approach to tackle the Taliban issue, then the dangers to the world remain.

Recently, there have been many talks about Taliban reconciliation and reintegration into the government. Much of this process has been led by the international community and its purpose is to serve the agenda of withdrawing their troops as quickly as possible. But that is a mistake. It is another short-term quick fix that will do nothing to solve the world's problems, only store them up and make them worse for another day.

The Taliban will argue that their form of conservative Islam is the only form of government Afghanistan needs, and that they alone can bring stability to the country. But it has been clearly demonstrated that their interpretation of education and health-care policy greatly oppresses at least half the population. And their views on security and justice bear no resemblance to what most people want or expect. Should they be given a political voice? I suppose that under the type of democratic system I believe in, everybody has a say in politics. But that is the point: politics is about talking, reasoning and persuading. It is hard to see how the Taliban will ever sit in a parliament along-side female politicians like me.

The Taliban frequently try to murder me by any means possible. And not only me. They make regular attempts on the lives of many other Afghan men and women—intellectuals, journalists, opponents and friends of the West. Are the Taliban people who will ever under-stand or respect what democracy means? I doubt it. Will they really be willing to share power with those who do not share their ideals? Will they sit in debates with us and try to reach a common ground? Will they support new legislation or ideas put forward by me or other women? The answer is no. And it is naive of the international com-munity to think this is possible. So much has been done in recent years to support and enhance the overall progress of Afghan women. Bringing the Taliban back into the government will undo all of that.

As I drive through Kabul, I always smile when I see the beauti-ful sight of little girls dressed in the school uniform of black *shalwar kameez* and white head scarves. Within the past decade, hundreds of thousands of little girls, including my own daughters, have gained the opportunity to be educated. This not only gives them the chance of a future but also improves the future economic and physi-cal health of their families. This in turn helps our entire nation grow stronger and powerful. If the Taliban return, these little girls will once again be forced back indoors and silenced underneath their burkas and a set of arcane laws that accord women fewer rights than dogs. Our nation will once again slide backwards into darkness. To allow this to happen would be a betrayal of the highest order.

In October 2010, I won a second term in the parliament. I had not let my people down and, despite widespread fraud and cheating on the part of some of my opponents, I got even more votes than I did the first time.

I was also thrilled that my elder sister Qandigul (known as Maryam to her family) was elected as an MP. She is the sister who was beaten by the Mujahideen the night my mother refused to show them where my father's weapons were hidden. She was illiterate and did not attend school as a child (I was the only female member of my family allowed to do so). But after she married and had children, she watched as I gained my education and saw what I had achieved. She too wanted to serve our country and do something important with her life. So she decided to educate herself. She started by going to night school to take computer and literacy classes and a few years later she graduated with a university degree. Now she is an MP like me and the latest member of the Koofis to take her place in the family business of politics. I am immensely proud of her achievements and I know she will work hard in her new role.

During the latest elections, there were even more threats on my life: gunmen trailing my car, roadside bombs laid along my route, warnings that I would be kidnapped. On the day of voting, two people were arrested who admitted they had planned to kidnap me, take me to a different district and then kill me. They had links to another local politician. That much was obvious because one of those arrested was the politician's relative. This man has since been released while the other remains in custody. I cannot explain why one of these men was released without charge after admitting his evil project. I can only say that due to my outspokenness, I cannot always rely on the support of our national security forces as much as I would like. Often I don't know who my would-be assassins are, whether they wear civilian clothes or official uniforms. At times in Kabul, I have had my car pulled off the road and been intimidated by our national intelligence forces, always without reason or explanation. This has become such a daily part of my life now. I will not say I am used to it—no one can ever get used to such threats—but I have learned to live with it.

Like my father before me, I am proud to say that I am known as an honest politician who is not afraid to speak out on difficult issues where needed. I have proven that I can deliver services and direct funds to those in need. Of course the people I represent are still among the world's poorest, and much work still needs to be done. But I know I have improved their lives by bringing roads, schools, jobs and mosques. Recently I championed the building of a series of women's mosques in some remote and very conservative villages. The mosques are a place to pray, and no man would deny his wife the chance to leave home for an hour a day to worship God. Sometimes it is the only opportunity these women have to get out of their homes. So the mosques I built will make other services accessible to women. In these centres of religion, women can now get advice on nutrition and hygiene or take literacy classes. Just one building like this can transform the dynamics of a poor village almost overnight.

Today, I am probably the best known of all the female politicians in Afghanistan and am extremely popular with the public, both men and women. The Afghan public now see me as a politician first and a woman second. This is something I am deeply proud of.

My supporters have suggested I run for president. I will not lie and say that the role of leading my nation is not something I would love to do. Of course I would. Name me a serious politician anywhere in the world who wouldn't want the top job if offered it. And I know it is a job I am capable of doing well. But in truth, I do not think the time is right. I don't think my country is ready to accept a woman in this role. Of course, I hope this will change one day. Until recently, no one thought a black man could be president of the United States but it happened. Other Islamic countries have had female heads of state. Megawati Sukarnoputri was president of Indonesia from 2001 to 2004, Begum Khaleda Zia was the first female prime minister of Bangladesh and in neighbouring Pakistan, Benazir Bhutto was also prime minister and was on the verge of being elected president when she was killed. I think about my early political heroines, Margaret Thatcher and Indira Gandhi. They are women who are remembered not for their gender but for their policies and their strength as leaders. And I know it could one day be possible in Afghanistan.

For far too long, politics in my country has been conducted at gunpoint. It has had more to do with who has got the most soldiers or the best tanks than with policy, plans or reforms for our future. This must change. But changes will take time. But while these changes germinate, take root and grow, so too will the economy. A stable Afghanistan will sprout opportunities for its people. Whether it is the farmer who can use better and safer roads to get to market, the budding entrepreneur building an import-export business or the hundreds of thousands of Afghans living abroad, many of them highly educated, the building blocks for a better future will begin to present themselves.

I don't wish to understate the challenges that lie ahead for my country. There are many problems to be overcome. Afghanistan is awash in corruption, flawed religious extremism and a river of money from the sea of opium poppies grown on our farmlands. But through the generations of suffering this land has endured, there is a strength and resolve in the people that has never been broken. I believe and pray that the time is approaching for all Afghans to put aside the past and look to the future. After so many years of war and oppression, we are left with virtually nothing. The only choice we have is to rebuild, and I believe that's what the majority of my countrymen and women genuinely want. They just need the framework to do it in. And they need a strong and decisive leadership to help turn a range of divided ideas and opinions about our nation into a cohesive whole. A leader who can bond our nation together and bring us success.

And if we can achieve that, my darling daughters, then perhaps some day your children's children will grow up free in a proud, successful, Islamic republic that has taken its rightful place in the developed world.

This is what I live for.

And it is what I know I will die for.

If this should happen, my darling daughters, then I want you to know that every word in this book was written for you. I want and need you, as well as all the boys and girls of Afghanistan, to understand and learn from my struggle. My dreams for this nation will live on in all of you.

And if the Taliban don't succeed in killing me? Well, Shuhra, maybe I will try to beat you to the post of first female president of Afghanistan. And maybe together we will form a new dynasty of powerful Islamic female leaders who bring good to the world.

I know as I write these final words my mother Bibi jan is definitely smiling in heaven.

A Historical Timeline
of Afghanistan

1919—Afghanistan regains independence after a third war against British forces trying to bring the country under their sphere of influence.

1933—Zahir Shah becomes king and Afghanistan remains a monarchy for the next four decades.

1973—Mohammed Dawoud seizes power in a coup and declares a republic.

1978—General Dawoud is overthrown and killed in a coup by the leftist People's Democratic Party.

1979—A power struggle between leftist leaders Hafizullah Amin and Nur Muhammad Taraki in Kabul is won by Amin. Revolts in the countryside continue and the Afghan army faces collapse. The Soviet Union finally sends in troops to help remove Amin, who is executed.

1980—Babrak Karmal, leader of the People's Democratic Party Parcham faction, is installed as ruler, backed by Soviet troops. But anti-regime resistance intensifies with various Mujahideen groups fighting Soviet forces. The United States, Pakistan, China, Iran and Saudi Arabia supply money and arms.

1985—Mujahideen come together in Pakistan to form an alliance against Soviet forces. Half the Afghan population is now estimated to be displaced by war, with many fleeing to neighbouring Iran or Pakistan.

1986—The United States begins supplying the Mujahideen with Stinger missiles, enabling them to shoot down Soviet helicopter gunships. Babrak Karmal is replaced by Najibullah as head of the Soviet-backed regime.

1988—Afghanistan, the Soviet Union, the United States and Pakistan sign peace accords and the Soviet Union begins pulling out troops.

1989—The last Soviet troops leave, but civil war continues as the Mujahideen push to overthrow Najibullah.

1991—The United States and the Soviet Union agree to end military aid to both sides.

1992—Resistance closes in on Kabul and Najibullah falls from power. Rival militias vie for influence.

1993—Mujahideen factions form a government with ethnic Tajik Burhanuddin Rabbani, who is proclaimed president.

1996—The Taliban seize control of Kabul and introduce a hard-line version of Islam. Rabbani flees to join the anti-Taliban Northern Alliance.

1997—The Taliban are recognized as the legitimate rulers by Pakistan and Saudi Arabia. Most other countries continue to regard Rabbani as head of state. The Taliban now control about two-thirds of the country.

2001—Ahmad Shah Massoud, a legendary guerrilla and leader of the main opposition to the Taliban, is killed, apparently by assassins posing as journalists.

2001 OCTOBER—The United States and Britain launch air strikes against Afghanistan after the Taliban refuse to hand over Osama bin Laden, held responsible for the September 11 attacks on America.

2001 DECEMBER 5—Afghan groups agree to a deal in Bonn forming an interim government.

2001 DECEMBER 7—The Taliban finally give up the last stronghold of Kandahar, but Mullah Omar remains at large.

2001 DECEMBER 22—Pashtun royalist Hamid Karzai is sworn in as the head of a thirty-member interim power-sharing government.

2002 APRIL—Former king Zahir Shah returns, but says he makes no claim to the throne.

2002 MAY—The UN Security Council extends the mandate of the International Security Assistance Force until December 2002. Allied forces continue their military campaign to find remnants of al-Qaeda and Taliban forces in the southeast.

2002 JUNE—The *loya jirga*, or grand council, elects Hamid Karzai as interim head of state. Karzai picks members of his administration, which is to serve until 2004.

2003 AUGUST—NATO takes control of security in Kabul, its first-ever operational commitment outside Europe.

2004 JANUARY—The *loya jirga* adopts a new constitution that provides for a strong presidency.

2004 OCTOBER-NOVEMBER—Presidential elections: Hamid Karzai is declared the winner, with 55 percent of the vote. He is sworn in, amid tight security, in December.

2005 SEPTEMBER—The first parliamentary and provincial elections in more than thirty years are held.

2005 DECEMBER—The new parliament holds its inaugural session.

2006 OCTOBER—NATO assumes responsibility for security across the whole of Afghanistan, taking command in the east from a U.S.-led coalition force.

2008 NOVEMBER—Taliban militants reject an offer of peace talks from President Karzai, saying there can be no negotiations until foreign troops leave Afghanistan.

2009 OCTOBER—Hamid Karzai is declared winner of the August presidential election, after second-place opponent Abdullah Abdullah pulls out before the second round. Preliminary results had given Karzai 55 percent of the vote, but so many ballots are found to be fraudulent that a run-off was called.

2009 NOVEMBER—Hamid Karzai is sworn in for a second term as president.

2010 JULY—A major international conference endorses President Karzai's timetable for control of security to be transferred from foreign to Afghan forces by 2014.

Acknowledgements

I WOULD LIKE to thank the following people:

My daughters, for their patience and the time they gave me during the writing.

Nadene, who has been extremely helpful in co-writing and narrating the book.

Elsa, who has been a great support in shaping the stories, managing the team and editing the book so many times and with patience.

My brother Ennayat, who spent his one week off travelling with Nadene and me to the remote mountainous area of Badakhshan to remind ourselves of childhood stories.

The security people in my district for providing required security to all of the team during the trip to our village.

Kaka Yatim, the brave driver who drove us on some of the most difficult roads in Afghanistan non-stop for two days and nights.

FAWZIA KOOFI IS a supporter of BEHZ Creations, which funds literacy projects in remote areas of Afghanistan. You can read more on www.fawziakoofi.org.

FAWZIA KOOFI worked with UNICEF and various NGOS as a women's and children's advocate before becoming a member of parliament and Afghanistan's first female deputy speaker in 2005. In 2009, she was chosen as a Young Global Leader by the World Economic Forum. She will run as a presidential candidate in 2014. Koofi is a supporter of BEHZ Creations, which funds literacy projects in remote areas of Afghanistan. She wrote this book with Nadene Ghouri, an award-winning BBC journalist and former Al Jazeera reporter who specializes in the Middle East. You can read more on www.fawziakoofi.org.